Chapter Headings

Royal National Institute for the Blind

Blind and partially sighted children in Britain: the RNIB survey

Volume 2

Errol Walker

Michael Tobin

and Aubrey McKennell

London: HMSO

This report was designed and printed by HMSO to specifications supplied by RNIB to ensure that it is legible. As the survey shows, the majority of blind and partially sighted people can read print which is clear and well designed. This report is set in 12½pt on 15pt Helvetica Regular.

The report is also available in braille and on audio tape. Enquiries about these editions should be sent direct to RNIB Customer Services, PO Box 173, Peterborough PE2 6WS, UK.

HMSO publications are available from:

HMSO Publications Centre
(Mail, fax and telephone orders only)
PO Box 276, London, SW8 5DT
Telephone orders 071-873 9090
General enquiries 071-873 0011
(queuing system in operation for both numbers)
Fax orders 071-873 8200

HMSO Bookshops
49 High Holborn, London, WC1V 6HB 071-873 0011
(counter service only)
258 Broad Street, Birmingham, B1 2HE 021-643 3740
Southey House, 33 Wine Street, Bristol, BS1 2BQ (0272) 264306
9-21 Princess Street, Manchester, M60 8AS 061-834 7201
80 Chichester Street, Belfast, BT1 4JY (0232) 238451
71 Lothian Road, Edinburgh, EH3 9AZ 031-228 4181

HMSO's Accredited Agents
(see Yellow Pages)
and through good booksellers

Contents

Foreword

This report presents the findings of the first ever nationwide survey of blind and partially sighted children in Great Britain. Its publication follows that of **Blind and partially sighted adults in Britain: the RNIB survey, Volume 1**, which was issued by HMSO in 1991.

Both surveys were commissioned by RNIB to provide a more detailed picture of our 'clients' than existing statistics could provide. We wanted to know the numbers of adults and children with visual impairments, their personal circumstances and needs, and the extent to which those needs were being met. As the country's largest voluntary organisation in this field we need to plan our own services with a real understanding of visually impaired people's needs.

This survey, conducted in 1988, took the form of lengthy, detailed interviews with the parents of 285 visually impaired children aged three to nineteen years. The children were identified from the records of a sample of local education authorities in Great Britain, and the interviews with their parents were conducted by professional interviewers.

The findings of the survey provide a detailed insight into the lives of families with a visually impaired child. The most striking finding to emerge is that more than half of these children have one or more additional disabilities such as impaired hearing or speech, physical handicaps or learning difficulties. The survey also illustrates the struggle families have to obtain information and advice about their child's condition; special counselling is shown to be rare yet nearly three-quarters of parents said they would have welcomed it.

This report has major implications for all those who provide services for disabled children, from education authorities to the health service, social services departments and voluntary bodies. RNIB is urgently reviewing its own policies and provision of services in the light of these findings and we will be encouraging others – not least central and local government – to do the same.

With the publication of this, the second volume of our survey of blind and partially sighted people, we have amassed an enormous bank of information, the full implications of which will take some time to digest.

But what is clear from this survey is that visual impairment has been an under-reported disability and that adults and children alike have a multiplicity of unmet needs. Now we must press for action to ensure that visually impaired people gain the resources and consideration they so desperately need.

John A Wall MA (Oxon)
Chairman, RNIB

Acknowledgements

Social surveys of this scale and complexity are possible only with the advice, support and encouragement of many individuals and organisations. First, however, our sincere thanks must go to the parents and visually impaired children who allowed us to intrude on their lives, and who coped with our lengthy questions with patience and good humour. We hope that this study will result in substantial improvements to the quality and availability of services to their children, themselves and all children with disabilities.

Our grateful thanks go to the many local education authorities who took part in the pilot and main surveys. Without their cooperation we could not have undertaken this study.

We are greatly indebted to our advisers and consultants whose experience of survey work and of policy issues contributed so much to our study. Our special thanks go to Roger and Gill Hinds who prepared the initial document which highlighted the topic areas for the study, and David Griffiths for his work in the development stage of the research.

The fieldwork was carried out by the British Market Research Bureau. We thank them for the immense amount of work they put into the questionnaire design and fieldwork itself.

Professor Gerald Hoinville of City University and Elizabeth Hoinville of the University of London worked respectively on the sampling and computational work on the sample selection. Jane Fielding and Dr Chris Fife-Schaw helped to set up the data on the computer at the University of Surrey.

An advisory committee was set up by RNIB under the Chairmanship of Ian Bruce to advise on the survey. Its members were Dr Tim Cullinan, Dr Henry Heath, Dr Adrian Hill, Colin Low, Tom Parker and Elizabeth Twining. The knowledge, experience and enthusiasm they brought to the design and development of the survey is gratefully acknowledged. We also thank the many RNIB officers who contributed their advice and experience, particularly Louise Clunies-Ross and the many RNIB Education Advisers who answered our questions. Jean White of RNIB provided invaluable support on the drafting and typing and RNIB's Publications Manager, Hilary Todd, finally got us into print.

Advice was sought from a number of individuals on issues to be included in the survey. They represented a wide range of disciplines and backgrounds and brought a wealth of specialist expertise to our work for which we are most grateful.

We owe very special thanks to Duncan Watson who, as RNIB Chairman when the survey was commissioned, gave every support and encouragement, and to Ian Bruce, RNIB's Director-General, whose vision and determination made this all possible.

Photographic credit: front cover
Lee Harrod has been blind since birth. He is 10 years old and lives in Norwich with his parents. HMSO and RNIB are very grateful to Mr and Mrs Harrod and Lee for their help and co-operation in providing the photograph.

Any errors and omissions are entirely the responsibility of the authors.

Errol C Walker
Aubrey C McKennell
Michael J Tobin

Notes on the Tables and Abbreviations

1   Percentages have been rounded to the nearest whole number; 0.5% is rounded up. As a result many of the tables will not add to 100%.

2   # = less than 0.5%.

3   Single or multiple answer questions.
Where a total % base, 'Total 100', is shown, only single answers have normally been allowed to the question.
Where the population base is shown as 'Base = 100%', multiple answers have been allowed, and single responses in the body of the table cannot be added together. In a number of tables a summary figure is given which adds the informants giving a group of answers; this represents the total number of informants giving these answers, not the total responses themselves.

4   'Base' refers to the number of people actually interviewed who form the base of the column concerned. For example, 285 is the total number of people interviewed for the survey.

5   Not all questions apply to every child. Where informants have not been asked a question, the total number of informants is given as a note to the table together with a reason for their inclusion or omission. In a number of cases, informants simply failed to answer a question, and where applicable it is also noted.

The question(s) that generates the answers given in a table normally forms part of the table. Where a subsequent table simply repeats the data, the question is not repeated. Also, where the question is simply a 'why' or 'who' question it is not given.

Abbreviations specific to the tables

Hi	High residual vision
Lo	Low residual vision
NOD	No other disability
NR	Non-registered
OD	Other disability
Ord	Ordinary school
R	Registered
Spcl	Special school

General abbreviations

BMRB	British Market Research Bureau
CAB	Citizens Advice Bureau
CCTV	Closed-circuit television magnifier
CSO	Central Statistical Office
DES	Department of Education and Science
DHSS	Department of Health and Social Security (now DOH)
DLS	Daily living skills
DOH	Department of Health
ERS	RNIB Express Reading Service
GHS	General Household Survey
GP	General Practitioner (family doctor)
HA	Housing Association
HB	Housing benefit
LA	Local authority
LVA	Low vision aid
NHS	National Health Service
NLP	No light perception
NR	Non-registered
OPCS	Office of Population Censuses and Surveys
RNIB	Royal National Institute for the Blind
RV	Residual vision
RVL	Residual vision level
SSD	Social services department
STL	RNIB Student Tape Library
VI	Visually impaired

Part A

Summary and Implications

1 Summary and Implications

Chapter 1 provides a summary of the main findings. The report is written as a descriptive narrative of the data with limited interpretation. This chapter, as well as summarising the findings for chapters 3 to 17, which cover the main topics investigated, provides more interpretative commentary and highlights some of the implications of the findings.

The report is based on interviews conducted with 285 parents of visually impaired children aged 3 to 19 years, who were identified from the records of a representative sample of 33 local education authorities in Great Britain.

Chapter 2, Background and objectives

This chapter provides the background to the survey and the objectives. It also provides a definition of the terminology adopted in the report and gives some guidance as to the analysis and presentation of the results. A brief review of previous surveys of visually impaired children, that have guided our study, is also given.

Chapter 3, The onset of visual impairment

The causation and age of onset of blindness or severe visual impairment can be significant factors in a child's, and the family's, success in reducing its potentially handicapping consequences. Knowing the cause and nature of the impairment can be of great help to the family in accepting and adapting to the circumstances. In those cases where there is an hereditary or genetic factor, such knowledge may be essential for the purposes of family planning. In other instances, decisions about the efficacy and timing of medical or surgical treatment will be dependent on the family's evaluation of the likely benefits and drawbacks; in yet others, the parents' expectations of the child's early development will need to be set against an understanding of how visual difficulties may impede the reaching of important developmental milestones (the beginning of crawling and walking, for example). The five-year old who has had useful residual sight for the first year or two of life may have better spatial awareness, may be more facially expressive and may have gained more from his/her visually mediated ability to imitate adult behaviour than his or her congenitally blind counterpart. The disadvantages are not likely to be permanent, but the age of onset of a child's disability will almost certainly affect the family's attitudes and its needs for practical and psychological help.

As will be shown in other sections of this report, most families are desperate for information and advice, a situation which has not changed materially since Langdon published the findings of his interviews with 183 parents of blind children in eight Midlands counties (Langdon, 1970). In that earlier survey, it was reported that 'many parents complain that they never received the simple explanation of the nature and cause of the child's visual disability to which they feel they are entitled' (ibid., p.288).

From the present survey it is evident that although most parents know the name of their child's visual impairment and its cause, there is still a considerable amount of uncertainty among many of them about other factors associated with the visual impairment. Twenty-seven percent said that they did not know the medical name of the condition because the doctors themselves did not know it, and yet in only 19% of cases is it reported that the doctors did not know the cause of the impairment. This discrepancy suggests that there are still failures or inadequacies in the communication system between parents and professionals.

Some 80% of the children were reported to have had their sight problem from birth, but in only 27% of cases was it actually suspected and confirmed at or soon after birth. By the age of one, a further 26% of children had had the condition confirmed, and by the second birthday 60% had been confirmed as being severely visually impaired. It is inevitable, given the difficult technical problems involved in some diagnoses, that there will be delays between initial suspicion and final confirmation of the existence of an impairment, and in this respect it is of interest to note that in 58% of the families it was someone in the home, a relative or a neighbour who first suspected the child's visual disability.

The fact that the label 'visual impairment' covers a diverse range of conditions is brought out by the finding that over half of the children had experienced a change in sight level since the onset of the condition. It was not intended to explore the cause of such changes in the survey but one non-controversial conclusion can be stated: regular monitoring must be carried out to ensure that appropriate treatment is available at the optimal time to improve, or prevent the deterioration of, whatever remaining sight the child may have.

Chapter 4, Visual impairment: aids and treatment

For many children, the visually disabling consequences of their impairment can be alleviated by the prescription of lenses and low vision aids which serve to clarify or enlarge the images falling upon the retina. For some people, the improvement in near vision brought about by spectacles and contact lenses can mean being able to use print rather than braille as the medium for reading and writing. For others, the improvement in distance vision can result in their being independently mobile rather than dependent upon sighted guides, guide dogs or electronic mobility devices. Some defects of vision are not amenable to correction by lenses; and for those children with no perception of light, the wearing of glasses would be solely for cosmetic purposes. If the number of children is reduced by the exclusion of the 29 with this severity of impairment, the survey reveals that some three-fifths of the remainder make use of glasses and/or contact lenses, with somewhat greater use being made by those children with no other disabilities and by those in ordinary schools. Although three-quarters of informants reported no problems in obtaining glasses and lenses, just over one-fifth had experienced long waiting periods, difficulties with fitting or problems over costs and obtaining spares.

Low vision aids, ranging from simple hand-held magnifiers to relatively expensive closed-circuit television devices (CCTV), make it possible for many additional tasks to be tackled by those who have poor sight. Only about one-third of the children were reported as using such aids, which increased to about two-fifths for those whose residual vision was better than 'no light perception'. Once the most severely visually impaired children had been excluded, no further differences were found on the basis of degree of residual vision. It is, perhaps, not surprising that most use was reported by the subjects who had no additional disabilities or who were aged 12 years and above. Nevertheless, the question must arise as to whether younger and additionally handicapped children are being sufficiently challenged, and encouraged, to use whatever sight they may have to assist in their learning. The role of the schools and local education authorities is brought out by the finding that almost three-fifths of users obtained their low vision aids from their schools, with nearly one-third reporting the assistance of hospitals in this respect. So far, the local and regional voluntary associations have played little part in this kind of provision; only 1% of users reported help from this source.

It is now generally recognised that it is important to optimise the visual environment, and one of the least expensive ways of achieving this is by means of well-placed lamps and special light-fittings. Only one-fifth of informants indicated that they had had any extra fittings installed at home for their children, with older children being twice as likely to have benefited from additional lighting. Most parents believed that it would not be of help to their children; clearly, there is a need for more expert advice from specialist advisory teachers and ophthalmic opticians.

Elsewhere in this report attention is drawn to parents' expressed needs for information and advice from medical and other professionally qualified specialists. As would be expected, almost all informants (97%) confirmed that their children had been seen at some time by an 'eye specialist' at a hospital or clinic; there was a sharp distinction between the other/no other disability groups, with more of the latter reporting that opticians, school doctors, family doctors and health visitors had been consulted about the children's eyesight problems. The school doctor, optician, and eye specialist were the advisers most likely to have been seen in the past six months. With increase in age, the pattern of visits and consultation changes. Older children are less likely to see specialists, such as health visitors and family doctors, about their visual problems.

Although there was generally a high level of satisfaction expressed over the medical care and treatment of visual impairment, a significant minority (14%) were dissatisfied. Among these, and others who reported any kind of dissatisfaction, the reasons given were the apparent inability of professionals to be of help, their lack of medical knowledge and their failure to answer parents' questions in ways they understood. Both the main survey and pilot work demonstrated that some parents were not merely expressing discontent with poor communication but also with the apparent impossibility of a cure for their child's visual impairment.

Almost two-fifths of parents said that their children had had special operations on their eyes, and sizeable minorities, 15 and 18 percent respectively, were expecting further surgery or were unsure as to whether it would be undertaken in the future. Here, again, was evidence of the long-term worries and anxieties experienced by families whose children have a severe visual impairment.

Chapter 5, Registration

To be registered with a local authority's social services department as blind or partially sighted requires (a) confirmation by a consultant ophthalmologist that certain criteria to do with visual acuities and fields of vision have been met and (b) the agreement of the person concerned to be placed on the register. For adults, registration as a blind person brings entitlement to various statutory rights, such as income tax allowances, social security benefits, free post for embossed literature, reduced television licence fees and instruction in communication and daily living skills. Registration is not, however, an essential prerequisite for access to special educational facilities for children of school age and young people still in education.

Identification of the children involved in this survey was undertaken by their local education authorities and therefore all of them have been recognised as having special educational needs as a result of their visual condition. Registration is not essential for access to special education provision, and this is brought out by the finding that 54% of the parents interviewed had not even heard of the registration system. Ten percent had heard of it, but this had not led to their children being placed on the social services department registers. Among the minority who had been registered, there was a clear-cut tendency for these children to have additional disabilities, to have lower levels of functional residual vision as defined for the survey, and to be in special rather than ordinary schools. Closer analysis of the returns shows that this trend is due almost entirely to the patterning among the registered blind rather than among those children listed on the partially sighted registers.

In the previous chapter, attention was drawn to the diverse range of conditions covered by the label 'visual impairment'. Another aspect of this is highlighted by the fact that the survey's ad hoc, functional definition of levels of residual vision results in some registered blind children being rated as having relatively high levels of residual sight and some registered partially sighted children as having relatively low levels. As long as a child's needs for appropriate low vision aids, for expert tuition in braille or print, and for other specialist input on mobility, daily living and other skills are being met, then the lack of concordance between LEA and social service department records is not important. There must, nevertheless, be a possibility that such discrepancies could result in occasional failure to co-ordinate the inputs of professional advisers (ophthalmologists, educational psychologists, peripatetic teachers). For the child, such a failure could mean a delay in gaining access to the kinds of service that would reduce the handicapping consequences of his/her disability. Registration should be examined to determine whether it should be more extensively 'advertised' and explained. Closer liaison between education and social services departments and a better match between their records could have more than merely administrative advantages.

Of the 104 children who were registered, nearly two-thirds of the blind children had been placed on the registers by the time they were five, but only one-third of the partially sighted had been recorded by the same age. From the parents' viewpoint, there are thought to be few benefits arising from registration (56% could not cite specific examples). Only 9% referred to the provision of educational resources and 7% mentioned the availability of talking books and cassettes. Registration is not seen by most parents as a key or triggering device for obtaining services or support.

Chapter 6, Other disabilities

Fifty-six percent of the sample have other disabilities, and as these additional problems are associated with various physical, mental, sensory and social handicaps, it is clear that this is not a homogenous group of pupils for whom a common curriculum and common teaching methodology will be easy to devise and implement. Even within the minority who have no additional disabilities, there are significant differences in the severity of the visual disability, with some being totally dependent upon touch and hearing for learning and most having useful levels of residual vision. The survey has revealed also a clear-cut tendency for those children who have poorer sight to be more likely to have additional impairments, especially in the areas of communication (hearing and speech), physical integrity and mental functioning. Our still imperfect understanding of how these disabilities interact with one another makes drawing up each child's Statement of educational needs extremely difficult.

In organisational terms, the differences in the number of additional impairments are carried over into school placement: 72% of the children in special schools have multiple disabilities; in ordinary schools, only half that proportion of visually impaired pupils have additional disabilities. The more disabilities a child has, the greater is the likelihood of special school placement, with 46% of children in special schools having 3 or more disabilities, compared with only 4% in ordinary schools.

For over half of the sample, the identification of other disabilities had been made before the first birthday. Eighty percent had been noted as having multiple impairments by their fifth birthday. The importance of early action to mitigate the educationally handicapping sequelae of congenital disabilities is now well recognised. With such a high proportion of these children being identified before the official age for compulsory schooling, it should now be possible to arrange pre-school playgroup and/or nursery provision for the great majority of them in order to assist their perceptual and cognitive development.

The central role of the paediatrician in monitoring non-sight-related problems is brought out by the finding that 48% of the total group of 285 subjects had been seen by a paediatric specialist. This proportion is probably an under-estimate since nearly one-third of the sample had been examined in a hospital assessment unit where paediatricians normally have supervisory responsibilities. With over a quarter of the group having seen a speech therapist and about one-third having been seen by a physiotherapist, we have further evidence of the severity of additional communication and mobility difficulties among these visually impaired children. Closer analysis of the data reinforces the contention that visually impaired childen fall into two distinct groups: those with and those without other disabilities. Among children without other disabilities, only 7, 3 and 9 percent respectively had been seen by speech therapists, occupational therapists and physiotherapists: the corresponding proportions among children with additional non-sight-related disabilities were 42, 25 and 49 percent.

What it has not yet been possible to measure is the efficacy of any treatments that have been provided, even if only in the sense that the child has subsequently been able to receive his/her education in an ordinary school. It would be reassuring to think that the 47% who had seen a speech therapist at some time, but who had had no contact for 12 months or more, were now regarded as not in need of further help. Satisfactory levels of communication skills are essential for academic learning as well as for social and vocational independence. Access to skilled speech therapists with additional, practical experience of the communication problems arising from poor or no vision, is of great relevance to the work being done by parents and teachers, and yet only one-third of those children who had required speech therapy had been seen within the past two weeks, whereas 60% of those requiring physiotherapy had been seen within the same period. Given informants' high level of satisfaction with the quality of health care received by the children, the question arises as to whether more use should be made of the health visitor professionals. In principle, their practice of home-visits can do much to ensure that other experts are called upon when required. Only one-fifth of all the children who had ever been seen by a health visitor had received such a visit in the past six months, and 63% had not been seen for over a year.

Only one-half of the parents stated that they had received an explanation of their child's disability in language they could understand, when they had first been given the news. Only 60% claimed ever to have had an explanation in terms that they could understand. Of the other 40%, three-quarters could not judge whether the disability was ever satisfactorily explained and one-quarter were adamant that it had never been fully laid out and expounded. This is, of course, a matter of great complexity, compounded by the experts' own uncertainty in some areas of causation and prognosis, by the difficulties associated with the place and timing of the explanations, and by the families' own experience and ability in 'cross examining' the experts. While further training of the professionals may be indicated – to bring about a closer match between their technical expertise and their powers of communication – it is vital that parents should feel that they have been helped to understand as fully as possible the nature and implications of their child's disabilities, together with the likely educational and other handicapping consequences. Perhaps what is indicated is a need for an advocate or adviser, drawn from the specialist teacher or the health visitor services. What is surprising, given their 'primary care' role, is how little is done in this respect by family doctors. These findings and those in Chapters 3, 4 and 15 clearly suggest the need for improved communication of information from the various social, health and education professionals to parents of children with disabilities.

Despite the number and severity of the other disabilities among the 159 multi-impaired children, nearly two-fifths of their parents still rated the eyesight problem as the one causing them most current concern. This was over three times as great as the next most frequently reported area of concern – physical handicap. This may reflect the parents' evaluation of the consequences of the visual disability for future learning, social acceptance and vocational success.

Chapter 7, Counselling and advice

More than 60% of parents said that they had nobody knowledgeable to talk to when they first learned of their child's problems; and over 80% said that this was what they had needed most at that time. Health professionals were most likely to be available to talk to. Of the 40% of respondents who had had an early opportunity to discuss the situation, nearly one-third had talked to an eye specialist, a quarter to a paediatrician, and about one-fifth to a health visitor (some parents having seen more than one of these professional advisers). Social workers, education advisers and psychologists had rarely been involved at this stage, and this is presumably because of the generally very early onset of the disabilities when it is the health professions that have the central role. When the topic of special counselling was explored, only 16% of respondents had received such help, with little difference between those whose children had additional disabilities and those where there were no significant complications. Of those families lacking this kind of counselling, nearly 70% reported that they would have welcomed it, and one-third of the families declared that they would still wish to have such help if it were available.

The mis-match between the desire for help and its provision was also revealed in the responses to questions about advice received on problems to do with feeding, toilet training, early mobility and language development. Only 27% of the 233 respondents for whom this was relevant had had such help. Frequency of contact with advisers ranged from weekly (one-third of those who had had this kind of help) to less than once a month (37%), with a tendency for more frequent support for families with a multiply disabled child.

It is the case that people sometimes forget having had help or have not recognised that it was being provided. Nevertheless, this pattern of response is extremely disturbing. It reveals levels of dissatisfaction that must be addressed by the statutory authorities, the various voluntary bodies and the relevant professional organisations. The registration of young children as disabled and/or their placement within the case-load of a health visitor, social worker, physiotherapist, education or other professional adviser are clearly insufficient in terms of ensuring that skilled advice and guidance will be given to the family on a regular and intensive basis, despite the large number of different medical, welfare and education professionals with interest and responsibilities. It may be that improvements are in fact taking place, as suggested by the finding that greater satisfaction with the services is expressed by the parents of the younger children in the sample. An extension of the Warnock Committee's 'Named Person' proposal (DES, 1978) would be one way of enabling parents to activate the kinds of help called for as their child's needs intensify and change.

Few parents (20%) had received genetic counselling, with advice slightly more common in families where the child was multiply impaired or had low residual vision. This is an interesting finding since in most of the special schools and colleges for visually impaired learners, group lectures and individual counselling are provided as part of the 'additional' curriculum for the older students. In other words, the low level of positive response from the parents does not seem to match the advice and knowledge available to their children (at least to those attending schools and colleges for visually impaired children).

The benefits to be derived from contact with other families where there is a disabled child are considerable, and indeed many of today's nationally celebrated organisations, e.g. the Spastics Society, were started by parents banding together for mutual support. The present survey reveals that 60% of parents had met others who had children with sight problems, and three-quarters of these informants had made such contacts by the time their child was 5 years of age. Poorer vision, additional handicaps, and the child's attending a special school were all associated with an increased probability of the parents having met other families like themselves and of their being members of self-help groups. The central role of the school in facilitating these contacts was brought out very clearly in the survey: both numerically and in percentage terms, the special school was most likely to have been the meeting place. With the move towards integrated education, the question must be addressed of how to make the ordinary neighbourhood schools as effective in this respect as the special schools. There have been recent moves to bring regionally-based parent groups together into some kind of loose federation, and this may be a useful mechanism or structure for informing the large minority (40%) of isolated parents about what they may gain from sharing their knowledge and worries with one another.

The final question in the advice and counselling section of the survey asked parents to reflect upon their experience, and list the kinds of support they would have found helpful at the beginning. In an earlier, specific question as to whether they would have liked special counselling, nearly 70% of parents who had not had this help declared they would have liked it. To this final question, only 25% of the total sample answered by mentioning counselling. However, related themes – such as talking to others, explanation of the disabling condition, prediction of what was likely to happen – were all touched upon. This surely highlights the need for all the professional bodies with responsibilities in this field to examine their procedures and their training systems. Such a re-appraisal should take account of how they can enable parents to be of assistance to one another; perhaps this may be most effectively achieved by listening to what existing parents have to say. The fact that only 5% of parents had received all the help they needed is dispiriting in the extreme.

Chapter 8, Daily living skills

Mobility and daily living skills, generally acquired by fully sighted children easily and without the need for formal instruction, are vital for visually impaired children if they are to compete and co-operate successfully with their peers. The developmental nature of some skills (e.g. using stairs, feeding) would be expected to be apparent among the youngest children only and it is predictable therefore that, when the under-fives are excluded from the analysis, there is little difference in competence on the basis of increasing age. Where there is a superiority by children aged 12 and over, as in the ability to make themselves a hot drink and to be independent in bathing, it is no doubt partly due to their age and experience but also to the reluctance of parents to allow younger children to undertake these potentially dangerous tasks unsupervised.

If age is of relatively minor significance in most of the daily living skills surveyed, the effects of other disabilities and poorer vision are, on the other hand, very clear. The handicapping consequences of multiple disabilities are brought out by a numerical index based upon all the eleven tasks examined: the 'index of competence' for children without other disabilities is 96%, compared with 65% for multiply-disabled children. The same index calculated in relation to level of vision is 88% for children with high residual vision and 65% for their low vision counterparts.

As will be shown in Chapter 10, there are strong correlations between school placement (ordinary compared with special schools) and the presence/absence of other disabilities and having higher/lower levels of residual vision. These are reflected here in the relationship between school placement and daily living skills, the index of competence for mainstream school placement being 91% as opposed to 65% for special school placement. The special schools are dealing with children who are on average much less adept in these important skills. This is highlighted in another way: one-quarter of all the special school pupils could carry out fewer than 4 of the 11 tasks; all of the mainstream pupils were able to do four or more of the tasks.

The interaction between additional disabilities and low residual vision is brought out clearly when the indices of competence are compared. While children with better vision but with other disabilities have a lower index (80%) than their counterparts without other disabilities (95%), we see that poorer sight itself reduces the index only slightly (to 93%) for those with no other disabilities, but quite markedly (to 53%) when in conjunction with other disabilities.

The survey indicates that there is in effect an additional, hidden curriculum that has to be provided for visually impaired learners, especially those with other disabilities, in order to equip them to pursue the conventional academic curriculum. Formal mobility instruction is possibly the only part of this extended curriculum that is generally recognised and explicitly timetabled. Public acknowledgement of the other components of the agenda might serve to underline the need for adequate staff/pupil ratios and the importance of the availability of teachers with specialist qualifications.

Chapter 9, Mobility

At the time of the survey, all the 285 children in the sample were aged 3 years and above. Eighty-eight percent of them were reported as being able to walk (85% unaided, 3% with the use of some form of aid). As shown earlier (Chapter 6), 56% of visually impaired children had at least one other handicap, and it is amongst these 159 subjects that we find the non-ambulant children, with one-fifth of the additionally disabled being unable to walk at all (some being able, however, to move around by crawling). The restrictions on learning are compounded further by the clear-cut tendency for these children to have lower levels of residual vision. For the child with severe visual disability, an understanding of what his or her world comprises – the objects and events in it and their qualities and functions – will depend upon his or her ability to feel it, hear it and to smell it.

In the absence of good sight, the child's own active exploration of his world is crucial, and delay in crawling and walking may constitute a secondary handicap. For the sighted infant, the motivation to crawl and walk is triggered to a large extent by visually-perceived stimuli, and most fully sighted children without any physical disability are able to walk by 18 months of age. In our sample, about one-third of the subjects were still not walking by two years of age. Among those without any other disabilites, 24% of those with high residual vision were walking by the age of 12 months, compared with 11% of those with low levels of residual sight, and there is still a difference by the time the second birthday has been reached (90 compared with 79 percent). The presence of other disabilities is also associated with later walking: only 47% of these children were able to walk by the time of their second birthday, compared with 87% of those without additional problems. While formal mobility training is out of place for the very young child, the data now available may suggest that there is a need for more advice and input from paediatricians and physiotherapists to help families to stimulate and encourage crawling and walking in these children as soon as the appropriate skeletal and musculature maturity has been reached.

Over the years, many kinds of visual mobility aids (traditional white canes, guide dogs) and non-visual ones (wheelchairs, walking sticks and frames, crutches) have been designed. Thirty-four percent of the children were reported as using some form of mobility aid, made up of 10% using visual and 24% using non-visual aids, the latter usually being wheelchairs (14%). The survey shows that most of the children, especially those with better residual vision and no other disabilities, do not use mobility aids for physical support or for signalling their impaired sight. However, nearly half (47%) of those with other disabilities do make use of this kind of support, with children with poorer sight among this group making most use of such devices.

While 95% of the children surveyed are said to go out accompanied by an adult every week, and 80% every day, we see the restricting effects of poor residual vision and additional disabilities when there is no adult in attendance. While 58% of those with better vision go out alone at least once a week, only 17% of those with poorer residual vision have this degree of freedom. Fifty-seven percent of those without additional disabilities go out alone at least once a week, compared with only 23% of those with additional disabilities. A similar pattern is seen in relation to going out in the company of other children. Sixty-eight percent of children with higher residual vision go out with other children at least once a week, compared with only 32% of those with poorer sight. Of those without other disabilities, 71% go out in the company of other children at least once a week, compared with only 33% of those with other disabilities. As would be expected, the frequency of travelling unaccompanied by adults increases with the age of the child, but again better vision and the absence of other disabilities are crucial factors. Eighty percent of those aged 12 and over and with high residual vision go out unaccompanied by adults at least once a week, compared with only 27% of the lower vision group of the same age. In the same age group, 75% of those having no additional disabilities go out alone at least once a week, in comparison with only 31% of the children who have other disabilities.

Over the last 25 years, mobility training for blind people has become systematised and there is a profession of mobility instructors (now also called rehabilitation workers). Most special schools for blind children have their own fully-qualified instructors, but some children of secondary school age are taught by mobility officers employed by their local authority's social services department. Twenty-six percent of visually impaired children in our sample had had formal instruction, those with low residual vision being more than twice as likely to be trained than those with better vision (38 and 17 percent); those aged 12 and over were more than twice as likely to have been trained than younger children. Most training had been provided by mobility officers based on the school (67%), and/or by officers employed by the local authority (35%). The role played by the special schools is brought out by the finding that 40% of children in special schools had had mobility training as opposed to 9% in ordinary schools. This is no doubt a reflection of the fact that special schools have a higher proportion of pupils with poorer vision and multiple disabilities than ordinary schools.

Among the parents whose children had not had special training, there were many (52%) who were not in favour of it. Parents may believe that such training is unnecessary for all but totally blind children. The modern urban environment, however, has many dangers for pedestrians, and especially for those with visual impairments. Instruction and practice in the optimal use of residual sight has proved beneficial for many classroom-based tasks, and parents may need to be alerted to the possible advantages of similar skills-training in the outdoor environment.

Chapter 10, School and careers

Historical background

The first school in Great Britain for blind children (and adults) was set up in Liverpool in 1791, and during the next 100 years many other private and charitable foundations were established. In 1889, the Royal Commission on the Blind and Deaf recommended that elementary education be made compulsory for blind children between the ages of 5 and 16, and this was implemented in two Acts of Parliament: the Education of Blind and Deaf Mute Children (Scotland) Act, 1890, and the Elementary Education (Blind and Deaf Children) Act, 1890, for England and Wales. It was not until the twentieth century that special provision was made for partially sighted learners, and by the mid-1930s a Board of Education Committee of Inquiry was specifically asking that such children should be taught in ordinary schools whenever possible and not in classes for blind children. The Handicapped Pupils and Special Schools Regulations 1945, following the Education Act, 1944, made partially sighted children a new and separate category of handicapped pupils. The 1945 Regulations (amended in 1959) defined these children as pupils whose defective vision prevented them from following the normal regime of ordinary schools 'without detriment to their sight'. Until the 1970s, many multi-impaired blind children assessed as having severe additional mental disabilities and/or behavioural problems were in the care of health authorities. The Education (Handicapped Children) Act of 1970 empowered the local education authorities to take over the care of these children who now became entitled under the Act to special education. The next significant advance came when the Warnock Committee (DES, 1978) recommended that the statutory categorisation of handicapped pupils should be abolished, with educational provision being based henceforth upon a detailed description of the child's educational needs. Where possible, these needs were to be met within ordinary schools. These, and related, matters were addressed in part in the 1981 Education Act. The present survey may be seen as picking up some of the changes and consequences arising from the 1981 Act and its immediate predecessors.

Type of school attended

At the time of the enquiry, 271 of the children surveyed were at school, only 13% being weekly or whole-term boarders. Fifty-three percent were in some form of ordinary school, e.g. the neighbourhood school, or a local school with a little specialist support in the form of equipment and visits from a specialist teacher, or an area school further away from home where there were other visually impaired pupils, equipment, and specialist teacher(s). Twenty-two percent were in special day or residential schools for visually impaired pupils, and 24% were in other kinds of schools specialising in the needs of handicapped children.

The survey has shown that the degree of residual vision and the presence of additional disabilities are key factors in school placement. Sixty-five percent of the pupils in ordinary schools are rated as having higher levels of residual vision, whereas 69% of those in some form of special schooling are assessed as having lower levels of vision. Seventy-six percent of the visually impaired pupils in ordinary schools have no other disabilities, while 64% of those in special schools have at least one additional disability. It can be argued that the two types of schooling (ordinary and special) are still catering in large measure for two different categories of children.

There may be some tentative evidence of a changing pattern, perhaps as a result of the 1981 Education Act. Among the older children, aged 12 and over, for whom special schooling was likely to be the norm when they started their education, only 22% of those rated as having poorer vision are in ordinary schools; among the younger children, who started school after the 1981 Act, 39% of those with poorer vision are in ordinary schools. It may be the case that primary schools are being influenced by the move towards integrated education and are now slightly more willing to accept children with greater impairment of sight.

Most non-disabled children change schools at some time, usually between the ages of 10 and 12 when they transfer from primary to secondary education. Seventy-five percent of the children sampled for this investigation had attended at least one other school before their current one. Of these, 16% at present in an ordinary school had transferred from a special school whereas 39% now in a special school had previously been in an ordinary school; in other words, there was a somewhat greater likelihood of a transfer from ordinary to special than the reverse.

In answer to a question about the preferred school placement for their children, some form of ordinary schooling (either neighbourhood or area school with special resources) was chosen by a majority of parents, with a sizeable minority of 35% opting for a special school placement. Parents preferring an ordinary school usually gave a social justification (to do with opportunities for mixing with sighted children), while those

16

preferring a special school mentioned the availability of specialist teachers and equipment. Parents whose children were more severely disabled were more likely to cite the specialist provision/resources argument, and as already shown, more children with multiple disabilities attend special schools.

Two-thirds of the parents were of the opinion that they had had some influence in the choice of school for their children but there was still a sizeable minority (24%) who considered that their own views were given little or no attention. Overall, two-thirds also reported that they were very satisfied with their child's placement – 60% among those with children in ordinary schools and 75% among those with children in special schools.

Mode of travel

Of the 237 day pupils, 60% get to school in 20 minutes or less and 81% within half-an-hour. About one-quarter of day pupils normally travel to school on foot, and over half travel by transport that has been provided ('school bus or taxi'). All the boarders use some form of motorised transport. Most of the children are accompanied when going to school, one-third of the day school attenders travelling with a family member or friend, and 40% with an escort. Perhaps surprisingly, 29% of boarders usually travel unaccompanied. Among day children and boarders the proportion travelling alone, as would be expected, rises with age: 12% among those in the youngest group, 27% among the 8 – 11 year olds, and 47% among those aged 12 and over. The demands on family members are greatest when the child is young: 55% of the 3 – 7 year olds are accompanied by someone in the house, the figures falling to 33% among the 8 – 11 year olds, and 12% among children aged 12 and over.

Statement of educational needs

The Statement (Record in Scotland) is the means by which a child's education needs are defined. Its relatively recent introduction is perhaps made clear by the finding that 50% of the parents of children aged 3 – 11 knew what a formal Statement was as opposed to only 39% of the parents of older children. Overall, no more than 45% of the sample claimed to know about the Statementing procedure. The situation is not quite so pessimistic as this figure suggests, since 63% had in fact received documents showing that an assessment of need had been made. Families where the child had other disabilities, and/or poorer vision, and/or was in a special school were more likely to have had a written record of assessment. The Statements, from which recommendations regarding educational placements are made, can be appealed against if parents are dissatisfied with the outcome. It is, of course, useful to have someone outside the family with whom to discuss the matter. Most of those who had received a written assessment of their child's needs knew of the appeal procedure (68%); however, most (59%) had not discussed the Statement's implications with people outside the family such as educational psychologists and advisory teachers.

Sports, pastimes and friendships

Eighty-three percent of parents reported that their children participated in some form of sports activity at school, with swimming the most frequently mentioned (45%). Higher levels of participation were reported among children with other disabilities and lower levels of residual vision; this is largely explicable in terms of the schools attended, since 59% of children in special schools went swimming as opposed to 29% in ordinary schools. The ordinary schools were also less successful in arranging non-sporting hobbies and pastimes: 46% of their pupils were reported as having no school-organised interests as against 34% in the special schools, the main difference being the extra opportunities offered in the special schools for listening to music. Some 25% of the children took part in clubs and activities organised by their schools during out-of-school time, and among the reasons parents gave for non-participation the most frequently cited was the absence of any such activities (32%), with ordinary schools being more frequently mentioned in this respect than the special schools.

Seventy-six percent of the children had close friends at school. The absence of other disabilities, higher levels of residual vision, and attendance at an ordinary school are all factors associated with an increased likelihood of having a close friend at school, and of playing with such a friend outside school hours and during school holidays. We see here some of the socially handicapping concomitants of severe disabilities and some of the outcomes of attending a special school located outside the child's home area.

Parental involvement and satisfaction with resources

Contacts between parents and schools were frequent, with 59% of parents reporting contacts occurring at least once a month; fewer than 10% of them expressed dissatisfaction with the amount of contact they had with their child's teachers.

For the 151 children with additional disabilities, parental satisfaction with the school's resources for meeting the special needs of the children differed markedly with type of school placement. Fifty-nine percent of parents whose multi-handicapped children attended an ordinary school were fairly or very satisfied with the level of resourcing; the corresponding figure for parents of children in special schools was 83%. It seems clear that there is still considerable scope for

18

improvement in the quantity and quality of resources available to many of those multi-handicapped children for whom an ordinary school placement is the preferred option.

Probably the most important 'resource' is the teacher with specialist qualifications. Sixty-five percent of the children were said to be taught by a specialist, with a larger proportion (72%) in special schools than in ordinary schools (56%). Most of the specialists operating in ordinary schools were said to be visiting teachers, i.e. they were not based in the school itself, and although 73% of children in special schools saw the specialist every day, only 10% of those in ordinary schools had such a high frequency of contact.

Prospects for the child at school and work

The parents had positive attitudes towards their children's future careers at school and work. Two-thirds reported that their children either already had taken or were expected to take public examinations. The parents' expectations for children with additional disabilities, with poorer vision, and placements in special schools were less optimistic, but even within these categories the survey revealed that between 29% and 45% of parents were expecting their children to take some form of public examination at school. Among the pupils who had taken or were expected to take these examinations, 66% were considered by their parents as likely to go on to some form of further education after the end of compulsory schooling. Parents of children with additional disabilities expressed somewhat less confidence about the prospects of their children going on to further education; 58% of them had such expectations as opposed to 71% of the parents of children without any other disabilities.

Parents of children aged 11 and over were asked about help from careers advisers. Twenty-six percent reported that their children had seen a careers adviser, another 26% did not know, and the remaining 48% said their children had not had such advice (presumably the schools would say it was too soon for the youngest adolescents). Many parents (37%) were unable to choose between a normal and a sheltered workplace when asked which type they considered would be most suitable for their child. While 10% favoured a sheltered setting for the child, the majority, 54%, considered that a place where most people did not have sight problems or other disabilities would be best. No other disabilities, better vision, and attendance at an ordinary school were all factors closely associated with a preference for a normal work place. The long-term stress felt by parents whose children had additional disabilities is no doubt being expressed among the 59% of them who could not decide which type of placement would be best.

Desired features and effects of schooling

When given a list of items concerned with features of schooling and the possible outcomes of a good education, 55% of respondents attached great importance to class work suited to the child's own rate of working, 54% to the presence of teachers with an understanding of visual handicap, 42% to good opportunities to integrate into the community when leaving school and 38% to their child having the chance to grow up with friends in the locality. Despite the anxieties and difficulties that most parents must have experienced about the welfare of their disabled children, it is perhaps noteworthy that 'sheltered surroundings' within the education system were considered by 47% of all parents as being least important for their child.

Chapter 11, Reading and writing

Given that the criteria for being registered as blind range upwards from no sight whatsoever to 3/60 Snellen (or even higher on the Snellen scale if there is a significant restriction in the size of the field of vision), it is perhaps not surprising that some 60% of the children in the survey were reported as being able to read or write print. The patterning within the sub-groups is clear. The proportion of children in ordinary schools who read and write print is more than twice as great as in special schools (82 and 35 percent respectively). Double the proportion of children with no additional disabilities can read and write print compared with their multiply-disabled counterparts (79 and 38 percent respectively), and there is a similar preponderance of those who can read and write print in the higher residual vision group (75 compared with 37 percent in the lower residual vision group). Some of the multiply-disabled children are effectively debarred from reading print because of their mental handicaps rather than their impaired sight. A larger proportion of older (63%) than younger (50%) children can read and write print.

The relatively large proportion of children (43%) with low residual vision who were reported to be print readers testifies to the importance of distinguishing between distance and near vision acuities when decisions are being made in infant and junior schools as to the selection of the optimal reading medium (braille or print). Indeed, the eye's powers of accommodation in children make it quite feasible for many of these visually impaired learners to tackle print of normal size. In the survey, it is shown that 41% of the total sample (69% of the print readers) could read normal-sized print. Further evidence of the different 'populations' being catered for in the ordinary and the special schools was to be seen in the different proportions of users of normal print: 68% in ordinary schools and 18% in special schools.

Fourteen percent of the children were braille readers. Among those aged 3 – 11 the proportion was 11%, and this increased to 18% among the older children. Poorer residual vision and attendance at a special school are factors associated with a higher likelihood of using braille: only 3% of the higher residual vision group could read braille compared with 26% of those with poorer sight (including, of course, those who were completely blind); 5% of the children in ordinary schools read braille, compared with 22% of those in special schools. Although so few pupils were braillists, it is interesting to observe that the parents of a sizeable minority of the non-braillists (17%) expected their children to learn the code in due course, with greater probabilities among children in special schools and with poorer residual vision. In many cases this expectation must be based on a prognosis of deteriorating sight. Since braille makes bigger cognitive and perceptual demands on the learner, the question must be asked as to whether it would be advisable for these children to be started on the code at an earlier age, even if this might entail learning print and braille simultaneously.

The teaching of braille is not evenly distributed between the two types of schooling: braille is reported as being taught in their schools for 5% of pupils currently in mainstream schools and for 47% of pupils in special schools. It should not be inferred from this that the opportunities for learning braille are less favourable in ordinary schools; the disparity is more likely to be due to the higher proportion in these schools of children who do not need braille on account of their better vision. Nevertheless, there may be some grounds for concern, or at least for monitoring the availability of braille teaching, in the light of those responses which show that braille is not currently being taught in schools where 11% of the pupils are said to be likely to need it in due course, and in those where 22% of informants are not sure as to whether braille will be needed at some time in the future. It is crucial that the teaching of braille, by qualified, skilled and experienced teachers, should be readily available in ordinary schools for any child who has a need for it.

One-fifth of the children are reported as using a typewriter at home, no other reading or writing aid being cited as frequently as this. Much more extensive use is made of such devices within the schools, with age now becoming a key factor: about two-fifths of children aged 12 and over used a typewriter at school as opposed to one-tenth of younger children. Either the availability of the devices or their need must account for the significantly greater use in special schools where 54% of pupils used some form of braille or print reading and writing aid compared with 25% in ordinary schools. There is also a clear-cut tendency for children with poorer vision to make greater use in school of typewriters, wordprocessors, closed-circuit television magnifiers and braille-writers. The presence or absence of other disabilities was not a determining factor in the use of aids.

There is much argument as to whether the age of micro-computer technology will have beneficial repercussions on the employment prospects of disabled people. The survey shows that 36% of this sample of visually impaired children are already using computers in their own homes, another 6% having them but not using them. Within the schools, there is an even greater proportion (68%) using these devices. There is little difference between types of school, but 17% of parents of children in special schools reported not knowing whether their children use computers at school, and this contrasts with only 6% 'don't knows' among parents of children in ordinary schools. More 'don't knows' were also to be found among parents of children with poorer vision and with other disabilities, presumably because more of these children were to be found in special than in ordinary schools.

Chapter 12, Leisure and holidays

Fewer than half (48%) of the children were reported as participating in sporting activities outside their schools, contrasted with 83% engaged in such activities at school. Swimming was again the most favoured sport. Overall, just under one-third pursued this particular pastime, and there were no significant differences between the sub-groups, a finding which is in contrast to the significantly higher participation in swimming during school hours by the more severely disabled, poorer vision children and those in special schools. For the second most frequently reported activity, rugby/soccer, where 16% were reported as participants, there were significant differences, with greater participation being reported for children with no other disabilities, higher residual vision, and placement in an ordinary school.

A wide range of other out-of-school hobbies and interests was highlighted by the survey, but only one reached a double figure percentage, viz. listening to music, listed for 15% of children. Overall, the most clear-cut difference was between those without and those with additional disabilities, 80% of the former compared with 58% of the latter having at least one out-of-school hobby or pastime. The same pattern of greater involvement was found among children with high compared with low residual vision (72 and 63 percent respectively) and in ordinary compared with special schools (74 and 63 percent respectively). There were also the expected age-related differences in both sports and other hobbies, the greater maturity and independence of the older children allowing them more opportunities to participate in, and choose from, the variety of activities.

Over three-quarters of the children were said to have close friends at school (Chapter 10) but this falls to 63% for friends living in the home locality. Differences within the groups are large; children with no other disabilities, better vision, and in ordinary schools have more locally-based friends than their sub-group counterparts (81 and 49 percent; 78 and 46 percent; and 85 and 44 percent respectively). Attendance at a residential special school for visually impaired pupils was shown in

Chapter 10 to be more common for children aged 12 and over than for younger children; this may account for the finding that a larger proportion of younger than older children have friends living locally (63 compared with 47 percent). Within the local community, there is no evidence to suggest that visually impaired children are segregated from their fully-sighted peers, since only 2% of informants reported that all their children's neighbourhood friends were themselves visually impaired.

While 98% of the children go on visits outside the home with their families, this drops to 35% when accompanied by friends only, and to 22% for totally unaccompanied journeys. Families take their visually impaired children on many kinds of outings, shopping being the most frequently mentioned activity (88% of informants). However, only 21% of the children go shopping, for example, with their friends and without adults in attendance; those with additional disabilities, poorer sight, and in special schools are much less likely to do this. There are also differences related to the presence of other disabilities and lower residual vision for visits with friends or alone to playgrounds, swimming pools, sports centres and cinemas. As could be predicted, there is a massive increase in friends-only and totally unaccompanied visiting among children aged 12 and over, but even here poorer levels of residual vision and additional disabilities are seen to impose constraints upon the children's independence.

A majority of parents (58%) reported experiencing problems when visiting places with their children, and these were more common for children with poorer sight. Within this sub-group 71% of parents stated that their children had problems. 'Unfamiliar surroundings' was the single most frequently cited problem within each group (14% overall). This is probably seen as primarily a problem for the child, whereas some of the others may be problems as much for the families themselves; among these would be 'people's behaviour', 'behaviour tantrums', 'having to watch', and 'feeding/special food'. For the child with no other disabilities, 'getting close to see' was mentioned more than any other problem (15%). It cannot be the case that this is a trivial problem for the multiply-disabled (3%) and the lower residual vision (6%) sub-groups but rather that there are even graver difficulties for them – to do with physical access, safety, and the feeding and behavioural problems – that have to be coped with by the parents.

Thirty-seven percent of the children are said to belong to some kind of neighbourhood club or society, with the main difference being between the no other disabilities sub-group (44%) and their multiply-disabled counterparts (31%). Brownies/cubs and similar organisations are attended by 12% of the children, those without other disabilities (18%) being more likely to be members than those with additional problems (8%). There is also a higher membership of the Physically Handicapped and Able Bodied (PHAB) clubs among more severely disabled children.

Among the substantial minority (37%) who go to local clubs and societies, four-fifths are members of what might be called integrated associations, i.e. not exclusively for disabled people; but even here there is a preponderance of children without other disabilities, with higher levels of residual vision and with placements in ordinary schools.

Only 6% of all informants reported having had problems in gaining membership of an association for their child, 44% responding with a straight 'no', and 50% saying that they had not applied for membership. It is not entirely clear whether there is a reluctance to seek membership of integrated clubs on the part of parents of children with additional disabilities, but among the few who have encountered difficulties, an unwillingness by the club to accept responsibility for the child appeared to be the cause of the rejection.

Eighty-two percent of informants had taken their children on holiday, a larger proportion of children without other disabilities (91%) than those with other disabilities (76%). Most holidays comprised some kind of self-catering (including camping and caravanning). Perhaps something of the difficulties experienced by families with multiply disabled children is expressed by their lower use (18%) of guest house and hotel holidays, compared to their counterparts whose children have no other disabilities (34%).

Well over half the children (57%) had been on holiday without their parents, those aged 12 and over being more than twice as likely to have done this than their younger counterparts. The most commonly mentioned organiser of such holidays was the child's school, and of the 57% who had had holidays without their parents, 57% had gone with their schools. Special schools (66%) were more likely to be the arrangers of these holidays than ordinary schools (42%). Relatives (17%), friends (4%), and organisations like the Scouts (8%) were also mentioned as the providers/arrangers of holidays and they tended to take those children without additional disabilities. Organisations for the blind and for other disabilities were each responsible for providing holidays for about 3% of the children who had been away without their parents. Hospitals and residential homes (6%) were notable for the fact that they concentrated solely on those children who had other disabilities, poorer vision, and placement in a special school.

Knowledge of the kinds of special holiday provided by social services/ educational authorities and organisations for disabled people was reported by only 38% of the informants, with greater familiarity shown by families whose children were multiply disabled, had poorer vision, and were in special schools. Even among the minority who knew of such holidays, no more than 28% had availed themselves of the service. These represented about 11% of the total sample. Another 31% of the whole group thought that such holidays would be suitable for their children, with greater endorsement coming from the families with more severely disabled children. There is an obvious need for greater publicity to be given to this facility.

Only 28% of parents reported using holiday play schemes available in their localities, and there was a tendency for these facilities to be used rather more by children with other disabilities and in special schools. The main providers were the local education authorities and the social services departments. Few facilities were provided by local voluntary societies for handicapped people, and even fewer by local societies for visually impaired people. There is massive scope for the extension of these facilities.

The importance of 'respite care' – having the child looked after while the family takes a holiday or other break from the daily routine and strain of caring for all of his/her basic needs – requires no emphasizing. About half (49%) of the families in the survey said that they had opportunities for such breaks. The greater the severity of the child's disability, visually and otherwise, the more likely was the family to have been given some sort of break from care. Of those who had received this kind of help, one-quarter (35 families) reported it as coming through the local social and welfare services departments, whose services were provided mainly for the additionally disabled, those with poorer vision, and in special schools. However, the main providers of respite care are relatives, and the pattern of service is slightly different from that provided by statutory welfare departments; that is, relatives provide rather more help for families whose children have fewer additional disabilities and who are in ordinary schools. Among those families that had never received help through the statutory welfare services, the majority (76%) said that they did not want such help, and this is more noticeable in families whose children are less severely disabled.

Chapter 13, Special toys and games

Toys and games serve many purposes in a child's development. They are part of a child's external physical world which has to be understood, manipulated and controlled. The ways in which children use them can also tell us much about their changing emotional and social needs. For the blind child, many features of the physical environment are difficult to apprehend: the totality of a car, the height of a tree, the distances between objects cannot be taken in in a single 'glance'. Those toys (such as dolls, toy cars and animals) which are in effect models of real-life objects allow the child to perceive the relationships among the component parts of their full-scale counterparts. They may be an important intermediate stage in the process by which children learn that external phenomena can be variously represented, by means, for example, of words, models and two-dimensional drawings. Even with the youngest babies, parents typically use toys to attract attention, to encourage interest in and curiosity about the world beyond the body and to develop early receptive language skills. The importance of these activities for blind or severely visually impaired children cannot be over-stated. Restricted access to objects and events beyond their immediate tactual reach may result in delays in arriving at some developmental milestones, and reduced opportunities for the kind of casual, unstructured learning available to their fully-sighted peers. Toys and the willingness of parents to use them can help to overcome or avoid these potentially handicapping consequences of the disability.

Help and advice about suitable toys and games are reported as having been received by a significant minority (41%) of parents. There are marked differences within the groups, with more parents of multiply disabled, low vision, and special school children stating that they had received such support. However, only in the multiply-disabled sub-group does the proportion of those getting advice exceed half (52%), and this is increased within the combined low residual vision, multiply-disabled sub-group where 57% of parents reported having been helped. The most frequently cited sources of advice are peripatetic teachers (21%) and schools (20%). Given the importance of early support for reducing the handicapping effects of congenital visual and other impairments, it is questionable whether school-based sources are adequate since they will rarely be involved in relation to children below the age of two years. The evidence is that there is considerable scope for improvement in the provision of both advice and services. The expansion of toy libraries, development of LEA visual impairment advisory services and the establishment of appropriately supported parents groups would all contribute to this improvement.

If attention is directed to use, as opposed to advice, then 55% of all families reported not having used special toys, and a further 3% didn't know. Within the groups, there is evidence that the families whose children have other disabilities, poorer vision, and placements in special schools make more extensive use of these toys, the respective sub-group totals being 47 and 36, 53 and 31, and 53 and 28 percent.

Only one (puzzles and jigsaws) of the eight categories of toys specially designed for children with sight problems had been used by as many as 25% of the families, and the overall figure, based upon use of at least one of the categories, is 42%, with higher overall use reported for children in special schools, with low residual vision, and with additional disabilities as compared with their sub-group counterparts.

Ordinary toy shops were the main source of toys and games for 32% of the families, with RNIB (25%) being the individual supplier most frequently reported among that large minority of families (42%) who had used special toys and games. Two-thirds of users had bought the toys, the other one-third having borrowed them from their education and social services authorities, schools and toy libraries. Among these users, one-third said that they had experienced difficulty in getting them.

Chapter 14, Radio, television, tape players and telephones

Very high proportions of the children in all groups are reported to like listening to the radio (88%) and watching/listening to television programmes (92%). On the radio, all groups show an overwhelming preference for music as compared with 'talks' programmes. The popularity of television is such that almost 100% watch it among children without additional disabilities, with high residual vision, and in ordinary schools. The somewhat lower proportions (87, 86 and 86 percent) among their sub-group counterparts still show the great attractions of this communication/entertainment medium, but here we are seeing significantly more families reporting either that their children do not watch/listen to television or that they do not know what the situation is.

Audio tape-recorder devices provide opportunities for learning and entertainment, and over four-fifths of the children use one or other of these machines. Talking books, used by 6% of the children in all, tend to be used more by children with low residual vision (11%) than by children with high residual vision (1%), but there is no difference between them in their use of the various kinds of conventional cassette devices. Among the possible explanations of the lower use of radio cassettes and music centres by children with multiple disabilities is the greater complexity of the controls and switches. Ordinary cassette players and walkman devices seem to be used equally by both these sub-groups. As might be expected, the older children listened to their tape machines more often than the younger ones, but more frequent use was also made of them by pupils in special schools (77%) compared with 56% in ordinary schools, and by those with poorer vision (78% compared with 56% with high residual vision).

Having looked at preference for music and talks on the radio, we also examined usage in relation to tapes. Eighty-eight percent used their tape machines for listening to music and 57% were reported as using them for listening to stories; only 2% specifically mentioned educational use. There was a trend for the low vision children to use their tapes more for listening to stories (63%), compared with 52% of children with high residual vision. Possibly the latter have somewhat easier access to stories in print. This may also be the explanation for the reduced use of tapes for listening to stories by children in ordinary schools (53%) as compared with their peers in special schools (64%). Such inferences must, however, be regarded with some caution because they do not fully accord with the finding that those using tapes very frequently, i.e. on a daily basis, do not listen to stories as often as those who use tapes rather less frequently (53 and 64 percent respectively).

As yet, only a minority of parents overall (29%) record materials for their children to listen to. Among those families with children having poorer vision, the proportion rises to 38%, but is lower (21%) among their counterparts whose children have better sight. Television and radio programmes, school lessons, house and garden sounds and people talking are the content of most of these specially recorded programmes; in each particular case, the families with children with poorer vision are more likely to make such recordings. Children who use tape players every day are also more likely to have these kinds of recordings made for them. Presumably, the children's needs/demands increase the range and frequency of recording of materials prepared; alternatively, families interested in doing these things, and convinced of their value, may be encouraging their children to make greater use of tapes.

Parents reported using a variety of suppliers of tapes, the most frequently mentioned being commercial organisations (86%), a figure that is probably an underestimate since 34% state that family and friends also give tapes, many of which would have been obtained from local retailers. One difference that emerged was between the two residual vision sub-groups: 13% of children with low residual vision obtain tapes from the RNIB Talking Book Service whereas no more than 3% of those with high residual vision make use of this source.

Eighty-seven percent of the families reported having a telephone in the home. In these homes, 55% of the children telephoned out and took calls; a further 17% took calls, and 2% used it only for making calls. Overall, then, 74% of the children in families where a telephone was installed used it. The handicapping consequences of the disabilities are brought out very starkly: 80% of children without additional disabilities made and received calls as against only 36% of those who were multiply disabled. A similar pattern was found among the residual vision sub-groups (67 and 43 percent) and the school placement sub-groups (73 and 41 percent): those with better vision and in ordinary schools are in the majority in each case.

Chapter 15, Information

The importance of adequate and timely information – medical, welfare, management, educational – cannot be over-stated. Children's needs are continually changing, and the absence of good information about how to meet these needs can entail not only an immediate disadvantage to the child but also intense frustration to the parent seeking to understand what is happening and to prevent any potential long-term handicap. The ideal solution would be the appointment of a single 'named person' for each disabled child, such a person being one of the various professionals who have a specific responsibility for some aspects of the child's well-being. The named person would be accessible by the family and would act both as a source of immediate information as well as a means whereby other information sources could be reached and activated. In the absence of such a key person, families are currently obliged to spend, and perhaps waste, time and energy as they try to discover the information they may need desperately.

The survey has revealed that the local education authority and the child's school are the most frequently mentioned purveyors of information, 46% of the informants citing this particular source. This is more clearly the case for those families whose children have not been registered as visually impaired. When parents were then asked to list the most important sources of information, talking to teachers and talking to medical experts were given equal prominence, 61% of informants citing each of these two groups. It may seem surprising that the medical experts were mentioned by larger percentages of parents whose children were less severely disabled and not registered than by parents of children with more severe disabilities and who had been registered with the authorities.

Other parents were another significant source of information, with almost half (49%) of all informants mentioning this. Parents of younger children and those with more severely disabled children were likely to obtain knowledge and advice in this way, and the large disparity between ordinary and special schools (36 and 59 percent respectively) is probably due to there being fewer parents with similarly disabled children in most mainstream schools (see Chapter 10). The increase in the numbers of parent support groups in recent years may explain why parents with younger children are exchanging information with one another more extensively than families with older children.

Less than half (45%) of informants mentioned books and leaflets as ways of informing themselves, but these are more commonly used by parents of non-registered children (51 compared with 33 percent); their less frequent contact with the social service workers may account for their greater reliance upon printed materials. That there is an inadequate supply of such materials is shown by the fact that 57% of parents said that they would like more information in printed form, which increased to 74% among parents with younger children.

RNIB is listed by no more than 16% of families, but those whose children have poorer sight (21%) rely upon it more than those whose children have higher levels of residual vision.

In his paper 'Parents Talking' (Langdon, 1970), the author quotes one couple's complaint: 'We felt that we have always had to do the searching to find out all that is available . . . there may be quite a few people who wouldn't know where to start.' This was taken up in the present survey and 76% of the respondents felt that they had had to go out and search for everything themselves. Medical advice, information about special education provision and entitlement to benefits were the most frequently mentioned subjects about which the respondents considered that they had had to go out and search for advice. There is clearly still much to be done to ensure that parents have the kinds of information they need; in addition to expert advice direct from the specialists, there is perhaps room for more pamphlets/leaflets dealing with particular topics.

Only 17% of informants reported finding any organisations useful to them for learning about their children's problems, RNIB being the only spontaneously named organisation by 16 people. When presented with a list of specific ways of obtaining information, a rather different pattern emerged.

Sixty-seven percent had visited a hospital, 44% a school for handicapped children, 29% an assessment centre, and 8% a centre run by RNIB; 'talking to experts' had been in the list and 50% of the sample said that this had been a means of acquiring information, while 'talking to families with similar children' was noted by 36%. A 'visit to a school for handicapped children' showed marked differences within the groups. Parents of children with multiple disabilities, with poorer vision, and in special schools are much more likely to have used this particular source than their group counterparts, and the biggest difference is in the school placement category: over three-fifths of parents with children in special schools have used this source of information, compared with only a fifth of parents whose children are in ordinary schools.

It is worth noting that when informants were presented with a list of possible sources of information, some 86% said that they had used at least one of them, whereas to the earlier, unprompted, open-ended question no more than 17% said that they had found any organisation of help.

As to the actual usefulness of these sources of information, 82% of those visiting a special school, 74% of those visiting a hospital, 68% of those visiting an assessment centre, and 33% of those going to an RNIB centre had found the visit useful. Seventy-nine percent of those who had talked to experts and 85% of those who had talked to other families had found these talks useful. About half who had seen a special film considered it to be useful.

Seventy-four percent of informants said that they knew of RNIB before being invited to participate in the survey, with greater familiarity shown by parents of children with lower levels of residual vision (80%) as opposed to parents whose children had better vision (68%). Precise knowledge of what RNIB does or provides varies in extent and accuracy among the 74% who know of it at all. Nearly one-third of this group knew about the supply of gadgets and aids, 27% knew about schools and training centres, while less than 20% spontaneously mentioned each of general advice/help, Talking Books, braille services, and training for blind and partially sighted people. Twelve percent thought, wrongly, that RNIB provided/trained guide dogs. Parents of more severely disabled children tended to be more knowledgeable about RNIB services.

When presented with a list of services available from RNIB and elsewhere for children with impaired vision, 85% of the sample thought RNIB provided braille books, 76% special toys and aids and 68% schools. The other correctly identified provision recognised by more than half of the informants was the further education and training service. Fifty-five percent incorrectly named guide dogs for blind children as an RNIB service.

Awareness and knowledge of an organisation's services are not necessarily identical with their use. Some 37% of the sample do use one or more RNIB services, users being more likely among children with low residual vision and in special schools than among their group counterparts. Being registered as visually impaired is also associated with greater use of the various services provided by RNIB.

What is now obvious is that there is still considerable scope for increasing the awareness of RNIB's services among the families of visually impaired children, and not just among those families whose children have poorer levels of residual vision or have placements in ordinary schools. About one-fifth of those who knew of these services had gained this information from the general media (radio, television, newspapers); the next most frequently mentioned sources, among many, were social and welfare workers and schools and teachers. Only 7% of those knowing about these services had been directly contacted by RNIB staff. It is worth noting that 75% of those who reported being aware of RNIB declared that they did not expect RNIB to contact them with offers of help and advice.

Chapter 16, Accommodation

Just under half (48%) of informants had been in their present dwelling for 7 years or more, and two-thirds had moved since the discovery of their child's disabilities. The most frequently mentioned reason for moving was the desire for a larger house or more space, with relatively few people spontaneously giving reasons to do with the child's disabilities. When prompted with child-related reasons, 41% cited one or more of those that were used as examples. Informants with children having other disabilities and/or lower residual vision were much more likely to attribute the move to an attempt to meet the children's needs than were those whose children were not so severely disabled. A similar pattern of response emerged in connection with changes made to the house to make life easier for the child; one-quarter of all respondents stated that they had made such adaptations.

These findings suggest that severe disabilities have consequences for the family as a whole, not the least of which are the financial burdens that may arise owing to the need to move or adapt the dwelling place.

Chapter 17, Demographics, social security benefits and income

The families participating in the enquiry are similar to the general population in terms of the proportions buying and renting their homes. As in all households with dependent children, there are few (8%) where the house is already owned outright, with no encumbering mortgage. Most respondents (81%) were married, the rest being single (3%), widowed (4%), or separated/divorced (13%).

The ethnic origin of the respondents, but not of the children, was recorded, and this showed that 93% were 'white', 1% 'black, Afro-Caribbean', 4% 'Asian, Indian/Pakistani' and 2% 'other'.

In about one-fifth of the households there was at least one other person with a visual disability.

The OPCS surveys of disability (e.g. Meltzer, Smyth and Robus, 1989) show generally greater prevalence of disability among boys than girls (60 and 40 per cent respectively). The present enquiry shows a similar distribution for visual impairment (64 and 36 percent), with a markedly greater disparity among those aged 12 years and over (70 and 30 percent).

Various kinds of social security and other benefits/allowances are available to individuals and households. Ninety-one percent of informants confirmed that they were in receipt of child benefit; if this particular allowance is excluded, some two-thirds of the families received benefits of one kind or another (housing, supplementary, unemployment, invalidity, attendance, mobility, etc.). Some of these benefits are, of course, not related to the specific needs of the visually impaired child in the family, but it seems likely that the most frequently mentioned allowances, attendance and mobility, are being paid as a result of the child's disabilities. Nearly half (48%) of the families received these two allowances, with greater take-up observed in families with younger children (aged 3 – 11), and where the children are registered as visually impaired, have other disabilities, lower levels of residual vision and are in special schools. The survey has shown that with child benefit excluded, four-fifths of families whose children fall into the most severely disabled categories are receiving some form of financial support.

At the time of the fieldwork (1988), at least three-fifths of the households reported incomes (salaries and allowances after the deduction of any taxes) below the then UK average of £233 per week, and 64% had savings of less than £1,000. It is impossible to quantify with any great precision the additional financial costs that are incurred by a family with a disabled child; nevertheless, there is evidence here that a majority of the families can be described as coping with below average financial resources.

Chapter 18, Method

Wide-ranging discussions within RNIB and with external consultants were carried out to determine the topics and themes to be explored in the survey, and pilot interviews were undertaken to validate the content and the methods. Parents were designated as the target population on the grounds of their intimate knowledge of the development and changing needs of the children concerned. However, the stratified sampling procedures adopted were based upon local education authorities and upon children identified by them as visually impaired. The major variables selected for classificatory and analysis purposes were chronological age, level of residual vision, type of school attended, the presence of other disabling conditions and formal registration as blind or partially sighted.

Chapter 19, Estimates of the prevalence of visual impairment among children

Although there are medico-legal criteria for classifying a child as blind or partially sighted, and although the Department of Health publish statistics showing the numbers of people officially registered with their local social service departments, it is recognised that many children meeting the criteria do not become registered. In addition, there are many others with defects of vision sufficiently severe to interfere with their learning and independence.

Estimating the numbers of children with these varying degrees of visual impairment is fraught with difficulties. For the purposes of this enquiry, local education authorities were asked to list children whom they had identified as visually impaired. Considerable variations in prevalence rates were noted among the authorities, suggesting the application of different criteria and/or differences in recording procedures.

On the basis of the data obtained from the local education authorities, it is estimated that there are 10,000 children in Great Britain with visual impairments that these authorities would regard as being significant for educational purposes. However, this figure is massively lower than the estimate of 21,000 children with a 'seeing disability' derived by the Office of Population Censuses and Surveys from their surveys of disability in Great Britain. It is concluded that the disparity is due to large-scale under-identification by the LEAs. If an extrapolation to the whole country were to be made from the LEA with the highest recorded prevalence, a population of 25,000 visually impaired children would be indicated. The population estimate from our survey is thus, at 10,000, the most conservative of these three, being founded upon an average of all the local education authorities.

Chapter 20, Methodological appendix

This chapter is a detailed exposition of the methodology and procedures adopted for the survey. It also examines the variations in the prevalence rates of visually impaired children recorded for the individual LEAs. Guidance is given on the interpretation of the percentages presented in the report.

Part B

Background

2 Background and Objectives

2.1 Objectives

This report is the second in a two volume set on blind and partially sighted people in Great Britain. The first report looked at adults; this volume looks at children through interviews with their parents or guardians.

The objectives of these reports were first detailed in the June 1986 edition of the *New Beacon* magazine. They were to:

1. Provide information which will enable RNIB to evaluate, promote and develop its services.

2. Identify problems in obtaining information about services or access to them.

3. Provide a national picture of the characteristics of the visually impaired population.

4. Examine how the needs of the visually handicapped population are being met from whatever source, including other service providers.

5. Give evidence of significant unmet needs so that RNIB or other agencies can take steps to ensure that those needs are met.

6. Identify areas for further investigation.

7. Extend and complement the information about severely visually impaired people gathered in the OPCS disability survey.

In addition, the survey of children aimed to:

8. Provide information on the education process, looking at the needs of both parents and children.

2.2 Sample

This report is based on interviews carried out in April and May 1988 with parents of 285 visually impaired children randomly selected from 33 local education authorities in England, Scotland and Wales. The education authorities were selected to provide a representative sample of local education authorities in Great Britain.

The subjects of the survey are blind and partially sighted children identified by local education authorities as having a visual impairment. Each education authority completed a short pro forma providing basic details of the children that they had identified in their area as having a visual impairment. A sample of children was identified from these forms; the local education authority then contacted the parents on behalf of RNIB to ask them to take part in the survey.

The interviews were carried out in the homes of the parents and therefore generally cover those living in private households. The domicile of the child was not of concern in the selection of the sample.

The age of the children ranged from three to nineteen years. The upper age limit effectively covered those children who continued to be the responsibility of the local education authority where the child/young person was still in education.

Parents were interviewed rather than the children for several reasons (see section 18.1), including the fact that in many areas the survey asked about events and situations in the early formative years of the child's life. The children themselves would not have been able to provide this information.

The main discussion on population projections is to be found in Chapter 19. The sampling method used allowed the application of a simple weighting factor to numbers in the sample in order to arrive at an estimate of population numbers.

2.3 Topics and fieldwork

Parents were questioned on the following topics: residual vision; onset; registration; other handicaps and health; counselling; mobility; daily living skills; school and careers; accommodation; reading and writing; radio, television, tapes and telephone; toys; leisure and holidays; sources of information.

The topic areas were derived from a study of previous research (section 2.6) and also from a specially commissioned report from two experienced workers in the field of visually impaired children. Their report identified a series of topic areas which were used as a guide for in-depth conversational interviews with nine parents. These interviews, previous research, the commissioned report and discussion with other experts helped us to identify the topics which formed the basis for the structured questionnaire design.

Interviewing of the parents was contracted out to the British Market Research Bureau (BMRB). The questionnaire went through several draft stages. The expertise of RNIB, BMRB and others, along with the information gained from the interviews with the selected parents, was used to progress the drafts, which were then tested in the field on a small cross-section of parents. From these field pilots a finalised questionnaire was constructed.

2.4 Analysis

The report breaks down the response to the questions by a series of 'standard heads'. These define the main characteristics on which differences in response to individual questions could be expected to occur (see section 18.4).

Only where the standard head bears upon the analysis is this shown in the tables and commented upon. If a particular standard head has not been shown it can usually be assumed that the percentage difference between the analysis sub-groups shows no statistically significant difference (see section 20.5).

2.5 Terminology

The terms 'impairment', 'disability' and 'handicap' have clear meanings. Impairment concerns the functional loss e.g. sight; disability, the restriction or inability to perform an activity due to the impairment; and handicap the social consequence of the functional loss. Martin et al. (1988), provides a discussion of the meanings attached to each. However, the three terms are often used interchangeably. In this report we have tried to be consistent by using the term visual impairment in preference to disability or handicap when referring to blind and partially sighted children. Non-visual impairments are usually referred to as disabilities.

Children with low residual vision can be considered as more severely disabled than those with high residual vision, likewise children with other disabilities compared with those without other disabilities. As a short hand the term 'more severely disabled' is used collectively to refer to children with low residual vision or to those with other disabilities.

We use the term 'less severely disabled' to refer to children with high residual vision, or to those with no additional disabilities. We are able to refer to these groups in this way because of the strong association between low residual vision and the presence of additional disabilities (see Chapter 6).

The term 'comparative sub-group' is often used in the report to save repetition in describing the sub-groups that make up the standard heads used in our analysis (see sections 2.4 and 18.4). For example, the residual vision comparative sub-groups are children with high and low residual vision.

Throughout this report we refer to the individuals interviewed as 'informants' for two reasons. First, for the most part they are providing information on the visually impaired child. Second, although most of the informants are the parents of the child, in a few cases they are not. In our generalisations, however, we refer to parents.

2.6 Previous major surveys of visually impaired children

The OPCS surveys of disability in Great Britain included a sample of disabled children: Bone and Meltzer (1989); Smyth and Robus (1989); and Meltzer, Smyth and Elliot (1989). These children were identified in the course of the massive and costly screening of private households which the OPCS mounted to locate their adult sample. Because of this sampling base the OPCS data provide the best source for national projections of prevalence of all disabilities, including visual disability.

The RNIB surveys were designed to complement the OPCS surveys. We made use of the OPCS results in our own population projections (Chapter 18). But while the OPCS questionnaire was particularly detailed with respect to the financial circumstances of families with disabled children living in private households, other topic areas are much more extensively covered in the present survey. This is particularly so for visual disability. The unprecedentedly wide range of types of disability covered by the OPCS surveys meant that the information collected on the special needs of people with a visual disability was necessarily very limited. The number of visually disabled children available for refined analyses is also limited in the OPCS survey. (OPCS interviewed the parents of 1,359 disabled children but only 6% of these, that is 82, were visually disabled.)

A number of other surveys, mostly of restricted geographical coverage, were found helpful in designing our own questionnaire. The study by Langdon (1970) was useful because of the extensive quotes reported from case histories. Several surveys with an educational focus, particularly around the integration/segregation issue – notably those by Colborne-Brown and Tobin (1983), Thomson et al. (1985), Jamieson et al. (1977) – helped us to understand these issues and how best to frame questions on parental opinions about them.

A major finding at the sampling stage of our own survey was the wide variation between LEAs in the recorded prevalence of visual impairment (see Chapters 19 and 20). Stockley's (1987) survey of declared LEA policies and provision amply substantiates our own finding of very wide diversity, and is a useful source for further enquiry into its nature.

Part C

Aspects of Disability

3 The Onset of Visual Impairment

3.1 Cause of the sight problem

3.1.1 Medical name for the eye condition

A complete medical assessment of the cause of the child's sight problem was not an objective of the survey. Questioning was therefore confined to three simple questions dependent on the awareness and knowledge of the informants.

Table 3.1 shows that overall the medical names most frequently reported for the child's eye condition were 'cataracts' (15%), 'nystagmus' (8%), 'optic nerve atrophy' (7%), and 'albinism' (5%). No other condition was reported by more than three percent of informants: conditions included 'glaucoma', 'high myopia', 'astigmatism', 'retinal dysplasia', and 'coloboma microphthalmos'. Few of the eye conditions showed significant differences between the sub-groups. There was a tendency for conditions such as cataracts (21 and 11 percent) and nystagmus (12 and 6 percent) to be reported more frequently for children with no other disabilities compared with children with other disabilities.

Registration status likewise showed little difference for most of the medical conditions reported. However, 'optic nerve atrophy' was reported for a larger proportion of the registered compared with non-registered children (13 and 3 percent respectively).

The main finding from this questioning was the large number (27%) of informants who reported that they did not know the medical name of the condition because the doctors did not know the cause. A slightly smaller number (22%) reported that they simply did not know the medical name of the child's condition. We will see later (see Chapter 6) that a large percentage of informants felt that they were never given an explanation of their child's condition in a language that they could understand.

3.1.2 Cause of the eye condition

When the informants were asked if they knew the cause of the child's sight condition, the most frequently mentioned cause was 'hereditary/

Table 3.1 Medical name of sight condition – by other disability, residual vision, type of school and registration status

'Do the doctors know the medical name for . . . (child's) eye condition? If 'yes', what is the name?' (S3Q1)

	Other disability		Residual vision		Ordinary or special school*		Regist-ration status		Total
	NOD	OD	Hi	Lo	Ord	Spcl	R	NR	
	%	%	%	%	%	%	%	%	%
Cataracts	21	11	15	16	19	13	15	15	15
Nystagmus	12	6	7	10	10	11	9	8	8
Optic nerve atrophy	7	6	7	6	6	7	13	3	7
Albinism	8	3	5	5	7	3	6	4	5
Glaucoma	4	3	1	5	3	3	4	3	3
High myopia	4	3	4	2	5	2	0	5	3
Strabismus	2	3	4	1	4	1	0	4	3
General handicap	1	5	3	4	2	5	8	1	3
Retinal dysplasia	2	3	2	2	1	3	3	2	2
Coloboma microphthalmos	2	2	1	2	2	2	2	2	2
Retinoblastoma	3	1	1	3	2	3	5	1	2
Astigmatism	2	1	2	1	2	1	1	2	1
Macular degeneration	0	1	0	1	0	1	1	0	1
Retrolental fibroplasia	1	1	0	2	2	1	2	1	1
Others	3	8	6	7	3	7	3	7	5
No, doctors don't know	29	27	30	25	26	28	27	28	27
Don't know	19	25	23	21	20	24	14	27	22
Base = 100%	126	159	145	140	129	155	104	181	285

(* 1 child was not at school)

genetic' (21%), followed by 'brain/vaccine damage' (10%), 'rubella', (6%), 'infection during pregnancy' (5%), 'illness just after birth', and 'too much/little oxygen' (4% each). Other reasons given by no more than 3% of informants were 'parents incompatible/related', 'accident/ failed operation', 'premature birth', or that it was a 'congenital' occurrence (see Table 3.2).

Again only a few of the causes reported clearly showed statistically significant differences between the sub-groups. More informants with children with no other disability reported causes as 'hereditary/genetic' (30 and 15 percent). A greater degree of uncertainty as to the cause was also expressed for children with no other disabilities compared with those with other disabilities; informants reporting 'no, doctors don't know cause' (26 and 13 percent).

'Brain/vaccine damage' was reported only for children with other disabilities (17%). The consequence of the strong association of other disabilities with low residual vision and children in special schools (see Chapter 6) means that this cause was also reported more for children with low residual vision (14 and 6 percent), and children in special schools (15 and 2 percent) compared with their sub-group counterparts.

For children with high residual vision informants more frequently reported that the doctor did not know the cause, compared with the response for children with low residual vision (23 and 14 percent).

Table 3.2 Cause of sight condition – by other disability, residual vision, type of school and registration status

'Do the doctors know what caused the eye condition? If 'yes', what did they say?' (S3Q2)

	Other disability		Residual vision level		Ordinary or special school*		Regist-ration status		Total
	NOD	OD	Hi	Lo	Ord	Spcl	R	NR	
	%	%	%	%	%	%	%	%	%
Hereditary/genetic	30	15	21	22	26	18	23	20	21
Brain/vaccine damage	0	17	6	14	2	15	9	9	10
Rubella	5	6	6	5	5	6	2	8	6
Infection during pregnancy	4	5	3	6	4	5	8	3	5
Illness just after birth	2	6	3	6	4	5	3	6	4
Too much/little oxygen	4	3	1	6	3	4	5	3	4
Congenital	5	2	4	2	4	3	4	3	3
Accident/failed operation	1	3	2	2	1	3	4	1	2
Parents incompatible/related	2	1	2	1	2	2	4	1	2
Premature baby	0	3	3	1	3	1	2	2	2
Never told	2	1	3	0	1	2	0	2	1
Others	6	7	7	6	7	6	4	8	6
No, doctors don't know	26	13	23	14	25	14	13	22	19
Clear reason as part of known cause given	17	21	19	19	17	20	21	18	19
Base = 100%	126	159	145	140	129	155	104	181	285

(* 1 child was not at school)

3.2 Onset

3.2.1 Age of onset

As regards the origins of the child's sight problems (S3Q4), 80% of children were reported as having had their sight problems from birth. For 3% (7 children) it was the result of an accident. For five of the seven children the accident had occurred by the time they were five years of age. 'Something else' was the response for 15% of informants and no further details were sought; 2% said they 'didn't know'. None of the sub-group analyses showed any statistically significant differences.

3.2.2 Stability of the sight level

Table 3.3 shows that for nearly a third (30%) of children there had been a perceived improvement in the child's sight since the onset of the eye condition. For 22% it had become worse, and for 43% it had remained the same.

Table 3.3 Change in sight level since onset by age, residual vision and type of school

'Have child's problems remained about the same since they began, or have they become better or worse?' (S3Q6)

	Age		Residual vision		Ordinary or special school*		Total
	3 – 11	12 +	Hi	Lo	Ord	Spcl	
	%	%	%	%	%	%	%
Stayed the same	43	42	36	51	36	48	43
Become better	36	24	39	21	36	25	30
Become worse	16	29	21	23	21	23	22
Don't know	5	5	5	5	6	4	5
Total %	100	100	100	100	100	100	100
Base	152	133	145	140	129	155	285

(* 1 child was not at school)

Only residual vision shows clearly statistically significant differences in the sub-group analysis. Fifty-one per cent of children with low residual vision were reported as having no change in their eye condition compared with 36% of children with high residual vision. Similar proportions of children with low and high residual vision were reported as experiencing a worsening of their sight, 23 and 21 percent respectively. For 39% of the children with high residual vision their sight had 'become better' compared with 21% of children with low residual vision.

Age showed a more mixed pattern: a similar number of younger and older children had had no change (about 42%). Thirty-six percent of the under-12s had an improvement in their sight compared with 24% of those aged 12 + ; conversely 16 and 29 percent respectively had 'become worse'.

The patterns for the school sub-groups reflected the larger proportion of low vision and older children in special schools compared with ordinary schools. The eye condition had not changed for 48% of children in special schools compared with 36% in ordinary schools; for 25 and 36 percent respectively the eye condition had 'become better'.

Table 3.4 shows that, overall, 50% of children had reached their present sight level by the time they were two years old. In fact, for 38%

Table 3.4 Age when sight problem reached its present level, by age and residual vision

'At what age did . . . (child's) sight problems become as they are now?' (S3Q7)

| | Age | | Residual vision | | Total |
| | 3 – 11 | 12 + | Hi | Lo | |
	%	%	%	%	%
At birth	41	34	29	47	38
After birth to 2 years	16	8	13	11	12
3 years to current age	21	35	30	24	27
Still changing	18	19	20	16	18
Don't know	5	5	8	1	5
Total %	100	100	100	100	100
Base	152	133	145	140	285

the sight level was set at birth, for a further 11% by the time they were a year old, and the final 1% by the age of two.

Nearly half (47%) of the children with low residual vision were born with their present sight level compared with 29% of children with high residual vision. Fifty-seven percent of under-12s had reached their present sight level by the time they were two compared with 42% of those aged 12 and over. The suggestion that those children who are not born with their present sight level continue to see a deterioration in their sight over the years is borne out by the fact that 21% of younger children reached their present sight level between the age of three and their current age compared with 35% of older children.

The sight level was still changing for about 18% of children across all the sub-groups.

Informants were asked about the doctor's expectation for the future (S3Q8). Fifty-eight percent reported that the doctors expected the sight to 'remain the same', 7% that it would 'become better', 12% 'become worse', and 22% reported as 'don't know'. The data suggest that younger children (11 and 4 percent), and children with higher residual vision (12 and 2 percent) were more often reported as likely to 'become better' than their sub-group counterparts.

3.3 Identifying the sight problem

3.3.1 Suspicion and confirmation of the sight problem

The time lag between first suspecting a sight problem and having it confirmed can be a period of great frustration for parents. The development work for the research suggested that parents did find this period very difficult, especially where there was some considerable time lag between suspecting a problem and its confirmation.

The sight problem was first suspected by the first birthday for 70% of children, including 44% where the sight problem was suspected at or soon after the birth. For 92% of children the sight problem was suspected before their sixth birthday. Eighty-six percent had had the problem confirmed by their sixth birthday. Twenty-seven percent had had confirmation at or soon after birth, a further 26% before the first birthday, and a further 7% before the second birthday.

Table 3.5 examines the period between suspecting the sight problem and its confirmation. Sixty percent of children had their sight problem confirmed at the same time that it was suspected. Whether the child was older or younger when the sight problem was first suspected made little difference to the time between suspecting and confirming the sight problem.

Table 3.5 Time between first suspecting the sight problem and its confirmation

'How old was . . . (child) when it was first suspected that he/she had an eyesight problem?' (S3Q9)

'How old was . . . (child) when it was first definitely confirmed by tests that he/she had an eyesight problem?' (S3Q12)

	Total
	%
Confirmed at the same time	60
Time between suspicion and confirmation:	
1 year after	18
2 years	6
3 to 5 years	9
5 to 10 years	3
All with a time lag between suspicion and confirmation	36
No data	4
Total %	100
Base	285

For the 36% of children where there was a gap between suspicion and confirmation, 50% had had a confirmation of the problem within a year, with 3% waiting between 5 and 10 years.

3.3.2 First suspicion of a sight problem

The results in Table 3.6 show that the person most likely to suspect the child's sight problem was 'someone in the house' (52%), followed by the 'paediatrician' (11%), 'health visitor/clinic' (7%), 'other relative' and 'teacher' (5% each). No other person was mentioned by more than 4% of informants: these included 'family doctor', 'eye specialist' (includes ophthalmologist), 'school doctor' and 'midwife'.

Table 3.6 Person who first suspected a problem with the child's sight – by other disability, school, and registration status

'Who first suspected or noticed that there was something wrong with . . . (child's) sight?' (S3Q10)

	Other disability		Ordinary or special school*		Registration status		Total
	NOD	OD	Ord	Spcl	R	NR	
	%	%	%	%	%	%	%
Someone in the house	55	50	52	52	62	46	52
Paediatrician	5	16	4	17	11	12	11
Health visitor/clinic	8	7	11	5	6	8	7
Teacher	6	4	8	2	2	6	5
Other relative	9	3	6	5	5	6	5
Family doctor	6	2	5	3	4	4	4
Eye specialist	1	6	3	9	4	3	4
School doctor	4	2	5	1	0	4	3
Other medical person	1	5	2	5	3	3	3
Midwife	2	1	1	2	2	2	2
Friend/neighbour	2	0	1	1	0	1	1
Optician	2	0	1	0	0	1	1
Child	0	1	0	1	0	1	#
Don't remember	1	3	0	4	3	2	2
Base = 100%	126	159	129	155	104	181	285

(* 1 child was not at school)

Sub-group comparisons revealed a number of small differences, most of which were individually too small to be statistically significant, but which together showed a consistent pattern. For children with no other disabilities 'other relative' (9 and 3 percent), and the 'family doctor' (6 and 2 percent) were mentioned more often compared with children with other disabilities. Conversely the 'paediatrician' (16 and 5 percent; statistically significant), and the 'eye specialist' (6 and 1 percent) were more frequently mentioned for children with other disabilities.

For children in special schools, compared with those in ordinary schools, 'paediatrician' (17 and 4 percent, statistically significant), and 'eye specialist' (9 and 3 percent) were mentioned more frequently as first suspecting the child's problem. For children in ordinary schools the 'teacher' (8 and 2 percent), 'school doctor' (5 and 1 percent) and 'health visitor/clinic' (11 and 5 percent) were mentioned more often than for children in special schools.

Registration showed little difference for any of the other persons except for 'someone in the house', where this was mentioned more often for registered compared with non-registered children (62 and 46 percent respectively). 'Teacher' (6 and 2 percent), and 'school doctor' (4% and none) were mentioned more often for registered compared with non-registered children.

4 The Visual Impairment: Aids and Treatment

4.1 Aids to vision

4.1.1 Glasses and contact lenses

Where the child had at least light perception, informants were asked a series of questions about the wearing of glasses and contact lenses, the use of low vision aids and additional lighting in the home.

Table 4.1 shows that overall 62% of children were reported as wearing either glasses or contact lenses or both. The residual vision sub-groups showed no difference. The only difference was that exhibited between children with no other disability and other disability (69 and 53 percent), and children at ordinary and special schools (68 and 53 percent).

Table 4.1 The wearing of glasses and contact lenses among visually impaired children, by other disability and type of school

'Does . . . (child) wear glasses† or contact lenses at all?' (S2Q14)

	Other disability		Ordinary or special school		Total
	NOD %	OD %	Ord %	Spcl %	%
Yes, glasses	60	47	56	50	54
Yes, contact lenses	5	3	6	2	4
Glasses and contact lenses	4	3	6	1	4
No, none	31	47	32	47	39
Total %	100	100	100	100	100
Base	121	135	128	127	256

(256 informants: 29 children with NLP were not asked)
† Includes sun and dark glasses

Four per cent of children wore contact lenses alone, and a further 4% wore both contact lenses and glasses.

The wearing of glasses includes children reported as wearing sun or dark glasses for cosmetic or protective reasons.

Twenty-two percent of children who had glasses or lenses were reported as having problems getting them. The main problems reported (actual number of informants shown in brackets) were 'long wait after ordering' (18), 'can't get them to fit properly' (7), 'needed spare or second pair' (6), and 'too expensive for us' (4). The most frequently mentioned problem was the long wait after ordering, although more than three-quarters reported no problems in getting glasses or contact lenses.

4.1.2   Low vision aids

Just under 40% of visually impaired children are reported as making use of low vision aids (S2Q17). Residual vision rather surprisingly showed no difference at all. Table 4.2 shows that the children making most use of low vision aids were those with no other disability and older children, 52 and 49 percent respectively. Twenty-seven and thirty percent respectively of children with other disabilities and younger children used low vision aids.

Table 4.2   Use of low vision aids by other disability and age

'Does . . . (child) use any low vision aids to help with his/her eyesight?' (S2Q17)

	Other disability		Age		Total
	NOD	OD	3 – 11	12 +	
	%	%	%	%	%
Yes	52	27	30	49	39
No	47	70	67	50	59
Don't know	1	4	3	2	2
Total %	100	100	100	100	100
Base	121	135	135	121	256

(256 respondents: 29 children with NLP were not asked)

Forty-five percent of children in ordinary schools were reported as using low vision aids, but this was not statistically different from the 33% in special schools using them.

A variety of low vision aids were used by the children shown in Table 4.3. A hand-held magnifier was the most popular, used by 60% of children, followed by 'closed-circuit television' (CCTV) (27%), 'hand-held telescope' (19%), 'magnifier on a stand' (17%), and 'magnifier attached to spectacles' (11%). A range of other low vision aids were also mentioned including a field expander and binoculars.

Table 4.3   Low vision aids used

'What low vision aids does he/she use?' (S2Q18)

	Children using low vision aids
	%
Magnifier, hand held	60
Closed-circuit television	27
Hand held telescope	19
Magnifier on a stand	17
Magnifier attached to spectacles	11
Magnifier, other	9
Monocular	8
Binoculars	8
Enhanced print/print writer	4
Field expander	2
Others	18
Don't know	1
Base = 100%	99

(29 children with NLP; 157 did not use any LVA)

Table 4.4 shows that by far the most common source of low vision aids is the school or local education authority (59%), followed by the hospital (28%). A 'low vision clinic', 'optician' and 'bought privately' (11% each) were the other sources mentioned by a significant proportion of informants.

Table 4.4   Source of low vision aids used

'Where does . . . (child) get his/her low vision aids from?' (S2Q19)

	Children using low vision aids
	%
School/local education authority	59
Hospital	28
Low vision clinic	11
Optician	11
Bought privately	11
Social services	5
RNIB	2
Local blind association/society	1
Others	3
Don't know/can't recall	2
Base = 100%	99

(29 children with NLP; 157 did not use any LVA)

Only the other disability sub-groups showed any statistically significant difference in the source of low vision aids, where 75% of children with other disabilities got their low vision aids from the 'school/local education authority' compared with 49% of children with no other disability.

Though not statistically significant, 4 of the 5 children who got their low vision aids from social services were registered, and all 5 were also in ordinary schools.

When asked if they had ever had problems getting the low vision aids used, 17% of informants said that they had (S2Q20).

The 17% translates to 17 actual informants. The sort of problems reported (actual numbers in brackets) were, 'long wait after ordering' (5), 'lack of information' (4), 'just not available' (3), 'school can't afford them/not enough aids for all pupils' (2 each), and 'nowhere to get them from/too expensive for us to buy' (1 each).

4.1.3 Lighting in the home

A simple aid to low vision is the provision of extra or correct lighting in the home. Informants were asked (at S2Q22) if they had had any extra or strong lights fitted in the home; only 1 in 5 informants said they had. Age was the only sub-group analysis to show a statistically significant difference, with 29% of informants with older children reporting additional lighting compared with 13% of those with younger children.

Those with no additional lighting were asked why they had none (S2Q23). Sixty-three percent said they 'didn't think it would help' and 19% that they 'never thought of it'. Relatively few informants offered reasons to do with non-benefit to the child's sight; 'don't like strong light' (6%) and 'doesn't need them' (6%) were the two reasons given here. Only 8% said it was because of the expense.

4.2 Medical care and treatment

4.2.1 Medical professional consulted

Chapter 6 looks at the medical professionals that the child may have consulted for their other permanent illnesses or disabilities. At question S2Q25 informants were asked about those professionals consulted specifically because of the child's eyesight problems; Table 4.5 shows the results.

Practically every child (97%) was reported as having seen an 'eye specialist at hospital or clinic'. Forty percent or more were reported as having seen one or more of the other professionals; 'optician' and

Table 4.5 Medical professionals consulted for eyesight problems, by other disability

'Can I just check, has your child ever seen any of these people about his/her eyesight problems?' (S2Q25)

	Other disability		Total
	NOD	OD	
	%	%	%
Eye specialist at hospital or clinic	98	96	97
Optician	68	48	55
School doctor	60	43	51
Paediatrician	44	43	43
Family doctor	52	36	43
Health visitor	48	33	40
Don't know	0	2	1
Base = 100%	126	159	285

'school doctor' were seen by 55 and 51 percent respectively, and about 40% had seen either a 'paediatrician', 'family doctor' or 'health visitor'.

Only the 'other disability' sub-groups showed any statistically significant difference for children reported as having seen one of the listed professionals for their eyesight problems.

A larger percentage of informants with children with no other disability reported the child as having seen an 'optician' (68 and 48 percent), 'school doctor' (60 and 43 percent), 'family doctor' (52 and 36 percent), and a 'health visitor' (48 and 33 percent) compared with their sub-group counterpart.

4.2.2 Last time a medical professional was consulted

A worried parent may seek advice or information from the many medical professionals that he/she comes into contact with in the child's early years. To better gauge the level of continued medical contact informants were asked (at S2Q26) when they last saw the medical professional reported at question S2Q25; Table 4.6 shows the results.

The majority of informants had moved on from the health visitor and family doctor as a contact about the child's sight problem; the health visitor or family doctor had not been seen for 12 months or more by 74 percent respectively. In fact nearly 40% of children had not seen either for five or more years. The paediatrician was also a lapsed contact, not having been seen by 54% of children for 12 or more months (24% for 5 or more years).

The remaining medical contacts about the child's sight, those seen within the last six months, were the optician (56%), eye specialist

Table 4.6 Time since last saw medical professional about the child's sight problem

'When did . . . (child) last see . . . (specialist at S2Q25) about his/her sight problem?' (S2Q26)

	Medical professionals					
	HV	FD	SD	P	OP	ES
	%	%	%	%	%	%
6 months or less	15	24	43	33	56	46
7 – 11 months ago	7	7	16	9	15	12
12 months to 4 years ago	34	26	27	30	35	29
5 or more years ago	40	37	7	24	5	11
Don't know	4	6	7	4	3	3
Total %	100	100	100	100	100	100
Base	113	123	145	123	156	276

HV = Health visitor, FD = Family Doctor, SD = School doctor, P = Paediatrician, OP = Optician, ES = Eye specialist

(46%), and the school doctor (43%). Overall, those not seeing any of this group for 5 or more years amounted to 11% or less.

While 33% had seen a paediatrician within the last six months, 24% had not seen one for 5 or more years.

4.2.3 Satisfaction with the medical professional

A general question (S2Q24) was asked on the overall level of satisfaction with the medical care and treatment the child had received for his or her sight problem. Seventy-six percent of informants were either 'very' or 'fairly' satisfied. Only 14% expressed overt dissatisfaction.

Asked about satisfaction with each of the medical professionals seen, the individual level of satisfaction expressed was very high, exceeding 70% overall.

The highest level of dissatisfaction was expressed by those who had seen a health visitor (20%), and an eye specialist (16%).

Table 4.7 shows that the single most frequent reason given for informants' dissatisfaction was that the person seen was not able to help. Forty percent of informants gave this reply, with over one-third referring specifically to the eye specialist.

Allied to this sense of frustration are the next two replies: 'lacked (medical) knowledge' (25%), and 'couldn't answer questions' (23%).

Table 4.7 Reasons for dissatisfaction with medical professionals

'And overall, how satisfied are you with the help your child gets/got from . . . (person at S2Q25)?' (S2Q28)

	Informants expressing dissatisfaction %
Couldn't help	40
Lacked (medical) knowledge	25
Couldn't answer questions	23
Pompous/dismissive	15
Not seen often enough	15
Didn't listen/wasn't interested	13
No patience with child	6
Other	28
Don't know	5
Base = 100%	83

(83 informants, those expressing dissatisfaction)

These replies quantify the responses that we found in the conversational interviews carried out in the development stage of the survey; here parents expressed frustration and hopelessness that the medical profession was not able to offer a cure or at least definitive reasons for the cause of their child's disability.

4.2.4 Medical intervention

All informants were asked about past and future eye operations (at S2Q29 and S2Q30 respectively). The questions were phrased to include all operations related to the child's sight. Thirty-eight percent of

Table 4.8 The likelihood of future eye operations, by other disability, residual vision and type of school

'Is . . . (child) likely to have an eye operation to do with his/her sight sometime in the future?' (S2Q30)

	Other disability		Residual vision		Ordinary or special school*		Total
	NOD %	OD %	Hi %	Lo %	Ord %	Spcl %	%
Yes	20	11	17	14	21	10	15
No	57	76	61	74	57	76	67
Don't know	23	13	23	12	23	14	18
Total %	100	100	100	100	100	100	100
Base	126	159	145	140	129	155	285

(* 1 child was not at school)

children were reported as having had such an operation in the past – 32 and 45 percent respectively of children with and without other disabilities.

Table 4.8 shows that while 15% of children were expected to have an operation in the future, 18% of informants expressed uncertainty as to whether the child would have any future operations.

Informants with more severely disabled children and children in special schools were the ones more certain that the child would not be having any operations in the future; on average 75% compared with just under 60% for their sub-group counterpart. There was a higher degree of uncertainty among those with no other disability and high residual vision (23% each) than among their sub-group counterparts (13% and 12%).

5 Registration

5.1 Legislation

Local authorities have an obligation to make arrangements for the keeping of registers of people defined under section 29 of the National Assistance Act 1948, and then to ensure that certain services are provided, including advice, support and rehabilitation. Registration on the part of the individual is voluntary and requires the completion of a form (BD8) by a consultant ophthalmologist; a failure to register does not exclude a person from receiving most services. Registration for children born with a visual impairment is not normally completed until they are two, and may be delayed in many cases (*In Touch 1990 Handbook*, 1990).

One factor of registration for children and young adults still in education is that the local education authority (LEA) takes much of the responsibility for meeting their needs. A commonly expressed view is that registration for children and young people of school age is not as important as it is for adults, and as a consequence it is believed that under-registration for children exceeds under-registration for adults.

5.2 Registration

5.2.1 Awareness of registration

Table 5.1 shows the results of asking informants if they had heard of registration with the local social services, making sure that no confusion could be made with any registers that the local education authority may hold. Overall, just under half (46%) of informants had heard of registration.

Residual vision showed the clearest difference between sub-groups: 56% of informants with children with low residual vision had heard of registration compared with 37% of informants with high residual vision children. A greater number of informants with children in special schools (52 and 40 per cent), or with other disabilities (52 and 40 percent) said that they had heard of registration compared with their sub-group counterparts. These latter differences are partly a consequence of children with low residual vision being more likely to have other disabilities or be in special schools (see Chapters 6 and 9).

The level of residual vision is the main factor in determining the awareness of registration among informants.

Table 5.1 Awareness of registration by other disability, residual vision, and type of school

'Some children are registered with their local social services for their sight problems. This is different from being registered with the local education authorities. Have you heard about registration with the local social services?' (S4Q1)

	Other disability		Residual vision		Ordinary or special school*		Total
	NOD	OD	Hi	Lo	Ord	Spcl	
	%	%	%	%	%	%	%
Yes	40	52	37	56	40	52	46
No	51	44	58	36	54	41	47
Don't know	10	4	6	8	6	7	7
Total %	100	100	100	100	100	100	100
Base	126	159	145	140	129	155	285

(* 1 child was not at school)

5.2.2 Registration as blind or partially sighted

Informants who had heard of registration were asked if their child was registered (S4Q2); of these 79% reported affirmatively. This increased to 89% for children with low residual vision and decreased to 64% for children with high residual vision.

Table 5.2 shows the registration status (blind or partially sighted) by residual vision level and type of school. Overall, just over half (56%) of all registered children were registered as blind, and 40% as partially sighted. The registration status of the remaining 4% was not known.

Table 5.2 Registration by residual vision, and type of school

'Is he/she registered as blind, or as partially sighted?' (S4Q3)

	Residual vision		Ordinary or special school		All registered
	Hi	Lo	Ord	Spcl	
	%	%	%	%	%
Registered:					
Blind	21	73	24	73	56
Partially sighted	71	26	68	25	40
Don't know status	9	1	8	2	4
Total %	100	100	100	100	100
Base	34	70	37	67	104

(181 children were not registered)

A single cause of sight loss can, within limits, give rise to differing levels of residual vision: e.g. two children with cataracts may have different levels of residual vision. By necessity the dividing line that we used to distinguish between children with low and high residual vision was a working definition. The basis of this definition is discussed in sections 18.5 and 18.6.

The residual vision sub-groups show how our sample is divided between those children registered as blind or partially sighted (Table 5.2). Seventy-three percent of children with low residual vision were registered as blind compared with 21% of the children with high residual vision. Conversely, 71% of children with high residual vision were registered as partially sighted compared with 26% of children with low residual vision.

The school type sub-groups also showed a clear split between those children registered as blind or partially sighted. Seventy-three percent of registered children in special schools were registered as blind, and 25% as partially sighted. Of registered children in ordinary schools, 24% were registered as blind and 68% as partially sighted. We also looked at the type of school the registered blind or partially sighted children attended. Of those who were registered blind, 17% were in ordinary schools and 87% in special schools. For children registered as partially sighted, 60% were in ordinary schools and 40% were in special schools. This evidence indicates that registered blind children are to be found in special schools rather than in mainstream ordinary schools.

Younger children were no more likely to be registered than older children. One would have expected that the high degree of association between low residual vision and the presence of another disability would have shown a significantly larger proportion of children with other disabilities being registered as blind; this was not the case. This confirms that registration is based on the level of residual vision, and that the presence of another disability, for example, does not greatly increase the chance of being registered.

Table 5.3 provides a summary of questions 1 – 3 on awareness and registration status based on the total sample.

Table 5.3, which summarises the responses to questions S4Q1, S4Q2 and S4Q3, shows that overall 50% of children with low residual vision were registered, with 36% registered as blind and 13% as partially sighted. However, possibly of more concern is the large number (44%) of informants with low residual vision who had not heard of registration. Nearly three-quarters of these children may be eligible for registration as blind (see section 5.2.2). Of the 63% of children with high residual vision where informants had not heard of registration, as many as one

Table 5.3 Awareness of registration, by other disability, residual vision, and type of school (S4Q1, S4Q2, S4Q3)

	Other disability		Residual vision		Ordinary or special school*		Total
	NOD	OD	Hi	Lo	Ord	Spcl	
	%	%	%	%	%	%	%
Registered:							
Blind	14	26	5	36	7	32	20
Partially sighted	14	15	17	13	19	11	15
Don't know	2	1	2	1	2	1	1
All registered	30	42	24	50	28	44	36
Heard of registration, but not registered	10	9	13	6	11	9	10
Not heard of registration†	60	48	63	44	61	48	54
Total %	100	100	100	100	100	100	100
Base	126	159	145	140	129	155	285

(* 1 child was not at school)

† Combines the 'no' and 'don't know' responses from Table 5.1

fifth could be eligible for registration as blind, and most of the remainder as partially sighted.

Of further concern is that nearly half (48%) of informants with children in special schools claimed not to have heard of registration.

5.2.3 Registration and LEA records

The pro forma sent to the LEAs (see sections 18.2.2 and 20.3) explicitly asked whether the child was registered as blind or partially sighted with the local social services. Thirty-six percent of the returned forms recorded the children as not registered in either category. However, the same percentage said that there was no information about the child's registration status in the LEA records.

We also obtained data on registration status directly from the informants. Working from published Department of Health (DOH) statistics (see note to chapter) we found that estimates of blind registration based on the informants' replies agreed with published estimates. However, on a rough estimate, it seems that about 1 in 5 children who were registered as blind, while being identified as visually impaired by the LEAs, did not have the fact of their registration with the local social services recorded on the LEA records.

The data on partially sighted registration behave differently. Population projections based on both the informants' replies and the returned pro-formas resulted in a one-third shortfall from published DOH figures. On the assumption that informants would know if their child were registered as partially sighted with the local social services, this indicates that many children so registered are not being identified as visually impaired by the LEAs.

5.2.4 Age at registration

As the sight level can change between onset and later life we asked informants with children currently registered as blind if the child was previously registered as partially sighted (S4Q4); 14% confirmed that they were.

Table 5.4 shows that overall 28% of registrations occurred by the time the children were two years old, and a further 28% by the time they were five. However, children eligible for registration as blind tended to be registered earlier compared with children eligible for registration as partially sighted.

Table 5.4 Age of registration as blind or partially sighted, by current registration status

'At what age was he/she registered blind?' (S4Q6)
'At what age was he/she registered partially sighted?' (S4Q7)

	Registration status		All
	Blind	Partially sighted	registered
	%	%	%
Age registered:			
Birth to 2 years	35	11	28
3 to 5 years	29	26	28
6 years and older	34	52	37
Don't know	2	11	7
Total %	100	100	100
Base	58	46	104

(181 children were not registered)

About a third (35%) of children registered as blind were registered before they were three years old; in total 64% were registered as blind by the time they were five. For children registered as partially sighted, 37% were registered by the time they were five.

As we have seen in Chapter 3, the sight problem was reported as occurring at or near birth for nearly half of the children with low residual vision, of whom nearly three-quarters may be eligible for registration as blind.

5.3 Benefits of registration

Table 5.5 shows that overall 56% of informants, including the 4% recorded as 'don't know', could not provide any specific examples of benefits that they received as a result of the child being registered. Asked a more general question (S4Q9) on how worthwhile they considered registration to be, half (51%) thought that registration was 'worthwhile', 28% felt it was 'not worthwhile', and 21% said that they 'did not know'.

Table 5.5 Advantages as a result of registration

'What advantages does . . . (child) get as a result of being registered?' (S4Q8)

	All registered
	%
Financial help from social services	12
Badge for car	11
Equipment	9
Educational resources	9
Bus pass/travel concessions	8
Talking books/cassettes	7
Non-financial help from social services	5
Other	6
None	52
Don't know	4
Base = 100%	104

(181 children were not registered)

'Financial help from social services' (12%), and 'badge for car' (11%), 'equipment', 'educational resources' (9% each), and 'bus pass/travel concessions' (8%) were the type of benefits informants mentioned specifically as coming from registration with the social services. The differences between those registered blind or partially sighted and the other sub-groups were not statistically significant, except for 'badge for car' which was solely reported by those with children registered as blind. Though it did not reach statistical significance, there was also some indication that more of the registered partially sighted compared with the blind sub-group felt that there were no benefits to registration, recorded as 'none' in the survey.

Note to Chapter 5

There were 259 children in our sample living in England. The DOH published figures for 1988 give 1,595 children aged between 5 and 15 registered as blind in England. The replies from informants indicated there were 39 such children (15%) of our relevant sample. Applying this percentage to the 10,000 children estimated to be on LEA records in Britain (see Chapter 19) gives a population projection that agrees sufficiently with the published figures. If we adjust the estimated number of those on LEA records to 9,000, since we are only considering England, the DOH published figure still falls well within the 95% confidence interval for our sample estimate. However, only 32 children were recorded as registered blind on the pro-forma that we obtained from LEAs in England. The implication therefore is that roughly 1 in 5 LEAs, while identifying registered blind children as visually impaired, are not recording their actual registration.

The DOH published figures for 1988 state that 1,679 children aged betwen 5 and 15 are registered as partially sighted in England. The replies from informants indicated that of our relevant sample there were 32 such children (12%). The LEA pro-formas revealed 31 such children. Applying these percentages even to the 10,000 children estimated to be on LEA records gives a population projection that is around one-third too low. If we can assume that informants knew whether their child was registered with the local authorities as partially sighted, the implication is that many such children are not being identified as visually impaired by the LEAs.

6 Other Disabilities

6.1 Types of other disability

Table 6.1 shows that over half (56%) of visually impaired children were reported as having another permanent illness or disability. This compares with the OPCS findings that 48% of all disabled children had a disability across more than one of the defined disability areas. For those children identified as having a seeing disability, 83% also had an additional disability (Bone and Meltzer, 1989). The larger proportion of visually impaired children with multiple disabilities identified by the OPCS may be due to a number of factors. First, that they prompted for more disability types than in this survey; secondly, we are looking for children that LEAs identified with a seeing problem. Our survey may also have missed a proportion of children who were so severely disabled in other areas that the sight problem was not identified. Therefore they were not included in our survey.

Table 6.1 Other permanent illness or disabilities, by age and residual vision

'I have already asked some questions about child's eyesight. I would like to check whether he/she has any other permanent illnesses or disabilities?' (S5Q1)

	Age			Residual vision		Total
	3 – 7	8 – 11	12+	Hi	Lo	
	%	%	%	%	%	%
Speech difficulties	25	30	24	15	37	26
Physical handicap	23	27	27	16	36	26
Mental handicap	19	29	27	12	38	25
Behaviour/social problems	23	11	21	15	24	19
Hearing difficulties	17	12	22	15	21	18
Epilepsy	17	16	15	8	24	16
Diabetes	4	1	2	1	4	3
Other medical illness	25	16	17	15	24	19
All with an additional disability	57	59	53	44	69	56
No other disabilities	43	41	47	56	31	44
Base = 100%	79	73	133	145	140	285

Table 6.1 shows that the most frequently mentioned disabilities were: speech (26%), physical handicap (26%) and mental handicap (25%).

Behavioural or social problems (19%), followed by hearing difficulties (18%) and epilepsy (16%) were the others mentioned.

6.1.1 Number of additional disabilities

Table 6.2 shows that overall, over half (56%) of the visually impaired children had another disability, just over a quarter (27%) had three or more other disabilities, and 29% one to two additional disabilities.

Table 6.2 Number of other disabilities among visually impaired children, by residual vision level and type of school

	Ordinary or special school*		Residual vision		Total
	Ord %	Spcl %	Hi %	Lo %	%
1 – 2	32	27	30	29	29
3 – 4	3	32	10	28	19
5 or more	1	14	3	12	8
One or more other disability	36	72	43	69	56
No other disability	64	28	57	31	44
Total %	100	100	100	100	100
Base	129	155	145	140	285

(* 1 child was not at school)

Table 6.2 also shows the association of additional disabilities with residual vision level. A larger number of children with low residual vision were reported as having another disability compared with children with high residual vision (69 and 43 per cent respectively). Therefore, the child with multiple disabilities is also likely to be more severely visually impaired.

A consequence of multiple disability is the type of school multiply disabled children attend. While 64% of children in ordinary schools were reported as having no other disability, the comparable figure for children in special schools was 28%. In fact nearly half (46%) of children in special schools had 3 or more additional disabilities, compared with 4% in ordinary schools. The implications of this are discussed further in Chapter 10. Because a larger proportion of children with additional disabilities attend special schools, the difference between those children who are more or less severely disabled translates into a difference between children in special and ordinary schools. This association needs to be borne in mind throughout this report.

Nearly 4 in 10 (38%) children were registered with the local authority for their additional disability. Registration was most likely for those children with a physical or mental handicap.

For the 74 children with a physical disability we enquired further about the severity of the disability; two-thirds (64%) were reported as having a 'total physical handicap', that is to say, wheelchair bound.

6.2 Age at which other disabilities became apparent

Table 6.3 shows that for two-thirds (65%) of the children who had additional disabilities, identification of the problems had been made by the time they were two years old. Identification had been made in over half of these cases before the first birthday, and a total of 80% had been identified as multiply disabled by their fifth birthday.

Table 6.3 Age at which other permanent illness or disabilities were identified

'How old was . . . (child) when the problem(s) were first identified?' (S5Q5)

	Age			All with other disability
	3 – 7	8 – 11	12 +	
	%	%	%	%
Age problem identified				
Birth to 2 years	69	74	58	65
3 – 5 years	24	12	14	16
6 – 10 years	2	12	17	11
11 – 15 years	0	0	9	4
Don't know	4	2	3	3
Total %	100	100	100	100
Base	45	43	71	159

(126 children had no other disability)

6.3 Medical professionals consulted for non-sight-related problems

Table 6.4 shows that 70% of children had consulted a medical professional for the non-sight problem. A correlation existed between whom they had seen, the age of the child and the presence of another disability. Eighty-six per cent of children with another disability had seen a medical professional compared with 48% of children without another disability. Younger children tended to be more likely to have seen either a health visitor or a paediatrician. However, the main difference exists between those with and without additional disabilities.

The professionals most frequently mentioned were paediatrician (48%), and health visitor (37%), followed by those in a hospital assessment unit (32%) and physiotherapists (31%). A variety of professionals could have been seen within a hospital assessment unit. A speech therapist was seen by 27% of children.

Table 6.4 Other specialist or medical professionals consulted for non-sight-related problems

'Apart from his/her sight problems has . . . (child) ever seen any of these specialists for health or medical care?' (S5Q7)

	Age and other disability				Other disability		Total
	3 – 11		12 +				
	NOD	OD	NOD	OD	NOD	OD	
	%	%	%	%	%	%	%
Paediatrician	34	65	21	62	28	64	48
Health visitor	33	53	13	42	23	48	37
Hospital assessment unit	17	43	15	46	16	45	32
Physiotherapist	6	50	11	49	9	49	32
Speech therapist	8	48	7	35	7	42	27
Occupational therapist	5	31	2	18	3	25	15
None/don't know	45	16	55	11	50	14	30
No information	45	16	58	11	2	#	1
Base = 100%	64	88	62	71	126	159	285

6.4 Last time a medical specialist was consulted

Table 6.5 shows that the health visitor and professionals in a hospital assessment unit had not been seen or visited for 12 months or more by two-thirds of the children who had used those services at some time. Those who had more recently seen one of these professionals were not necessarily the younger children.

Between a third and a half of children had not seen one of these professionals for 12 months or more: paediatrician (40%), speech therapist (47%), occupational therapist (39%) and physiotherapist (32%). Between a third and two-thirds had seen one in the last six

Table 6.5 Time since last consulted medical professional for non-sight problem

'When did . . . (child) last see . . (specialist at S5Q7)?' (S5Q8)

	Medical professionals					
	HV	HAU	P	S	OT	PH
	%	%	%	%	%	%
6 months or less	21	19	46	36	52	67
7 – 11 months ago	11	9	12	3	2	0
12 months or more	63	68	40	47	39	32
Don't know	5	4	2	15	9	1
Total %	100	100	100	100	100	100
Base	106	91	136	76	44	89

HV = Health visitor, HAU = Hospital assessment unit, P = Paediatrician, S = Speech therapist, OT = Occupational therapist, PH = Physiotherapist months. The physiotherapist (67%) and the occupational therapist (52%) had been seen most recently.

About a third of children seeing a speech and occupational therapist had done so within two weeks of our survey interview. About 60% of children seeing a physiotherapist had done so in the same period (not shown in the table).

The majority of children receiving continued 'treatment' from one of the therapist professionals are to be found among children with other disabilities.

Well over 80% of informants said that they were either very or fairly satisfied with the medical and health care the child had received. However, it is well documented that respondents, in such situations, are reluctant to express dissatisfaction where they are receiving a service or help for which they feel grateful.

6.5 Receipt of a clear explanation of the child's disability

Table 6.6 shows that half of the informants who had children with other disabilities (in response to S5Q10) felt that they were given an explanation they could understand when the problem(s) was first identified. A similar number (46%) felt that they were given an explanation they could understand about the child's sight problem.

Table 6.6 Explanation of disability in language parent could understand when first told about the problem(s)

'Thinking about **all** your child's problems, when you were first told about them, were you given an explanation in language you could understand?' (S5Q10)

'When you were first told about your child's **sight** problem, were you given an explanation in language you could understand?' (S5Q11)

'Have you ever been given an explanation in words you can understand?' (S5Q12)

	All problems (S5Q10)†	Sight problem (S5Q11)	Explanation at some time (S5Q10/11/12)
	%	%	%
Yes	50	46	60
No	47	43	11
Don't know	3	11	30
Total %	100	100	100
Base	159	285	285

† Only asked of children with other disabilities

Those who said this explanation was not given at the time the problems were first identified were asked (at S5Q12) if they had ever had such an explanation. Overall, 60% of informants felt that the child's problem had subsequently been explained satisfactorily to them, leaving 40% of informants still without a full understanding of their child's problems.

The circumstances surrounding this lack of explanation were not probed further. However, our development work in the early stages of the research suggested that some parents felt that either they were not given what they considered a full explanation of the child's problem, or that they wanted, but were not given, a specific cause of the disabilities.

Table 6.7 shows that the ophthalmologist (45%) and paediatrician (32%) were the most frequently mentioned professionals to provide this clear explanation. The only other notable percentages were a medical person/hospital (10%), and the family doctor (6%). Seventy per cent of informants who had children with no other disability said the ophthalmologist had provided a clear explanation of the sight problem. Where the child had other disabilities, the paediatrician (44%) and the ophthalmologist (32%) provided this explanation.

Table 6.7 Source of explanation of the disability in language the informant could understand

	Other disability		Total
	No other disability	Other disability	
	%	%	%
Ophthalmologist	70	32	45
Paediatrician	10	44	32
Medical person/hospital	8	11	10
Family doctor	2	9	6
Hospital professor/consultant	2	5	4
School doctor	3	3	3
Base = 100%	63	117	180

(105 informants were not given an explanation)

6.6 The disability causing most concern

Table 6.8 shows that 38% of informants felt that the child's eyesight problem was their major cause for concern. Although the survey revealed 47 children who were reported as having a 'total physical handicap', only 19 (12%) reported that the physical handicap was the major cause for concern. The mental handicap caused most concern for 11% of parents.

Table 6.8 Which of the current problems causes the parents most concern

'Which of the problems causes you most concern nowadays, the eyesight problem or the . . .?' (S5Q6)

	All with other disability
	%
Eyesight	38
Physical handicap	12
Mental handicap	11
Behaviour/social problems	9
Other medical illness	8
Hearing difficulties	4
Speech difficulties	3
Epilepsy	2
Can't say	13
Total %	100
Base	159

(126 children had no other disability)

7 Counselling and Advice

7.1 Counselling and advice

Ninety percent of informants agreed with the statement (at S6Q1) that what they needed most when they first learned about their child's problems was someone knowledgeable to talk to. In fact 82% 'agreed a lot' with the statement. Just under 40% of parents said that they had someone knowledgeable to talk to at that time.

Table 7.1 shows that eye specialist/ophthalmologist (31%), paediatrician (25%), and health visitor (22%) were by far the most frequently mentioned 'knowledgeable' person that they spoke to. The family doctor was mentioned by 11%. RNIB, school doctor, and educational psychologist were among the others mentioned by 3 or 4 percent of informants.

Table 7.1 Knowledgeable person parents had to talk to when they first learned of problem(s)

	All who had someone to talk to
	%
Eye specialist/ophthalmologist	31
Paediatrician	25
Health visitor	22
Other medical specialist	19
Family doctor	11
Social/welfare worker	4
RNIB education adviser	4
RNIB generally	3
School doctor	3
Educational psychologist	3
Base = 100%	110

(175 had no one to talk to)

When asked how often these knowledgeable people were being seen, 30% said they saw the person at least once a week; half were seen less than once a month.

7.1.1 The use of and demand for counselling

The agreement with S6Q1 on the need to talk to someone showed the overwhelming desire for some form of 'counselling'. When directly questioned on this, only 16% of informants had special counselling; an additional 4% had someone they could talk to. The results are shown in Table 7.2.

Table 7.2 Receipt of special counselling, by other disability

'Parents can be anxious and worried when they first learn their child has a handicap. In some areas social workers and other helpers spend time just listening and talking over people's worries and feelings. Have you had any special counselling like this to help you cope with your worries?' (S6Q5)

	Other disabilities		Total
	NOD	OD	
	%	%	%
Had special counselling	13	19	16
No counselling, spoken to someone	0	7	4
No counselling	86	74	80
No worries	2	1	1
Don't know	1	0	#
Total %	100	100	100
Base	126	159	285

Informants with children who had other disabilities were more likely to have received special counselling or to have spoken to someone about their problems compared with those where the children had no other disability (26 and 13 percent respectively).

Table 7.2 shows that only 1% of parents expressly reported that they did not have any worries in response to question S6Q5.

Table 7.3 shows that over two-thirds of those who had not had counselling would have liked it at that time. A third of them still felt the need for counselling at the time of the interview. This high level of demand continues, even among those with children aged 12 or over, where we know that nearly 80% of the children were born with their disabilities.

7.2 Special guidance and advice on bringing up a child with disabilities

Those whose children were not born with their sight problem were asked (at S6Q8) if they had received special advice or guidance on the particular difficulties they had encountered while bringing up a child with a sight problem. A lamentably low number of just over a quarter (27%) said they had received such guidance, as shown in Table 7.4.

Table 7.3 Past and present desire for special counselling among those who have not received it

'Given the opportunity, would you have liked to have special counselling to help you cope with your worries?' (S6Q6)

'And would you still like to have special counselling like this, if it were available?' (S6Q7)

	All who have not had counselling
	%
S6Q6:	
Yes, would have liked	69
No/don't know/had no worries	31
Total %	100
S6Q7:	
Would still like counselling	34
No current desire for counselling	64
Total %	100
Base	240

(45 informants have had counselling)

Table 7.4 Advice given on the special needs or problems of bringing up children with a disability, by age of child

'S6Q8 'Thinking back to . . . (child's) first three years, did anyone give you advice on how to bring up a child with problems such as . . .'s? I mean give you advice on special problems for . . ., on things like feeding, toilet training, reaching out for things, walking and talking. Please think about all the people you have already told me about as well.'

	Age			Total
	3 – 7	8 – 11	12 +	
	%	%	%	%
Yes	43	26	16	27
No	56	74	80	71
Don't know	2	0	4	2
Total %	100	100	100	100
Base	68	61	104	233

(52 children had their sight problem from birth)

Table 7.4 also shows a trend for parents of younger children to be more likely to have received such guidance. The number who had received guidance decreased as the age of the child increased; 43, 26 and 16 percent for the age groups 3 – 7, 8 – 11 and 12 + respectively. It may be that welfare and support services are becoming more aware of the need to provide this form of advice to parents in the early days. The increase in the number of those with younger children who said that they were receiving such advice suggests that there has been an increase in the provision of these services.

There was some indication that parents of more severely disabled children were more likely to have received such advice; though not statistically significant, it does seem logical.

Table 7.4 and the response to the questions on counselling suggest that for the vast majority of parents the support they received in terms of guidance and advice was minimal.

7.2.1 Sources of guidance and advice on bringing up a disabled child

Table 7.5 shows that advice was provided by a wide range of 'welfare' professionals, no one group predominating. The base for those with and without other disabilities was too small to show any statistically significant differences, but the trend did suggest some differences between the two groups.

The most frequently mentioned source was the 'health visitor/clinic' (26%), probably reflecting the almost mandatory contact a health visitor has with mother and newly born child. The physio- and occupational therapist and RNIB in general (16% each) are the next most mentioned sources, followed by teachers for the visually impaired and

Table 7.5 Sources of advice and guidance on bringing up a child with disabilities, by additional disabilities

	Other disability		Total
	No other disability	Other disability	
	%	%	%
Health visitor/clinic	24	27	26
Physio/occupational therapist	4	24	16
RNIB in general	16	16	16
Teacher for the visually impaired	12	14	13
Paediatrician	4	19	13
Eye specialist, ophthalmologist	8	8	8
Child's school	4	11	8
Teacher for other handicaps	0	11	7
Social/welfare worker	0	11	6
Social worker for blind	4	5	5
RNIB education adviser	8	3	5
Speech therapist	0	8	5
School doctor	0	3	2
Base = 100%	25	37	62

(62 respondents, only those who had received advice)

paediatricians (13% each). It is worth noting that both the physio- and occupational therapist and paediatrician are reported more frequently where the child is multiply disabled, reflecting the increased contact of that group with these professionals. Social workers are less frequently mentioned, reflecting the areas of responsibility of the education, health, and social services between the age groups.

7.2.2 Advice on making use of the senses available to the child

Informants were asked about two specific aspects of information they may have been given by the welfare professionals. The first was on the use of speech and sound to encourage the child; 61% said they were given this advice. Where the child had some residual vision (54 in this group), informants were asked (at S6Q12) if they were given advice on how to encourage the child to make best use of what sight he/she had. Exactly half said that they were.

7.2.3 Frequency of contact with welfare professional when child was an infant

Of the informants who said they had received some advice or guidance, a third (34%) said they were in contact with someone at least once a week; just over a third (37%) said they were in contact less than once a month. For children with multiple disabilities informants tended to report more frequent contact: 40% compared with 20% reporting at least weekly contact. This more frequent contact provided increased opportunity for the passing of information to parents.

A third (32%) of parents had maintained contact with the same person(s) since the child was an infant. Twelve of the 20 parents who still had contact saw the person(s) less than once a month.

7.3 Satisfaction with the level of support and advice received

When asked about their overall level of satisfaction with the advice and support they had received, 51% of informants said that they were either very or quite satisfied. Dissatisfaction was expressed by 31%. No real difference existed between the various sub-groups, such as those with other disabilities, and residual vision level. A small difference was discernible with age, more informants with younger children expressing a higher level of satisfaction; the percentages, in order of the increasing age ranges were 66, 48 and 43, possibly reflecting the point made in section 7.2 of an increased level of provision of welfare support services in more recent years.

7.4 Genetic counselling

We asked all parents if they had received any genetic counselling. Overall 20% of parents said that they had. A small difference existed for children with low compared with high residual vision (25 and 15 percent respectively), and those with and without an additional disability (24 and 15 percent respectively). Of course the provision of genetic counselling will depend on whether the disabilities are suspected of having a hereditary link.

7.5 Contact with other parents of children with disabilities

The sharing of experiences with others is often considered to be one of the ways in which those who are in some form of crisis situation learn to cope. Table 7.6 shows that 60% of informants had met other parents in a similar position. But more worrying is the 40% who said they did not have such contact. Furthermore, this proportion is similar for those whose children are aged 12 or more, where in many cases the onset of the problems would have occurred several years before the interview. Those parents had coped with the child, and any problems they encountered, in isolation without the knowledge, support and shared experience of others.

Table 7.6 Contact with other parents of children with disabilities, by residual vision, other disability and type of school

'Have you met parents of other children with problems like . . . (child)?' (S6Q17)

	Residual vision		Other disability		Ordinary or special school*		Total
	Hi %	Low %	NOD %	OD %	Ord %	Spcl %	%
Yes	50	69	50	68	42	75	60
No/don't know	50	31	50	32	58	25	40
Total %	100	100	100	100	100	100	100
Base	145	140	126	159	129	155	285

(* 1 child was not at school)

A clear pattern exists based on residual vision, the presence or absence of other disabilities, and the type of school the child attends. The parents of children with high residual vision, no other disabilities and attending ordinary schools are less likely to report contact with other parents than children with low residual vision, other disabilities and attending special schools. The percentages are 50 and 69, 50 and 68, and 42 and 75 respectively.

The level of sight and the presence of other disabilities are related to the type of school attended. Lower residual vision children and children with other disabilities are more likely to attend special schools (Chapter 6). The attendance at special schools provides the opportunity to meet other parents in a similar situation. Table 7.7 shows that the most frequently mentioned way of meeting other parents is through the child's school (58%).

Table 7.7 also shows that parents of more severely disabled children, with low residual vision or other disabilities, were more likely to report having met other parents through the child's school (65 and 67 percent respectively) compared with 48 and 42 percent for their sub-group counterparts. Twenty-five percent reported meeting other parents through self-help groups, and this varied little between the sub-groups. The other frequently mentioned form of contact was through the 'hospital since birth' of the child (17%). This was obviously while attending the hospital for treatment or rehabilitation.

Table 7.7 How parents of children with similar problems met, by residual vision, other disabilities and type of school

'How did you meet these other people?' (S6Q18)

	Residual vision		Other disability		Ordinary or special school		Total
	Hi %	Lo %	NOD %	OD %	Ord %	Spcl %	%
Through child's school	48	65	42	67	32	70	58
Self-help group	22	28	26	25	24	26	25
Hospital since child's birth	18	17	18	17	20	16	17
Through friends	3	13	10	8	9	9	9
Through counsellor or social worker	12	4	11	6	11	6	8
Through relatives	6	3	8	3	9	3	5
In hospital, when child was born	3	3	5	2	6	2	3
RNIB	0	3	0	3	0	3	2
Others	8	10	10	10	11	9	9
Base = 100%	73	97	62	108	54	116	170

(170, only those who had met other parents)

Though not statistically significant, there was a tendency for informants with less severely disabled children to report that this contact came through a 'counsellor or social worker', averaging 11 and 6 per cent compared with those with more severely disabled children. RNIB was mentioned only by the parents of more severely disabled children.

The difference between those at ordinary and special schools may also be seen here. Thirty-two percent with children attending ordinary schools, compared with 70% at special schools, said 'through the child's school', reflecting the possible isolation pointed out above. It may be worth noting that half of those who reported self-help groups also reported the child's school, thus reinforcing the importance of the school in providing the opportunity for shared experience.

7.5.1 Age of child when other parents were first met

Informants were asked the age of their child when they first met other parents. Three-quarters had met other parents with disabled children by the time their child was five years old; in fact, 42% had made contact by the time the child was two. There was a small tendency (not statistically significant) for parents with more severely disabled children to have made this contact while the child was younger.

7.5.2 Self-help parent groups

We asked (at S6Q20) those who had met other parents whether they were members of 'self-help groups', providing an explanation as to what we meant by the term: '. . . parents . . . who get together to talk and to organise things'. Twenty-one percent of those who had met other parents said they were members of self-help groups. Slightly fewer parents reported being actual members than reported simply meeting parents through self-help groups (21 and 25 percent respectively), showing greater participation though not necessarily 'membership'. It may be that for some groups there is no membership as such, more an informal meeting.

Table 7.8 shows that overall just 12% of all parents of visually impaired children were members of self-help groups.

Table 7.8   Membership of self-help groups among parents of visually impaired children, by type of school

'Are you a member of a self-help group of parents? By that I mean other parents whose children have problems, who get together to talk and organise things?' (S6Q20)

	Type of school*		Total
	Ordinary school	Special school	
	%	%	%
Member of self-help group	4	19	12
Met other parents only	38	56	47
All met other parents or members of group	42	75	60
Neither members nor met other parents	58	25	40
Total %	100	100	100
Base	129	155	284

(* 1 child was not at school)

Table 7.8 also demonstrates how the self-help groups are organised around the attendance at special schools. Not only may the children be getting specialised help at these schools, but parents are also receiving the support they need, so that they in turn may be able to offer better support to their children.

Twenty-one of the 35 parents (60%) who were members of groups said the group met on a monthly basis.

7.6 Support and advice most needed at onset of the child's problems

Having been questioned on all aspects of support and advice that they had been given, parents were then asked in summary what support or advice they would have liked most when their child's problems were first identified. The unprompted responses are shown in Table 7.9.

Table 7.9 Support and advice most needed at the onset of the child's problem(s)

'Thinking back to when you first found out about . . . (child's) problems, what sort of support and advice would you have found helpful at that time?' (S6Q22)

	All parents
	%
Counselling/talking it over	25
Chatting to others	17
Explanation of condition	16
Explanation of likely future	12
General advice on coping	9
Explanation of benefits/what was available	6
Carer to give break	2
Don't know what	15
Had all the help needed	5
Base = 100%	285

Counselling or talking it over (25%) was the most frequently mentioned, followed by chatting to others in a similar situation (17%). An explanation of the child's condition (16%) and of the future and what it might hold (12%) came next. Parents clearly wanted to discuss their feelings and fears. The four items most frequently mentioned were given by 52% of informants as the first of the four answers allowed to this question, and are an indication of the importance of this form of support to parents. This is in line with our findings in section 7.1.1 on the demand for counselling among parents.

Part D

Daily Living and Mobility

8 Daily Living Skills

8.1 Daily living tasks

Mastery of the school curriculum presupposes competence in many areas of functioning. Without these skills – autonomy and independence in spatial orientation, mobility, safety, hygiene and self-care – some scientific, craft, artistic, technological and physical education curricula cannot even be embarked upon, let alone developed to an acceptable standard. In this section of the enquiry, parents were asked to comment upon their child's ability to carry out eleven tasks using these basic self-care and daily living skills (DLS). Table 8.1 shows the percentage of children able to do each task.

Overall, 9% of children were reported as not being able to do any of the tasks listed. 'Make a hot drink' (43%) was the task the fewest number of visually impaired children were able to do. Only 24% of younger children aged 3 – 11 years were able to do this, possibly due to restrictions imposed because of the danger in young children handling hot water. However, it was also the task the fewest number of older children were able to do (65%).

'Wash all over or bath' (68%), 'comb and brush own hair' (73%), 'dress self' (75%), and 'feed self with a knife and fork' (77%) were the other tasks that less than 80% of children were able to do.

'Get in and out of bed on their own' (89%), 'feed self with a spoon' (89%), 'come down steps and stairs' (85%), 'clean own teeth' (82%), 'use toilet by self' (82%), and 'wash own hands and face' (81%) were the tasks over 80% of children were able to do.

8.1.1 Disability and the performance of daily living skills

The sub-group analysis in Table 8.1 clearly shows that the ability to do the individual tasks differs between those children with and without other disabilities and those with high and low residual vision. Consequently differences exist between children in ordinary and special schools. Children not able to do any of the tasks were exclusively children with other disabilities (16%). The same percentage also had low residual vision, and all were in special schools.

Table 8.1 The ability to perform daily living tasks, by other disability, residual vision, and type of school

'Now I would like to ask you about things that . . . (child) can do for himself/herself. I have here some examples of things people do. Please sort them into things . . . (child) can do, and things he/she can't, by placing them in a section on this board' (S8Q1)

	Other disability		Residual vision		Ordinary or special school*		Total
	NOD	OD	Hi	Lo	Ord	Spcl	
	%	%	%	%	%	%	%
DLS tasks							
Get in and out of bed on own	99	81	97	81	99	80	89
Feed self with a spoon	99	81	97	80	99	80	89
Come down steps and stairs	98	75	96	74	98	74	85
Clean own teeth	100	69	94	71	99	69	82
Use toilet by self	99	69	92	72	96	72	82
Wash own hands and face	98	67	92	69	98	66	81
Feed self with a knife and fork	96	62	90	64	91	66	77
Dress self	96	59	87	64	92	62	75
Comb and brush own hair	94	55	84	61	88	60	73
Wash all over or bath	98	67	81	54	84	55	68
Make a hot drink	63	28	57	29	53	35	43
Not able to do any of the tasks	0	16	1	16	0	16	9
Average % of those able to do tasks within each sub-group	96	65	88	65	91	65	77
Base = 100%	126	159	145	140	129	155	285

(* 1 child was not at school)

Calculating an average percentage (an index of competence) for each of the sub-groups gives an overall picture of the total number able to do the various tasks. The average is 65% in the other disability, low residual vision, and special school sub-groups; in their sub-group counterparts the average is close to or exceeds 90%, reaching 96% in the no other disability sub-group. Thus, more severely disabled children are less able to perform the tasks.

8.1.2 Additional disabilities and daily living skills

Table 8.2 shows how the presence of an additional disability combines with low residual vision to affect radically the ability to perform the tasks. For children with high residual vision the presence of another disability sees a reduction, in the average, from 95 to 80 percent in their ability to do one or more of the tasks. For children with low residual vision this proportion drops even more dramatically, from 93 to 53 percent.

Table 8.2 Children able to perform daily living tasks, by other disability within residual vision levels

	High residual vision		Low residual vision		Total
	Other disability		Other disability		
	NOD	OD	NOD	OD	
	%	%	%	%	%
Get in and out of bed on own	99	94	100	72	89
Feed self with a spoon	99	95	100	71	89
Come down steps and stairs	99	96	96	64	85
Clean own teeth	100	86	100	57	83
Use toilet by self	99	84	100	59	83
Wash own hands and face	99	84	98	55	81
Feed self with a knife and fork	95	83	98	49	77
Dress self	95	76	98	48	75
Comb and brush own hair	95	70	93	46	73
Wash all over or bath	94	65	86	40	68
Make a hot drink	68	43	52	18	43
Not able to do any of the tasks	0	3	0	24	9
Average % of those able to do tasks within each sub-group	95	80	93	53	77
Base = 100%	82	63	44	96	285

Another way of looking at this data is to compare the difference between those children with low and high residual vision who have no other disabilities and those with other disabilities. For children with high or low residual vision and no other disabilities, the average percentage able to do one or more of the tasks is about the same (95 and 93 respectively).

The data show that the ability to perform most of the tasks is affected more by the presence of an additional disability than by the level of residual vision. For children with both low residual vision and another disability the inability to perform the task is compounded. So while a relatively high percentage of children with high residual vision and other disabilities (80%) are able to perform the tasks, this is not so for those children with low residual vision and other disabilities (53%).

8.1.3 Age and daily living skills

Age played a lesser role in influencing the number of children able to perform the individual tasks. Only 'make a hot drink' showed a clear age difference, with 24 and 65 percent of younger and older children respectively reported as being able to do this task. 'Wash all over or bath' just showed a statistically significant difference between younger and older children (62 and 75 percent respectively).

The ability to carry out the individual tasks was looked at further by excluding those children aged five years and under from the analysis. The overall percentage of children reported as being able to do the individual tasks changed by no more than one or two points, confirming the lower influence of age on their ability.

8.2 Tasks the child is able to do

Table 8.3 shows that while 91% of children are able to do at least one of the tasks, only 41% can do all of them, with 34% able to do 8 to 10 tasks. It has already been noted (Table 8.1 and section 8.1.1) that the children least able to do any individual task are almost exclusively children with other disabilities, low residual vision and children in special schools (16% in each sub-group). About half this number again in the same sub-groups could only do between one and three of the tasks. Overall, this makes almost a quarter of children in these sub-groups unable to do more than three tasks.

About 90% of children with high residual vision, no other disability or in ordinary schools could do eight or more of the tasks compared with about 60% of their sub-group counterparts. (While only 6% of those children who could do 8 to 10 tasks were able to make themselves a hot drink, and 79% were able to 'wash all over or bath', it is worth noting that this may have as much to do with restrictions imposed by parents as restrictions caused by the child's disabilities.)

Table 8.3 Number of daily living tasks child is able to do, by other disability, residual vision, type of school and age

	Other disability		Residual vision		Ordinary or special school*		Age		Total
	NOD	OD	Hi	Lo	Ord	Spcl	3 – 11	12 +	
	%	%	%	%	%	%	%	%	%
Number of tasks able to do:									
None	0	16	1	16	0	16	9	8	9
1 – 3	0	8	3	6	0	8	4	5	5
4 – 7	3	20	8	17	7	16	17	7	12
8 – 10	36	32	34	34	44	25	47	19	34
All of them	61	25	55	26	49	34	23	61	41
Total	100	100	100	100	100	100	100	100	100
Base	126	159	145	140	129	155	152	133	285

(* 1 child was not at school)

The difference between children in ordinary and special schools is an important factor to note. Ninety-three percent of children in ordinary schools were able to do eight or more of the tasks, compared with the much lower 59% of children in special schools. These findings highlight the role of the school in trying to meet the formal educational needs of the child while also developing the other (self-care) skills. It is a responsibility that is recognised in both types of schools, and it can be seen to constitute the hidden or additional curriculum required by visually impaired learners. Finding time for it is a major problem for the teachers. Given the type of pupils in the special schools, with their higher proportions of children with additional disabilities and poorer vision, the job of providing the extended curriculum is formidable.

It has already been noted that age has less influence on the ability of visually impaired children to perform the individual tasks, but when all the tasks are taken together a larger age difference does appear. Eighty percent of older children are able to do eight or more tasks compared with 70% of younger children. However, the number of children able to do all the tasks is much greater among older compared with younger children (61 and 23 percent respectively).

8.2.1 Most easily achieved daily living skills

Table 8.4 examines the percentage of children able to do the tasks, based on the number of individual skills they are able to achieve. This gives a threshold showing which tasks are most easily achieved by children who can do only a few tasks compared with children able to do more.

Table 8.4 Overall number of tasks child is able to do

	Number of individual tasks child is able to do					Total
	None	1 – 3†	4 – 7†	8 – 10	All	
	%	%	%	%	%	%
Get in and out of bed on own	0	62	94	100	100	89
Feed self with a spoon	0	54	97	100	100	89
Come down steps and stairs	0	39	89	94	100	85
Clean own teeth	0	23	57	100	100	83
Use toilet by self	0	8	71	97	100	83
Wash own hands and face	0	8	49	100	100	81
Feed self with a knife and fork	0	0	37	95	100	77
Dress self	0	0	20	96	100	75
Comb and brush own hair	0	8	26	84	100	73
Wash all over or bath	0	0	6	79	100	68
Make a hot drink	0	0	3	6	100	43
Base = 100%	25	13	35	96	116	285

† Low base, percentages to be treated with caution

Table 8.4 gives some indication of which tasks are more difficult. Among the thirteen children able to do between one and three tasks, none of them were able to 'feed self with a knife and fork', 'dress self', 'make a hot drink', or 'wash all over or bath'. The number of children able to do 4 – 7 tasks (37, 20, 3 and 6 percent respectively) also found these difficult.

For children able to do 8 – 10 tasks, the same tasks again figure as difficult: 'make a hot drink' (6%) proved the most difficult, followed by 'wash all over or bath' (79%), and 'comb and brush own hair' (84%).

Among children able to do 8 – 10 tasks, some degree of difficulty was apparent with 'feed self with knife and fork', 'use toilet by self' and 'come down steps and stairs'.

8.3 Reasons why children were unable to do the tasks

It has already been suggested (section 8.1.2) that the presence of an additional disability compounds the child's difficulty in performing the tasks. Where the child was able to do a particular task, the informant was then asked whether the child had any difficulty doing it. Where the child had difficulty, or was earlier reported as not being able to do the task, the informant was asked whether the difficulty or the reason for not doing the task was mainly due to the child's sight problem or another reason. The results are shown in Table 8.5.

Table 8.5 Main reason why child has difficulty or is not able to do the daily living task (percentage across rows)

'Is the difficulty (not being able to do the DLS task) mainly because of his/her eyesight, or something else?' (S8Q4)

'Can't he/she . . . (do activity) because of his/her eyesight, or something else?' (S8Q5)

		Reason not able to do the DLS task					
		Sight	Other	Both	Don't know	Total	Base
Get in and out of bed on own	%	5	73	14	9	100	44
Clean own teeth	%	16	59	12	13	100	83
Feed self with a spoon	%	22	51	13	14	100	63
Feed self with a knife and fork	%	27	44	14	16	100	110
Dress self	%	32	38	14	16	100	121
Use toilet by self	%	14	49	18	18	100	77
Wash own hands and face	%	13	56	13	18	100	77
Make a hot drink	%	26	37	17	20	100	185
Wash all over or bath	%	16	51	16	16	100	104
Comb and brush own hair	%	24	48	14	15	100	109
Come down steps and stairs	%	28	46	11	16	100	83
Averaging % in columns		**20**	**50**	**14**	**16**	–	–

By averaging the percentages within the columns of the table, a summary is produced for each of the reasons given for the difficulty or problem over all the individual tasks. The average of the percentages shows that overall about 20% of children have difficulty with the tasks because of their 'sight' compared with 50% where 'other' reasons were reported. Similar percentages of informants reported 'both' or 'don't know' (14 and 16 percent).

For the majority of the individual tasks, the difference between those informants reporting 'sight' and 'other' was marked. The following are the tasks for which an 'other' reason was reported at least three times more frequently than sight as the single cause of the difficulty: 'get in and out of bed on own' (5 and 73 percent); 'clean own teeth' (16 and 59 percent); 'use toilet by self' (14 and 49 percent); 'wash own hands and face' (13 and 56 percent); 'wash all over or bath' (16 and 51 percent).

'Sight' and 'other' reasons respectively were reported by almost equal numbers for 'dress self' (32 and 38 percent) and 'make a hot drink' (26 and 37 percent) as the main cause of the difficulty.

This direct questioning confirms the conclusions drawn from the purely statistical analysis that the sight problem alone is not, in the parent's opinion, the single most important reason for the children not being able to perform the tasks. The deciding factor is the compounding effect of sight loss and other disabilities.

9 Mobility

9.1 Level of mobility

The mobility of visually impaired children is looked at on two levels. The first is simply the physical ability of the child to move around on his/her own, the second whether the child is capable of independent mobility and travel.

Table 9.1 shows the physical mobility of visually impaired children. Residual vision and age showed no differentiation. All children in our sample were aged 3 years and over and, in terms of the development of the non-disabled children, could be expected to walk independently.

Table 9.1   Mobility levels by other disability and residual vision

' . . . Can I just check first of all, can . . . (child) walk on his/her own, or with the help of aids?' (S7Q1)
'Did . . . (child) ever start to crawl or move about on his/her own?' (S7Q2)
'Can . . . (child) still crawl or move about on his/her own?' (S7Q3)
'Did . . . (child) ever start to walk?' (S7Q5)

	Other disability and residual vision				Other disability		Total
	No other disability		Has other disability				
	Hi	Lo	Hi	Lo	NOD	OD	
	%	%	%	%	%	%	%
Walk unaided	100	100	86	66	100	74	85
Walk aided			8	4	0	6	3
Walk unaided or aided	**100**	**100**	**94**	**70**	**100**	**80**	**88**
Cannot walk	**0**	**0**	**6**	**30**	**0**	**20**	**12**
All cannot walk:							
Can crawl or move on own	0	0	5	9	0	8	4
Mobility regression:							
Can crawl used to walk	0	0	2	3	0	3	1
Can't crawl or move, used to walk	0	0	0	3	0	2	1
Used to crawl or move, now none	0	0	0	1	0	1	#
Never crawled or moved	0	0	0	14	0	8	5
Total %	100	100	100	100	100	100	100
Base	82	44	63	96	126	159	285

The first point is that all children without additional disabilities are reported as being able to walk unaided. Of all those with another disability, 80% can walk either unaided or aided (74% unaided). Ninety-four percent of those with high residual vision and other disability can walk unaided or aided (86% unaided); 70% of children with low residual vision and other disabilities can walk unaided or aided (66% unaided). Overall 88% of visually impaired children can walk unaided or aided.

9.1.1 Children unable to walk

Table 9.1 shows that 5% (13 children) of visually impaired children are reported never to have crawled or moved. All thirteen children had an additional disability and low residual vision (forming 14% of children with low residual vision), reflecting the association between low residual vision and increased disability in other areas (see Chapter 6). Four percent had not progressed beyond crawling or moving. For just over 2% there had been a regression: from walking to crawling (1%); 'can't crawl or move, used to walk' (1%). One child who had crawled now did not move at all.

9.1.2 Age at which children started to walk

Table 9.2 shows the age at which visually impaired children are reported to have started walking. Overall, 87% with no other disability started to walk at under 2 years of age; in fact 97% were walking at under 3 years. The rest were walking by their fifth birthday.

Table 9.2 The age child started to walk, by other disability and residual vision

	Other disability and residual vision level				Other disability		Total
	No other disability		Other disability				
	Hi	Lo	Hi	Lo	NOD	OD	
	%	%	%	%	%	%	%
Under 1 year old	24	11	10	9	20	9	14
1 to under 2	66	68	49	31	67	38	51
Under 2 years	**90**	**79**	**59**	**40**	**87**	**47**	**65**
2 years, under 3	9	11	14	14	10	14	11
3 years, under 5	0	9	14	13	3	13	9
5 to 7 years	0	0	5	7	0	6	4
Never walked but crawled	0	0	5	10	0	8	5
Never crawled or moved	0	0	0	14	0	8	5
Don't know what age	1	0	2	2	1	2	1
No information	0	0	2	0	0	1	#
Total %	100	100	100	100	100	100	100
Base	82	44	63	96	126	159	285

For children with other disabilities walking was a more drawn out development. Overall just under half (47%) were walking at under two years: 59% of those with high residual vision and 40% with low residual vision. A third of children with other disabilities did not walk until after their second birthday. Twenty percent were reported as not walking at the time of the survey. What can be seen is the presence of another disability holding back the independent physical mobility of visually impaired children.

9.2 The use of mobility aids

As shown in Table 9.3 just over a third of visually impaired children used a vision mobility aid, including white cane or guide dog. The remaining 24% used a physical mobility aid, such as a walking stick, purely for physical support.

Children with other disabilities were two-and-a-half times more likely to use some form of mobility aid than children with no other disability (47

Table 9.3   The use of mobility aids, by other disability and residual vision

	Other disability and residual vision level				Other disability		Total
	No other disability		Has other disability				
	Hi	Lo	Hi	Lo	NOD	OD	
	%	%	%	%	%	%	%
Wheelchair	0	0	11	34	0	25	14
White or red cane	2	25	8	11	10	10	10
Pushchair	0	2	11	12	1	11	7
Walking frame	0	0	13	10	0	11	6
Walking stick	0	0	3	2	0	3	1
Crutches	0	0	3	1	0	2	1
Orthopaedic aids	0	0	5	1	0	3	1
Guide dogs	0	0	2	0	0	1	#
Other	8	5	3	5	7	4	6
All using vision mobility aids†	2	25	8	12	10	10	10
All using non-vision aids	9	7	27	43	9	37	24
All using any aids	**11**	**32**	**35**	**54**	**18**	**47**	**34**
No mobility aids	**78**	**55**	**56**	**38**	**70**	**45**	**56**
Don't know	11	14	10	8	12	9	10
Total %	100	100	100	100	100	100	100
Base	82	44	63	96	126	159	285

† A vision mobility aid is one specifically for visual impairment e.g. a white cane, compared with a mobility aid for support e.g. walking frame.

and 18 percent respectively). They were also four times as likely to be using a non-vision mobility aid (37 and 9 percent).

The use of a vision mobility aid was clearly split between children with low and high residual vision (16 and 5 percent respectively). Children with low residual vision were also more likely to be using one of the non-vision mobility aids (31 and 17 percent), reflecting the association between low residual vision and other disabilities.

Table 9.3 shows that, overall, children with high residual vision and no other disability were less likely to use any mobility aid; only 11% of this group used one. In comparison, the largest group of users of mobility aids (55%) were children with low residual vision and another disability.

9.2.1 Mobility aids used

Overall, the 'wheelchair' was used most frequently by 14% of the children with a visual impairment, followed by the 'white or red cane' (10%). A pushchair and walking frame were used by 7 and 6 percent respectively, while walking stick, crutches and orthopaedic aids were used by 1% each. A guide dog was used by one visually impaired child.

Within the overall figures, differences occurred between sub-groups. Wheelchairs were used only by children with other disabilities (25%). Within this group it was children with low residual vision who used them more than those with high residual vision (34 and 11 percent).

A 'white or red cane' was used by 16% of children with low residual vision, while only 5% of those with high residual vision used one.

9.3 How frequently children go out

Eight in ten children were reported to go out with an adult every day, and 95% went out at least once a week (table not shown). Barely one percent never went out.

Tables 9.4 and 9.5 show the frequency with which visually impaired children go out without an adult, either on their own or with other children. Table 9.4 shows that overall 30% go out almost every day on their own, increasing to 38% when those who go out at least once a week are included. Low residual vision and the presence of another disability reduce the frequency with which visually impaired children go out alone. The number of children with low and high residual vision reported as going out at least weekly are 58 and 17 percent respectively; for children without and with other disabilities the percentages are 57 and 23 respectively. In other words, about 75% of children with other disabilities or low residual vision never go out on their own compared with about 38% of those with high residual vision or no other disability.

Table 9.4   Frequency children go out on their own, by age, residual vision and other disabilities

' . . . how often, if at all, does he/she go out (-side the home) on his/her own?' (S7Q12)

	Age		Residual vision		Other disability		Total
	3 – 11	12 +	Hi	Lo	NOD	OD	
	%	%	%	%	%	%	%
Almost every day	23	38	47	12	42	20	30
At least once a week	3	14	11	5	15	3	8
At least once a month	0	5	1	4	5	0	2
Once in 2 – 3 months	0	0	0	0	0	0	0
Less often	1	4	0	4	2	2	2
Never	73	41	41	75	35	76	58
Total %	100	100	100	100	100	100	100
Base	152	133	145	140	126	159	285

Table 9.5 shows that 51% of visually impaired children go out at least once a week accompanied by another child but without an adult.

Table 9.5 shows that less severely disabled children go out more frequently with other children. Thus, more children with high residual vision are reported to go out 'almost every day' than children with low residual vision (53 and 21 percent respectively). The corresponding totals for children without and with other disabilities are 57 and 22 percent.

Table 9.5   Frequency children go out with other children but without an adult, by age, residual vision, and other disability

'How often, if at all, does he/she go outside the home with other children but no adults?' (S7Q11)

	Age		Residual vision		Other disability		Total
	3 – 11	12 +	Hi	Lo	NOD	OD	
	%	%	%	%	%	%	%
Almost every day	34	42	53	21	57	22	38
At least once a week	12	14	15	11	14	11	13
At least once a month	1	4	3	2	2	3	3
Once in 2 – 3 months	1	2	2	1	2	1	1
Less often	1	0	0	1	1	0	#
Never	51	38	26	64	22	63	45
Total %	100	100	100	100	100	100	100
Base	152	133	145	140	126	159	285

9.3.1   Visually impaired children aged 12 years and over

Age, not unexpectedly, influences which children are reported as going out on their own. Most responsible parents would not let a very young child out on his/her own, so while 82% of children aged 3 – 7 years never go out alone, this is reduced to 41% for those aged 12 and over. Table 9.6 looks at going out alone for children aged 12 and over, by residual vision level and the presence or absence of other disabilities. This takes into account the effect of those children who might, in normal circumstances, be too young to be allowed out by themselves.

Table 9.6 Frequency children aged 12 or over go out on their own, by residual vision, and other disabilities

' . . . how often, if at all, does he/she go out on their out (-side the home) on his/her own?' (S7Q12)

	Residual vision		Other disability		Total
	Hi	Lo	NOD	OD	
	%	%	%	%	%
Almost every day	60	19	52	25	38
At least once a week	20	8	23	6	14
At least once a month	2	7	10	0	2
Once in 2 – 3 months	0	0	0	0	0
Less often	0	7	3	4	2
Never	18	59	13	65	58
Total %	100	100	100	100	100
Base	60	73	62	71	133

Table 9.6 clearly shows that it is those children with low residual vision or those having another disability who are most frequently reported as never going out (59 and 65 percent respectively), compared with children with high residual vision or no other disability (18 and 13 percent respectively).

Children aged 12 and over go out just as often with other children and without adults as they do on their own (no table shown). For those with and without another disability, 15 and 58 percent never go out with other children; for those with low and high residual vision the corresponding percentages are 13 and 58.

9.4 Mobility training

Table 9.7 shows that, overall, only a quarter (26%) of visually impaired children have had mobility training. Mobility training was broadly defined in the question to make the informant aware of its special nature.

Table 9.7 The need for mobility training, by age and residual vision, and residual vision

'Has your child ever had any mobility training (that is special training about moving about in the home or outside)?' (S7Q15)

'Do you think your child should have had mobility training?' (S7Q16)

	Age and residual vision				Residual vision		Total
	3 – 11		12 +				
	Hi %	Lo %	Hi %	Lo %	Hi %	Lo %	%
S7Q15							
Had mobility training	12	22	23	48	17	38	26
No mobility training	85	69	74	43	80	58	68
S7Q16							
Should have mobility training	12	24	12	16	12	20	16
Should not have mobility training	73	45	62	27	68	38	52
Don't know at Q16	4	6	2	6	3	6	4
Don't know at Q15	0	3	2	3	1	3	2
Total %	100	100	100	100	100	100	100
Base	85	67	60	73	145	140	285

Table 9.7 shows that children with low residual vision were more than twice as likely to have had mobility training as those with high residual vision (38 and 17 percent respectively). Fifty-two percent of informants said that their child should not have any mobility training.

Sixty-eight percent of children with high residual vision were thought not to need mobility training, compared with 38% of children with low residual vision. Only an additional 20% of low residual vision children were thought to need mobility training; this comprised one-third of such children who had not had any.

Age also had a clear influence, with 36% of children aged 12 and over having had mobility training compared with 16% of those aged under 12. Those who felt the child should have mobility training were similar for the two age groups (14 and 17 percent respectively).

9.4.1   Other disabilities and mobility training

Table 9.8 shows that visually impaired children with other disabilities are more likely to have received mobility training (30 and 21 percent), and that informants felt that these children should have such training (19 and 12 percent). Children with no other disability are more likely to be reported as not needing mobility training (64 and 43 percent). This is a possible consequence of those children with no other disabilities also tending to have higher residual vision, and it is children with high residual vision who were said not to need mobility training.

Table 9.8 The need for mobility training, by other disabilities

	Other disability		Total
	NOD	OD	
	%	%	%
S7Q15			
Had mobility training	21	30	26
No mobility training	75	62	68
S7Q16			
Should have mobility training	12	19	16
Shouldn't have mobility training	64	43	52
Don't know at Q16	3	5	4
Don't know at Q15	0	3	2
Total %	100	100	100
Base	126	159	285

9.4.2 Source of mobility training

Table 9.9 shows that a mobility officer is clearly the main source of mobility training; 67 percent of informants said that training had been given by a mobility officer in the child's school. Thirty-five percent said it had been given by the mobility officer from the local authority. The physiotherapist was mentioned by 8%, though this person would not have provided mobility training as understood by those working in the field of welfare for visually impaired people. Others mentioned included peripatetic teacher (3%), mother, and pre-school project (1% each).

Table 9.9 Source of the mobility training (S7Q17)

	All who have had mobility training
	%
Mobility officer in school	67
Mobility officer from LA	35
Physiotherapist	8
Peripatetic teacher	3
Mother	1
Pre-school project	1
Others	1
Don't know	1
Base = 100%	75

(210 had not had mobility training)

Formal lessons were the medium by which half (51%) of the children received their mobility training, and 19% had been on some form of residential course. Just over a quarter (28%) were reported as only having had general advice, not proper lessons. All children reported as having been on a residential course for their mobility training were in special schools.

9.4.3 Mobility training and attendance at special schools

Table 9.10 shows that children who have had mobility training are concentrated in special schools rather than ordinary schools (40 and 9 percent respectively).

Informants with children in ordinary schools were more likely to express the opinion that the child should not have mobility training (74%) than those with children in special schools (34%) (no table shown).

Table 9.10   Mobility by type of school and age

'Has child ever had any mobility training (that is special training about moving about in the home or outside)?' (S7Q15)

	Age and type of school				Type of school		Total
	3 – 11		12 +				
	Ord %	Spcl %	Ord %	Spcl %	Ord %	Spcl %	%
Had mobility training	5	30	17	48	9	40	26
No mobility training	94	69	83	48	90	57	72
Don't know	1	1	0	4	1	3	2
Total %	100	100	100	100	100	100	100
Base	81	70	48	85	129	155	284

(1 child not at school)

Of the 67% of children who had been given mobility training by a mobility officer in school, 92% were attending a special school. Even among the 35% who were given training by a local authority mobility officer, 77% were in special schools (no table shown).

Part E

Schooling

10 School and Careers

10.1 Attendance at school

Table 10.1 shows that 95% of children were attending school at the time of the interview. Fourteen children were not at school: one was aged under 5, and 8 were aged 17 and over.

Table 10.1 Attendance at school, by age of visually impaired child

	Age			Total
	3 – 7	8 – 11	12 +	
	%	%	%	%
At school	98	100	91	95
Not at school	2	0	9	5
Total %	100	100	100	100
Base	79	73	133	285

10.1.1 Ordinary and special school attendance

Table 10.2 shows that just under half (46%) of visually impaired children attend an 'ordinary' school; 53% attend a 'special' school. The overall pattern is for younger children to attend a local ordinary school, with older children attending either a local or residential special school. So, while 61% of children aged 3 to 7 years are in ordinary schools, this decreases to 37% for those aged 12 and over. However, most of the difference in the type of school attended is based not on age, but on the level of residual vision and presence or absence of another disability.

Table 10.2 shows that within the two age groups the percentage differences between the two residual vision levels are in the same direction and of the same magnitude. The exception to this is the percentage of younger and older children in residential special schools, and those with low residual vision in an 'ordinary local school with little support'.

Table 10.2 Type of school, by residual vision within two age groups

'Which of these (show card†) best describes the type of school (child) goes to?' (S9Q9)

| | Age and residual vision | | | | Total |
| | 3 – 11 | | 12 + | | |
	Hi %	Lo %	Hi %	Lo %	%
Ordinary local school	39	15	37	13	26
Ordinary local school with little support	31	18	29	3	20
Area school with resources	7	6	8	6	7
Area special school for visually handicapped	1	21	6	19	11
Residential special school for visually handicapped	2	9	12	23	11
Area special school for all handicaps	18	30	10	36	24
Don't know	1	2	0	0	1
Total %	100	100	100	100	100
Base	84	66	52	69	271

(14 children were not at school)

†The definitions of the school types from the show card are given in the Appendix to Chapter 20

Table 10.3 shows the type of schools attended for children with and without other disabilities and with high or low residual vision.

Table 10.3 Type of school, by other disability and residual vision

| | Other disability | | Residual vision | | Total |
	NOD %	OD %	Hi %	Lo %	%
Ordinary local school	40	15	38	14	26
Ordinary local school with little support	28	13	20	20	20
Area school with resources	8	5	7	6	7
Area special school for visually handicapped	12	11	3	20	11
Residential special school for the visually handicapped	10	12	6	16	11
Area special school for all handicaps	3	41	15	33	24
Don't know	0	1	1	1	1
Total %	100	100	100	100	100
Base	121	150	136	135	271

(14 children were not at school)

Table 10.3 shows that 68% of children without other disabilities attended an ordinary school, compared with 64% of children with another disability who attended special schools.

More severely disabled children were to be found in special than in ordinary schools, whether or not the severity of disability is measured by the presence or absence of additional disabilities, or by the level of residual vision.

Fifty-eight percent of children with high residual vision were in ordinary schools, compared with 69% of children with low residual vision who were in special schools. Clearly therefore some allocation based on severity of disability is in operation determining whether children attend either a special or an ordinary school.

Tables 10.2 and 10.3 show the broad descriptions that we offered to parents as to the type of schools that the child attended. (The full descriptions, defining the schools, are given on the show card in the appendix to Chapter 20.) These descriptions were arrived at during the development stage of the research. Informants were asked (at S9Q10) whether the category they chose exactly described the type of school, and if not, to say how it differed. Seventy percent of informants said that it accurately described the school. Of the 27% who said the description differed (73 informants), 80% were placed in the broad category of 'special' schools. The main differences mentioned in the special school category were: 'no long journey involved'; 'not just for visually handicapped children'; 'for many handicaps'. For those who said the ordinary school differed from the category description, this was because more support was provided by the school than the description allowed, e.g. special teachers or special equipment.

10.1.2 Day school or boarding

The majority (88%) of children were day pupils; 13% boarded. As shown in Table 10.4 the proportion boarding was split fairly evenly between weekly and term boarding.

A greater proportion of children who had another disability, or had low residual vision (16 and 19 percent respectively) were boarders, compared with those without other disabilities or with high residual vision (8 and 6 percent respectively).

Of the 30 children attending a residential school for the visually handicapped, four were day pupils. Of those who went to an area special school, seven boarded.

Table 10.4 Day or boarding school attended, by other disabiity and residual vision level

'Does . . . (child) board at school, or is he/she a day pupil? If board is that weekly boarding, or boarding for the whole term? (S9Q3)

	Other disability		Residual vision		Total
	NOD	OD	Hi	Lo	
	%	%	%	%	%
Day school	92	84	94	81	88
Weekly boarding	7	7	3	11	7
Term boarding	1	9	3	8	6
Total %	100	100	100	100	100
Base	121	150	136	135	271

(14 children were not at school)

10.2 Getting to school

Table 10.5 shows that 72% of children lived within 30 minutes' journey time of their school, and also separates the boarders from day school children.

Table 10.5 Time taken to get to school, by whether day or boarding pupil

'How long does it take to get to school? (S9Q4)

	Day or boarding pupil			Total
	Day	Weekly board	Term board	
	%	%	%	%
10 minutes or less	36	5	0	32
11 – 20 minutes	24	0	0	21
21 – 30 minutes	21	5	7	19
31 – 45 minutes	7	5	7	7
46 – 59 minutes	4	0	0	4
1 – 2 hours	8	58	27	12
More than 2 hours	0	26	60	5
Don't know	1	0	0	#
Total %	100	100	100	100
Base	237	19	15	271

(14 children were not at school)

Eighty-one percent of day pupils had a journey time of 30 minutes or less, although 8% had a journey of between one and two hours. For boarders (term and weekly) 81% took more than an hour to travel to school, and half of these took over two hours. In Chapter 16 it is noted that relatively few parents reported having moved house to be near a particular school.

Eighty-two percent of children with high residual vision lived within a thirty minute journey of their school, compared with 61% of children with low residual vision. This is perhaps explained by the fact that 19% of children with low residual vision were boarders compared with 6% of those with high residual vision.

An age-related trend was aso discernible, possibly reflecting the fact that older children are more likely to board or travel further afield to a school that provides education to meet their special needs. While 51% of children aged 3 – 7 lived within a 10 minute journey of school, this decreased for those aged 8 – 11, and 12 + (38 and 17 percent respectively).

10.2.1 Mode of travel

Overall, just under a quarter (23%) of children walked to school. The rest travelled by train and bicycle (2 and 3 percent respectively) and by car or bus. Again it is sensible to look at this by day and boarding pupils, as shown in Table 10.6.

Table 10.6 Mode of travel to school, by whether day or boarding pupil

'How does . . . (child) normally travel to school' (S9Q5)

	Day	Boarders†			Total
		Week	Term	All	
	%	%	%	%	%
School bus/mini-bus	30	16	8	12	27
Taxi/mini-cab	23	68	40	56	27
On foot	26	0	0	0	23
By private car	19	21	47	32	20
Bicycle	3	0	0	0	3
Ordinary bus	3	0	0	0	2
Ambulance	2	0	0	0	2
Train	0	5	28	15	2
Does not travel to school	0	0	7	3	#
Base = 100%	237	19	15	34	271

(14 children were not at school)

†Small base: caution with percentages

None of the boarders made the journey on foot. A third (32%) travelled by private car, and over half (56%) by taxi or mini-cab. Only boarders reported travelling by train (15%), and a further 12% by school bus or mini-bus. This pattern of travel clearly corresponds with the longer journey time reported in section 10.2.

Day pupils used more varied methods of transport. Just over a quarter (26%) travelled on foot and 19% by private car. Over half (55%)

travelled by provided transport, school or mini-bus (30%) and taxi (23%) being the main forms.

10.2.2 Travelling to school accompanied or alone

Table 10.7 shows that just under a third of children were reported as going to school by themselves; 30% were taken by someone in the household, and 40% were escorted by someone outside the household.

Table 10.7 Who escorts child to school, by whether day or boarding pupil

'Who usually goes with . . . (child) to school, or does he/she usually go alone? (S9Q6)

	Day	Boarders†			Total
		Week	Term	All	
	%	%	%	%	%
Escort	40	42	27	35	40
Goes alone	32	37	20	29	32
Has to be taken by someone in the house	29	21	53	35	30
Has to be taken by a relative/ friend	3	0	13	6	3
Don't know	0	0	7	#	#
Base = 100%	237	19	15	34	271

(14 children were not at school)

†Small base: caution with percentages

Two-thirds of day school pupils were accompanied to school; 29% 'has to be taken by someone in the household' and 40% were escorted by someone who was not a friend, relative or neighbour. Boarders were fairly evenly split between being taken by a household member, escort, or going alone.

With increasing age, across the three age groups 3 – 7, 8 – 11 and 12 +, the numbers being taken by someone in the house decreased from 55 and 33, to 12 percent respectively. Conversely, children reported as going to school by themselves showed an almost mirror trend, increasing from 12 and 27 to 47 percent. Those who were escorted remained relatively constant for the same age groups, at 34, 44 and 41 percent respectively.

10.3 Visually impaired children in 'ordinary' schools

Where the word 'special' was not part of the description of the school categories on the prompt card, the schools were broadly classed as 'ordinary'. Fifty-three percent of children came into this category, and informants were asked a series of questions about these schools.

Ninety-eight percent of pupils had lessons with children who were sighted, and 8% said that there was a special unit in which visually impaired children were taught as a group.

The level of awareness of special schools for visually impaired children was checked (at S9Q14) among the parents of these children. Fourteen per cent of informants said that they had not heard of 'special schools for visually handicapped children'.

10.3.1 Presence of other children with a visual impairment in the 'ordinary' school

Table 10.8 shows that 6 in 10 children in a non-special or 'ordinary' school were reported as possibly being the only one with a visual impairment. Ony 41% of informants were able to say definitely that other visually impaired children were in the school.

Table 10.8   Visually handicapped children in ordinary schools

'Are there any other visually handicapped children in the school?' (S9Q18)

	Residual vision		Total
	Hi	Lo	
	%	%	%
Yes	39	48	41
No	39	38	39
Don't know	22	15	20
Total %	100	100	100
Base	103	40	143

(128 children were not at 'ordinary' school, 14 not at school)

Informants who said there were other visually impaired children in the school were asked (at S9Q19) how many: 44% said '1 or 2'; 20% said '3 – 5'; those reporting '6 – 10' and '11 – 50' were 9 and 10 percent respectively; 17% were unable to say how many.

10.4   Choice of school

Asked (at S9Q15) how they felt their views were considered in the choice of the child's current school, overall two-thirds (68%) of parents felt that they had had a positive influence, but a fifth (20%) felt that their views were given little attention or they were not asked at all. Table 10.9 shows the results.

10.4.1   Statementing

The Statementing procedure is the formal process by which the local education authority assesses the child's special educational needs. This process should involve the parents. As shown in Table 10.10,

Table 10.9 Parents' influence on the choice of the child's school, by other disability and residual vision

'Thinking about the school (child) goes to now, which of these phrases best describes how much you think your views were considered in this placement?' (S9Q15)

	Other disability		Residual vision		Total
	NOD	OD	Hi	Lo	
	%	%	%	%	%
Strongly influenced	39	28	33	33	33
Taken into account	26	43	29	42	35
Given little attention	6	3	5	3	4
Views not asked for	22	18	20	20	20
Had no strong views	7	5	7	5	6
Don't know	3	1	3	1	2
Total %	100	100	100	100	100
Base	121	150	136	135	271

(14 children were not at school)

Table 10.10 Knowledge of the Statement of special educational need, by age

'Do you know what a Statement† of special educational need is?' (S9Q73)

	Age		Total
	3 – 11	12 +	
	%	%	%
Yes	50	39	45
No	48	58	53
Don't know	2	3	2
Total %	100	100	100
Base	151	133	284

(1 child was not at school)

†In Scotland the Statement was referred to as a Record.

when asked directly if they knew what a Statement was, 45% of informants said that they did. The only difference in this knowledge was related to the age of the child. Informants with younger children were more likely to report knowing what a Statement was than those with older children (50 and 39 percent). There was some indication that where the child had another disability the parents might be more aware of the Statement, but this was not statistically significant.

Those who reported knowing what a Statement of special educational needs was, were then asked (at S9Q74) if they had had a Statement written about their child; 85% said 'yes'.

10.4.1.1 Documentation of the child's assessment

Our first question on knowledge of Statementing was quite open and used the term 'Statement' ('Record' in Scotand), making no attempt to explain the term. A better assessment of awareness of the Statement may come from our subsequent question, which asked about a written assessment rather than about a Statement. The question was: 'Can I just check, have you ever been given written documents to show that your child's educational needs have been formally assessed?' (S9Q75). The response is shown in Table 10.11.

Table 10.11   Receipt of documents to show that the child's needs have been formally assessed, by other disability, residual vision and type of school (S9Q75)

	Other disability		Residual vision		Ordinary or special school*		Total
	NOD	OD	Hi %	Lo %	Ord %	Spcl %	%
Yes	54	70	54	72	46	77	63
No	44	30	44	27	52	22	36
Don't know	2	1	2	1	2	1	1
Total	100	100	100	100	100	100	100
Base	126	159	145	140	129	155	285

(*1 child was not at school)

We now have 63% of informants reporting that they had been given a written assessment of their child's educational needs, compared to the 45% in response to the unexplained question about a Statement. As shown in Table 10.11, a greater number of the more severely disabled children had been 'formally' assessed compared with their relatively less disabled counterparts. A larger number of children with low residual vision and other disabilities, 72 and 70 percent respectively, had had a written assessment, compared with 54% each for children with low residual vision or no other disability. Because more severely disabled children attended special schools (see section 6.1.1), a larger number of children in special than in ordinary schools had had a formal written assessment (77 and 46 percent).

10.4.1.2 The right of appeal against the Statement's outcome

Sixty-eight percent of those who had been given a written assessment were aware that they could have appealed against the outcome (for the most part this would mean the school recommended). There was a small tendency, not statistically significant, for those with younger children (73 and 60 percent) to say that they knew about the possibility of appeal. It was the 1981 Education Act that required the formal assessment of each child's special educational needs. That it is the parents of younger children who are more aware of statementing may be a reflection of the statementing process not being fully implemented in the early years following its introduction.

10.4.1.3 Discussion of the Statement

Expert guidance in any decision-making process is useful. We asked informants (at S9Q76) whether they were able to get any independent advice about their child's Statement. The question was phrased to eliminate discussions within the family, but to recognise that not all the advice sought would be formal. Table 10.12 shows that 41% of parents receiving a written assessment had discussed it with someone outside the family.

Table 10.12 Discussion of the written Statement with someone outside the family

'Did you discuss this document with anyone outside your family?' (S9Q77)

	Ordinary or special school		Total
	Ord	Spcl	
	%	%	%
Yes	54	34	41
No	46	65	59
Don't know	0	1	1
Total %	100	100	100
Base	59	120	179

(106 had not received a written Statement)

Table 10.12 also shows that where the child attended an ordinary school informants were more likely to report having discussed the document. It may be that where the child was at a special school the parents felt more confident in their own knowledge. However, because the document may have come **before going** to the present school it is possible that where the special school was recommended the parents were quite happy with the outcome and so felt less of a need to discuss, or question, the outcome. The data do not allow one to do more than speculate.

Asked (at S9Q78) with whom they had discussed the document, a wide range of people were mentioned. Most frequently mentioned were: 'child's school', 36%; 'educational psychologist', 29%; 'peripatetic or visual handicap teacher', 16%; 'social worker', 11%; 'teacher for other handicaps', 8%; 'school doctor', 'paediatrician' and 'friend or neighbour', 7% each. Others mentioned by between 1 and 3 percent include: general practitioner; physio-, occupational and speech therapist; RNIB; parents of other handicapped children; and hospital-based social workers.

We asked all informants: 'Have you had a formal meeting with various specialists where they have talked about and decided what would be the best type of school or education for your child?' (S9Q79) Just under half (48%) of informants had such a meeting. Fifty-five percent of those with children in special schools had a formal meeting compared with 35% of those in ordinary schools. Quite clearly, not all those who had a written Statement said that they had attended a formal meeting.

Just 8% (11 informants) of those who had been to a formal meeting were accompanied by someone outside the family who helped them to put their case. Those mentioned were: 'social/welfare worker' (by 4 informants); 'educational psychologist' and a 'teacher or adviser' (each by 2); 'health visitor', 'paediatrician' and 'peripatetic teacher for the visually handicapped' (each by 1 informant).

10.4.2 Satisfaction with the current school

Given the relatively high number of parents who felt that they had some influence on the choice of school, a reasonable level of satisfaction with the school may be expected. This is indeed what was found. Ninety-two percent of parents said they were either 'very' or 'fairly' satisfied with the school (68% said 'very' satisfied).

No significant difference in satisfaction was found between children with or without additional disabilities and between those with high or low residual vision level.

Even among parents who said that they felt their views were not considered in the choice of school, nearly 90% were satisfied with the school.

The only discernible difference in satisfaction was among those expressing a very high level of satisfaction when looked at in terms of attendance at a special or ordinary school. As shown in Table 10.13, informants with children at special schools were more willing to express very high levels of satisfaction with the school (75 compared with 60 percent).

The five percent (12) of informants who expressed dissatisfaction were asked their reasons for this. They were evenly distributed between: 'failure to cope with child's handicap'; not providing 'academically for the child'; and 'not providing for the child's visual handicap'.

Table 10.13 Satisfaction with child's current school by type of school

'How do you feel about . . . (child's) present school?' (S9Q16)

	Ordinary or special school		Total
	Ord	Spcl	
	%	%	%
Very satisfied	60	75	68
Fairly satisfied	32	17	24
All satisfied	92	92	92
Neither	3	3	3
Fairly dissatisfied	1	4	3
Very dissatisfied	4	1	2
Don't know	1	1	1
Total %	100	100	100
Base	126	145	271

(14 children were not at school)

10.5   Sports, hobbies and interests at school

10.5.1   Sports

Table 10.14 shows that visually impaired children participate in a wide variety of sports; the most frequently mentioned were: 'swimming' (45%), 'rugby/soccer' (26%), 'athletics/running' (20%), and 'PE/PT' (17%). Only 17% of children were reported as not taking part in any form of sport at school.

Except for one or two sports, participation rates in the individual activities showed few statistically significant differences between the various sub-groups. However, the trend was for a larger number of less severely disabled children to be reported as participating in the individual activities. The exceptions to this were disability-related sports, e.g. 'wheelchair sport', and two specific activities: horse riding and swimming.

Table 10.14 shows that more children with another disability or with low vision took part in swimming (50 and 53 percent respectively), compared with their sub-group counterparts (38 and 37 percent respectively). Horse riding followed a similar pattern but at a lower level of activity, 1 and 5 percent for children with no other disabilities or high residual vision, compared with 15 and 12 percent respectively for those with other disabilities and low residual vision.

A possible explanation of this pattern is the fact that 59% of children in special schools were reported as taking part in swimming compared with 29% of those in ordinary schools. Horse riding is also reported

Table 10.14 Sports child participates in at school, by other disability and residual vision

'What sports, if any, does . . . (child) take part in at school?' (S9Q23)

	Other disability		Residual vision		Total
	NOD	OD	Hi	Lo	
	%	%	%	%	%
Swimming	38	50	37	53	45
Rugby/soccer	36	18	34	17	26
Athletics/running	28	13	18	21	20
PE/PT	20	14	24	10	17
Gymnastics	12	6	7	10	9
Horse riding	1	15	5	12	9
Rounders/baseball	11	4	13	2	7
Hockey	9	2	7	4	5
Cricket	7	3	7	2	5
Tennis/table tennis/badminton	8	2	9	1	5
Netball	7	3	7	2	4
Outdoor adventure	9	0	4	4	4
Physiotherapy-linked activity	2	3	2	4	3
Wheelchair sport	0	5	1	4	3
None	13	19	15	18	17
Base = 100%	121	150	136	135	271

(14 children were not at school)

more for children in special schools (16%), whereas it is not reported for any of the children in ordinary schools. Therefore, these are activities of special significance within special schools; swimming may have some physiotherapy basis. 'Wheelchair sport' was only reported for 5% of children in special schools. These sports may reflect a greater level of provision in special compared with ordinary schools.

10.5.2 Hobbies and interests

Asked (at S9Q24) what hobbies or interests (other than sports) the child followed at school, overall 40% of children were reported not to have any hobbies or interests organised by the school. Table 10.15 shows the responses.

The number of children without hobbies or interests differs between those attending ordinary and special schools (46 and 34 percent respectively), and between younger and older children (45 and 33 percent respectively). This latter difference may equally apply to non-disabled children.

Table 10.15 Hobbies and interests at school, by type of school

'What (other) hobbies and interests does . . . (child) have at school?' (S9Q24)

	Ordinary or special school		Total
	Ord	Spcl	
	%	%	%
Listening to music	3	23	14
Painting/drawing/art	9	8	9
Computing/games	7	8	8
Cooking	3	8	6
Playing music	6	4	5
Handicrafts, e.g. pottery	6	5	5
Reading	4	4	4
Writing stories	2	3	3
Singing	2	3	3
Acting/drama	4	3	3
Non-disabled physical activity	3	3	3
Listening to stories	2	2	2
Board games	3	1	2
Cubs/scouts/guides	0	3	2
Church activities	1	2	2
Active physical sport	2	3	2
Disabled physical activity	0	3	2
Fashion/clothes	1	1	1
Meeting/talking to friends	0	1	1
Playing generally	2	1	1
None	46	34	40
Base = 100%	126	145	271

(14 children were not at school)

A wide variety of activities was mentioned, with most responses varying between 2 and 5 percent. Only listening to music exceeded 10%. 'Painting/drawing/art', and 'computing' games were reported by 9 and 8 percent respectively.

There was little variation between sub-groups. Only one or two activities were clearly more popular among one sub-group compared with another. Listening to music was more frequently mentioned for children in special schools compared with those in ordinary schools (23 and 3 percent). A 'physical activity' for the disabled was only reported for children in special schools (3%), where the children in all cases had both low residual vision and another disability.

10.6 School-organised clubs outside school hours

Table 10.16 shows that a quarter of children were reported as taking part in some out-of-school hours activity or club organised by the school. Older children (35%) or those with no other disability (32%) were more likely to take part in such activities, compared with younger children (18%) or those with other disabilities (20%).

Table 10.16 Participation in school-organised clubs and activities outside school hours, by other disability and age

'Outside school hours, does . . . (child) belong to any clubs or take part in any activities organised by the school?' (S9Q28)

	Other disability		Age		Total
	NOD	OD	3 – 11	12 +	
	%	%	%	%	%
Yes	32	20	18	35	25
No	68	79	81	64	74
Don't know	0	1	1	1	1
Total %	100	100	100	100	100
Base	121	150	150	121	271

(14 children were not at school)

A wide range of activities was mentioned: from sports teams (18 children), youth clubs (12), religious groups (9), scouts/guides (9), music and drama, to computing.

10.6.1 Reason for not taking part in school-organised activities

Table 10.17 lists the reasons why the child did not take part in these school organised activities. The single most mentioned reason, reported by 32% of informants, was that no such activities were organised. This reason was reported more for children in ordinary than in special schools (39 and 25 percent).

Several reasons for non-participation applied particularly to children in special schools rather than those in ordinary schools: 'live too far from school' (30 and 6 percent respectively) was one. 'Too handicapped generally', 10%, 'too mentally handicapped', 6%, and 'too physically handicapped', 5%, all applied to children in special schools, but were not mentioned at all for children in ordinary schools.

Twenty-one percent of children in ordinary schools were said to be 'too young' compared with 7% in special schools. None of the children in special schools was said to be simply 'not interested', but this was said of 9% of those in ordinary schools.

Table 10.17 Reasons given for not taking part in out-of-hours school-organised activities, by type of school

	Ordinary or special school		Total
	Ord	Spcl	
	%	%	%
No such activities at school	39	25	32
Live too far from school	6	30	19
Child too young	21	7	14
Not interested	9	0	5
Too handicapped generally	0	10	5
Too mentally handicapped	0	6	3
Too physically handicapped	0	5	3
Activities, but no one to care for child	2	2	2
Child too shy	0	4	2
Not able to cope	2	2	2
No one to care for the child	2	1	2
Organiser can't cope	2	1	2
Other reasons (unspecified)	9	6	7
No reason given	19	21	20
Base = 100%	96	104	200

(71 took part in activities at school, 14 were not at school)

10.7 Friends at school

Three-quarters (76%) of children were reported to have close friends at school, as shown in Table 10.18.

Table 10.18 Children with close friends at school, by other disability, vision level, and special school

'Does (child) have any close friends at school?' (S9Q25)

	Other disability		Residual vision		Ordinary or special school		Total
	NOD	OD	Hi	Lo	Ord	Spcl	
	%	%	%	%	%	%	%
Yes	92	63	83	68	89	64	76
No	8	31	17	25	11	30	21
Don't know	0	6	0	7	0	6	3
Total %	100	100	100	100	100	100	100
Base	121	150	136	135	126	145	271

(14 children were not at school)

Thirty-one percent of children with another disability, and 25% with low residual vision, were reported as not having any close friends at school; this compares with 8 and 17 percent respectively for children with no other disability and high residual vision. Thirty percent of children in special schools, compared with 11% of those in ordinary schools, were reported not to have close friends. Including the 'don't knows' this increases those without close friends by 6% for each of the more severely disabled children. (This is based on the assumption that if there was a close friend the parents would be more likely than not to be aware of this fact.)

The data reveal that for more severely disabled children, more of whom are in special schools, the formation of close friendships is impeded. This finding confirms that the fears of isolation which some parents express about sending the child to a special school are justified. (See sections 10.11.4 and 5.)

10.7.1 Playing with school friends

Table 10.19 shows that for children with close friends at school, 51% did not play with them during the evenings or weekends, and 46% did not play with them during the holiday period.

It is more severely disabled children and those at special schools who were least likely to be reported as playing with friends outside school. The percentage difference was widest between children in special and

Table 10.19 Children playing with close friends outside school, by other disability, residual vision and type of school

'Does he/she play with these school friends in the evenings or at weekends as well as at school?' (S9Q26)

'And what about school holidays, does he/she play with school friends then? If 'yes' is that regularly or occasionally?' (S9Q27)

	Other disability		Residual vision		Ordinary or special school		Total
	NOD	OD	Hi	Lo	Ord	Spcl	
	%	%	%	%	%	%	%
S9Q26							
Yes	60	35	56	39	66	27	49
No/don't know	40	65	44	61	34	73	51
Total %	100	100	100	100	100	100	100
S9Q27							
Regularly	32	18	31	20	38	12	26
Occasionally	34	21	33	23	34	22	28
Regularly or occasionally	**67**	**39**	**64**	**43**	**72**	**34**	**54**
No	33	61	36	58	29	67	46
Total %	100	100	100	100	100	100	100
Base	111	94	113	92	112	93	205

(14 children were not at school, 66 had no close friends at school)

ordinary schools: 73 and 34 percent respectively did not play with friends outside of school during evenings and weekends.

Playing with school friends during the holidays shows a similar pattern, with more severely disabled children and those in special schools being less likely to play with friends during the holidays. Children in ordinary schools were twice as likely to play with school friends during the holidays (72 and 34 percent respectively).

Though not statistically significant, the percentage of children in all the analysis sub-groups who play with friends during the holidays is greater than the percentage who play with friends during the evenings and weekends.

10.8 Parental contact with the school

Table 10.20 shows that 87% of parents were in touch with the child's teachers at least once a term, with parents of younger children being in more frequent contact. Sixty-eight percent of parents of younger children were in contact at least once a month compared with 48% of those with children aged 12 and over. This may be partly due to the fact that more younger children were escorted to school, and that the older children travelled further to school, presenting less opportunity for the informal contact that occurs with the escorting of younger children.

Table 10.20 Frequency of contact with teachers, by type of school and age

'Overall how often are you in touch with (child's) teachers, for example by talking with them, or in such ways as a school diary?' (S9Q31)

	Age		Total
	3 – 11	12 +	
	%	%	%
Almost every day	27	11	20
At least once a week	18	20	19
Once a month	23	17	20
Once a term	25	31	28
Once a year	3	15	9
Less often	3	6	4
Don't know	1	0	1
Total %	100	100	100
Base	150	121	271

(14 were not at school)

Eighty-seven percent of informants said that they were either 'very' or 'fairly' satisfied with the level of contact with teachers; only 8% expressed any dissatisfaction and the rest could not say one way or the other.

10.8.1 Provision for children with multiple disabilities

Over half of visually impaired children had another disability. Any school provision would have to take this into consideration in making provision for the child's special educational needs.

Table 10.21 shows that 47% of informants with children with other disabilities said that they were very satisfied with the school provision to meet their non-sight needs. Twenty-nine percent were fairly satisfied. Twelve percent expressed dissatisfaction and the same number could not say.

Table 10.21 Satisfaction with the school to meet the non-sight needs of children with other disabilities, by type of school and residual vision

'You mentioned earlier that besides the sight problem . . . (child) also has (other disabilities). From this card, how satisfied are you overall that the school has sufficient resources, equipment and materials to meet your child's special educational needs?' (S9Q33)

	Ordinary or special school		Residual vision		Total
	Ord	Spcl	Hi	Lo	
	%	%	%	%	%
Very satisfied	41	49	52	44	47
Fairly satisfied	18	34	16	38	29
Neither	11	4	7	5	6
Fairly dissatisfied	9	6	9	5	7
Very dissatisfied	11	2	9	2	5
Don't know	9	6	9	5	6
Total %	100	100	100	100	100
Base	44	107	58	93	151

(14 children were not at school, 120 had no other disability)

It should be noted that satisfaction ratings in surveys usually have a positive bias, respondents appearing reluctant to express dissatisfaction with the services that they are asked to evaluate. This is particularly notable for satisfaction ratings with welfare services, where a high level of satisfaction is usually expressed.

For children in special schools, a higher level of satisfaction was expressed than for those in ordinary schools (83 and 59 percent respectively). A higher level of satisfaction was also expressed for children with low compared with high residual vision (82 and 68 percent respectively).

The expectation of high levels of satisfaction makes one reasonably confident that those in ordinary schools were experiencing a real and significant level of dissatisfaction with the provision to meet their children's needs.

10.9 Qualifications of the teaching staff

Table 10.22 shows that two-thirds (65%) of children were being seen by teachers whom informants reported as being specialists in teaching children with sight problems. This increased to 73% for children with low residual vision, and 72% for those in special schools. The percentages for those with high residual vision, or in ordinary schools were 57 and 56 respectively.

Table 10.22 Children taught by specialists, by type of school and residual vision

'When child is at school is he/she seen at all by a teacher or teachers who are specially qualified to deal with children with sight problems?' (S9Q34)

	Ordinary or special school		Residual vision		Total
	Ord	Spcl	Hi	Lo	
	%	%	%	%	%
Yes	56	72	57	73	65
No	40	17	38	18	28
Don't know	4	10	5	10	7
Total %	100	100	100	100	100
Base	126	145	136	135	271

(14 children were not at school, 120 had no other disability)

Table 10.22 reveals that for nearly three-quarters of children in special schools or with low residual vision, their sight problem was being attended to by a teacher whom the informant recognised as being a specialist in teaching children with a sight problem. While nearly 60% of those in ordinary schools or with high residual vision were being seen by a 'specialist', a significant minority were not.

10.9.1 Visiting or school-based specialist teacher

The other question was the frequency with which the child saw this specialist. In special schools, 73% of children who saw a specialist teacher reported that the specialist was based at the school. Twenty-three percent said that the teacher visited the school, and 4% could not say. The percentages were reversed for children in ordinary schools seeing a specialist. Only 14% had a specialist teacher based at the school; 86% had a visiting teacher.

It should be remembered that 39% of visually impaired children in an ordinary school were reported categorically as being the only child in the school with a visual impairment, and a further 20% of informants did not know if there were others in the school (section 10.3.1).

10.9.2 Frequency of contact with the specialist teacher

Overall, 47% of children saw a specialist teacher on a daily basis; this varied from 66% of those with low residual vision to 23% with high residual vision. Where the child was in a special school, 73% saw the teacher on a daily basis, compared with 10% of those in ordinary schools. In total 53% of children in ordinary schools saw the specialist teacher at least once a week.

The informants usually saw the specialist once a term. Overall, 11% reported not having seen the teacher at all.

10.10 Special or ordinary education

10.10.1 The choice of schools

For 71% of informants the child was in the only school that was considered at the time of choosing schools. As seen in section 10.4, 68% of parents felt that their views were at least taken into account when the current school placement was decided, and the level of satisfaction with the current school was very high. This suggests that parents had already had some 'debate' and come to a decision as to the type of school they wanted for their child, and the current placement was a reflection of this.

Table 10.23 Consideration of other schools, by type of school and residual vision

'Can I just check, did you consider any other school before you chose this one?' (S9Q38)

	Ordinary or special school		Residual vision		Total
	Ord %	Spcl %	Hi %	Lo %	%
Yes	23	32	21	36	29
No	77	68	79	64	71
Total %	100	100	100	100	100
Base	126	145	136	135	271

(14 children were not at school)

Those parents of children with low residual vision (36%) or in special schools (32%) were slightly more likely to have considered another school before the present one. This compares with 23 and 21 percent respectively for children in ordinary schools or with high residual vision.

Of those who had considered another school, three-quarters (76%) had actually made the effort to visit those under consideration.

10.10.2   Changing schools

Three-quarters of children currently in school had been at another school before the present one. As one would expect, as the age of the child increased the number reported as having attended a previous school increased; over the three age groups 3 – 7, 8 – 11 and 12 + the percentages were 60, 70, and 89 respectively.

Table 10.24 looks at children who had changed schools. This shows that 60% of children were previously in an ordinary school. This compares with 46% at the time of the survey in ordinary schools (section 10.1.1).

Table 10.24 Previous school attended, by other disability, vision level and type of school (currently attended)

'Thinking about the last school, which type of school did he/she go to before?' (S9Q42)

	Other disability		Residual vision		**Current school**, ordinary or special		Total
	NOD	OD	Hi	Lo	Ord	Spcl	
	%	%	%	%	%	%	%
Previous school							
Ordinary school	80	40	77	44	84	39	60
Special school	20	60	23	56	16	61	40
Total %	100	100	100	100	100	100	100
Base	102	103	102	103	95	110	205

(14 children were not at school, 66 had attended no previous school)

The numbers previously in ordinary and special schools, compared to the situation at the time of the survey, suggest a movement from ordinary to special schools.

What Table 10.24 shows is that the majority of children do not move across school types, i.e. children in ordinary schools will, for the most part, move to another ordinary school. While the majority of children in special schools came from another special school, there was a larger movement from ordinary into special schools. Eighty-four percent of children currently in ordinary schools came from another ordinary school, and 61% of those in special schools came from another special school. Nearly 40% had moved from an ordinary to a special school; the reverse move amounted only to 16%.

The other analysis sub-groups in the table simply demonstrate the observation that the level of disability had already determined the type of school in which the child was placed (see sections 10.1.1 and 10.10.3). Approximately 80% of children with no other disability or with high residual vision were previously in ordinary schools, compared with about 40% of those with other disabilities or with low residual vision.

10.10.3   Previous school and age

Tables 10.24 and 10.25 are similar, but the latter splits ordinary schools to distinguish between senior, and nursery and junior, and shows the data for children with high and low residual vision within two age groups. It also seeks to show that the separation into ordinary and special schools occurs early and is, to some extent, set by the time the child reaches his or her junior middle years.

Table 10.25 Previous school type attended, by residual vision within two age groups

'Thinking about the last school, which type of school did he/she go to before or was it something different?' (S9Q42)

	Age						All ages
	3 – 11			12 +			
	Residual vision			Residual vision			
	Hi	Lo	Total 3 – 11	Hi	Lo	Total 12 +	
	%	%	%	%	%	%	%
Previous school							
Ordinary school:							
Senior	44	28	36	78	40	57	47
Junior/nursery	31	20	26	0	2	1	13
All in ordinary school	75	48	62	78	42	58	60
Special school	25	53	38	22	58	42	40
Total %	100	100	100	100	100	100	100
Base	52	45	97	46	54	108	205

(14 were not at school, 66 had attended no previous school)

The totals for both age groups show that approximately 60 and 40 percent of younger and older children previously went to ordinary and special schools respectively. Looking at the two age groups separately, one can see the effect that both age and the level of residual vision have on the type of school previously attended. A greater number of children with high than with low residual vision were reported as having previously attended an ordinary school; 75 and 48 percent for those aged 3 – 11, and 78 and 42 percent for the 12 + age group. By looking within the two age bands separately (which acts to exclude the effect of age) it can be seen that the severity of the disability determines the type

123

of school the child attends. The results are paralleled if the exercise is repeated substituting the 'other disability' for 'residual vision' sub-groups in Table 10.25.

Looking within the age bands for younger children, the difference between those in ordinary junior or nursery schools is not statistically significant, though there may still be a real difference. This shows that unless a very young child is so severely disabled as to clearly need specialist help, special school placement may not occur. Separation into special and mainstream schools begins when the child moves away from the nursery setting.

10.11 The acceptable and ideal school

To gain some insight into what schools people might choose for their child, given a free choice, we first asked informants (at S9Q44) to look at a descriptive list of school types, and say which they would find acceptable. From the acceptable schools they were then asked (at S9Q45) which they would prefer.

10.11.1 Acceptable schools

Table 10.26 gives the results based on the schools informants listed as acceptable.

The summaries at the bottom of Table 10.26 show how the schools considered acceptable were divided between the broader categories of special and ordinary school. The area school with resources was kept separate as it fell between the two. Overall, there is little difference between the choice of ordinary (58%) and special (50%) schools. The percentage differences were not large enough to clearly state that one was preferred over the other.

Generally, where the child was more severely disabled (had low residual vision or an additional disability), a preference was shown for special school provision, and vice versa. Thus, while informants with children who had no other disability (79%) or high residual vision (76%), chose ordinary schools, those with other disabilities (64%), or low residual vision (71%) found special schools more acceptable.

It is notable, however, that ordinary schools were more acceptable to the parents of more severely disabled children than special schools were to the parents of those with less severe disabilities. The findings from the in-depth interviews, conducted at the development stage of the survey (see section 18.1) provide some insight into the reason for this. Parents want their children to mix where possible with 'normal' children and this could more easily be achieved within the ordinary school setting.

Table 10.26 Types of schools informants found **acceptable**, by other disability, residual vision and type of school

'I'd now like to move on to something a little different. Here are some cards showing a number of different types of school. We would like to know if you had a completely free choice, which schools you would find acceptable for (child) to go to, and which would be unacceptable . . .?' (S9Q44)

	Other disability		Residual vision		Ordinary or special school		Total
	NOD	OD	Hi	Lo	Ord	Spcl	
	%	%	%	%	%	%	%
Ordinary local school	37	15	38	11	47	6	25
Ordinary local school with a little support	74	40	70	40	89	26	55
Area school with resources	37	31	32	35	33	34	34
Area special school for visual handicap	22	28	10	40	12	37	25
Residential special school for visual handicap	16	21	11	26	9	27	19
Area special school for all handicaps	5	40	15	34	3	43	24
Summary groups							
All stating ordinary	**79**	**41**	**76**	**41**	**96**	**26**	**58**
Area school with resources	**37**	**31**	**32**	**35**	**33**	**34**	**34**
Special schools	**32**	**64**	**29**	**71**	**19**	**77**	**50**
Base = 100%	121	150	136	135	126	145	271

(14 children were not at school)

10.11.2 Preferred schools

Table 10.27 shows the response to the question asking which school would be most preferred given a free choice.

When informants were asked to make only one selection, overall, the ordinary school was marginally preferred. If we add the area school to the ordinary school choice, we have a clear preference for the ordinary school over the special school setting.

Table 10.27 gives a more detailed breakdown of the categories, which indicate a clear preference for education in an 'ordinary local school with a little support'. Thirty-five percent overall said that this would be their preferred type of school. About 45% of informants with more severely disabled children chose this type of school compared with about 24% of those with less severely disabled children. However, a significant minority of parents with more severely disabled children (other disability, 30%, low residual vision, 23%) preferred the 'area special school for all handicaps'. This is a clear signal, in these cases, that they considered some form of special school setting may provide the best for the child.

Table 10.27 Preferred school by other disability, residual vision and type of school

'And can I just check, if you had a completely free choice, which type of school would you most prefer . . .?' (S9Q45)

	Other disability		Residual vision		Ordinary or special school		Total
	NOD	OD	Hi	Lo	Ord	Spcl	
	%	%	%	%	%	%	%
Ordinary local school	16	5	18	2	21	0	10
Ordinary local school with a little support	48	23	45	24	62	11	35
Area school with resources	15	10	13	12	10	15	12
Area special school for visual handicap	11	8	2	16	2	16	9
Residential special school for visual handicap	7	11	6	13	2	16	10
Area special school for all handicaps	0	30	10	23	0	31	16
Summary groups							
All stating ordinary	**65**	**28**	**63**	**26**	**83**	**11**	**44**
Area school with resources	**15**	**10**	**13**	**12**	**9**	**15**	**12**
Special schools	**18**	**49**	**18**	**53**	**4**	**63**	**35**
Base = 100%	121	150	136	135	126	145	271

(14 children were not at school)

10.11.3 Current school type and the preferred choice of school

This section looks at the alignment of the current school the child attended and the school preference expressed by their parents. The current school was to some extent determined by the child's level of disability; so the more severely disabled child was to be found in a special rather than ordinary school setting.

Table 10.26 shows that 96% of parents with children in an ordinary school found the ordinary school setting acceptable, with 19 and 33 percent respectively finding the special school and the area school with resources acceptable. Where the child was in a special school, 77 and 26 percent respectively found the special and ordinary school acceptable. This suggested rather more willingness to consider the ordinary school among those in special schools, and less willingness among those in ordinary schools to move into special schools.

Looking at the preferred schools, there was a sort of retrenchment into the type of school the child currently attended. For informants with children in an ordinary school, the preference was for the ordinary school setting to the exclusion of the other categories; 83% preferred an ordinary school, 9% an area school, and 4% special schools. Where the child was currently in a special school, 63% maintained the preference for the special school, with 15% preferring an area school, and 11% an ordinary school.

These findings support those above showing the large number of people who felt that they had some say in the school the child attended (section 10.4), and the high level of satisfaction expressed with the child's current school (section 10.4.2).

10.11.4 Reasons for choosing preferred school

Table 10.28 shows the reasons given by informants when asked why they picked the preferred school. These have been broadly grouped into three categories: 'specialist provision', 'integration/social' reasons, and 'others'. A summary total has been given for the first two categories.

Table 10.28 Reason for choosing preferred school, by school

	Preferred school†			Total
	Ord	Spcl	Area‡	
	%	%	%	%
Specialist provision				
Specialist teachers	9	18	24	14
More specialist equipment/facilities	9	19	49	18
Multiple handicap provision required	0	2	0	1
Prefer boarding; can't handle at home	0	7	0	3
Want similar mix of children	2	16	30	11
All mentioning special provision	**20**	**62**	**100**	**47**
Integration/social				
Want normal school; mix with sighted	44	3	30	27
Wider social integration	3	0	9	3
Local to be with family	3	3	3	3
Wanted local school; no travelling	17	6	6	11
Normal school with special provision	4	0	0	1
All mentioning integration/social	**71**	**10**	**49**	**44**
Others				
Not need special school	11	0	0	5
Only school suitable	19	35	3	23
Independence/less dependent on family	1	3	3	2
Base = 100%	120	96	33	258

(14 were not at school, 13 did not pick a preferred school)

† 9 Respondents mentioned 'other' as choice of school: the percentages are not shown for this group, but the total of 258 includes their responses.

‡ Small base, caution with percentages

Sixty-two percent of those preferring special schools clearly considered the special provision as paramount in their choice. Just 10% who preferred special schools gave one of the integration/social reasons for their choice. Specialist equipment and facilities (19%), and the provision of specialist teachers (18%) were the main reason given, closely followed by the chance to mix with other children with similar disabilities (16%).

In contrast, those preferring the ordinary school considered the integration or social reasons as paramount in their choice, 71% stating one of these reasons. The most frequently mentioned reason for this choice was the desire for the child to be in a 'normal' school or mixing with sighted or non-disabled children (44%). This was followed by the requirement for a local school with little or no travelling (17%).

The 'area school with resources', a blend of the ordinary and special school, provides some evidence of parents' need for a mix of both. All the informants mentioned the specialist resources available, with just under half (49%) also mentioning one of the integration or social reasons, namely the need for mixing with non-disabled children (30%).

Table 10.29 examines the reasons for choice in terms of disability level. Where the child was more severely disabled (low residual vision, 56%, another disability, 53%) a larger number of informants gave a reason related to special provision, compared to those with less severely disabled children (high residual vision, 38%, no other disability, 40%).

Table 10.29 Summary of reasons for choosing preferred school, by other disability and residual vision

	Other disability		Residual vision		Total
	NOD	OD	Hi	Lo	
	%	%	%	%	%
Special provision reason	40	53	38	56	47
Integration/social reason	54	35	44	44	44
Base = 100%	119	139	132	126	258

(14 children were not at school, 13 did not pick a preferred school)

Integration/social reasons formed quite high priorities for parents of both more and less severely disabled children. Forty-four percent of parents with children with either high or low residual vision gave one of these reasons. However, where the child had no other disability, integration/social reasons seemed more important than for those where the child had another disability (54 and 35 percent).

Reasons based on 'special provision' were given a higher priority by parents with more severely disabled children: low and high residual vision, 56 and 38 percent; presence and absence of other disabilities, 53 and 40 percent.

10.11.5   Disadvantages of preferred school

Table 10.30 shows that when asked (at S9Q47) what disadvantages the preferred school may have, over half (54%) of informants did not offer any. Sixty-five percent of those who preferred an ordinary school could not think of any disadvantages, decreasing to 49 and 42 percent respectively for those preferring an area school with resources and a special school.

Table 10.30 Disadvantages of the most preferred school, by school

	Preferred school†			Total
	Ord	Spcl	Area‡	
	%	%	%	%
Distance/long journey	0	16	21	9
Lack of facilities/equipment	7	3	9	6
Won't make local friends	1	7	3	4
Not mixing with 'normal' children	1	8	3	4
Other children not aware	3	1	9	3
Teachers not aware	3	0	0	2
Child may be held back	1	2	3	2
Parents don't see child	0	3	0	1
No/none/nothing	65	42	49	54
Base = 100%	120	95	33	257

(14 were not at school, 13 did not pick preferred school, 1 no data)
† 9 respondents mentioned 'other' as choice of school; the percentages are not shown for this group, but the total of 257 includes their responses.
‡ Small base, caution with percentages

The distance involved in attending a special or area school was the most frequently mentioned disadvantage (16 and 21 percent respectively). Another issue of concern for children attending some form of special provision was the removal from the local or family support system. Eight percent with children in special schools mentioned the inability to mix with 'normal' children, and a further 7% that the child 'won't make local friends'.

For children in ordinary schools the disadvantages mentioned could be summed up as the child's special needs not being met by: lack of equipment or facilities (7%); a lack of awareness by teachers (3%) and other children (3%). For those in an area school, lack of awareness by other children (9%), and lack of equipment or facilities (9%) also caused concern.

These disadvantages were almost a mirror image of the advantages stated for the chosen school, indicating the weighing up that parents had to make in the choice of schools.

A recurring theme found in the in-depth interviews, in the development stage of the survey, was the removal of the child from the local environment and the family when special schools were being considered. This caused them to lack friends in the area where they lived, with a further removal from the family. (Section 10.7 on playing with friends illustrates this.) However, parents seemed to consider educational needs more important than the social need in the final choice. This may be given some credence by the relatively large number (25%) choosing a special school who simply reported that it was the only suitable school (Table 10.28).

10.12 Future prospects

10.12.1 The likelihood of taking public examinations

Table 10.31 shows that overall two-thirds of children were expected either to take public examinations (56%), or had already taken them (10%). This contrasted somewhat with the numbers in the general population, where only 55% of pupils left school in 1987/88 with some form of qualification (CSO, Social Trends 20, Table 3.14, page 56, 1990). The question was designed more to gauge expectations rather than to establish the 'facts'. However, large differences were evident, based on the level of disability of the children and the type of school they attended.

Table 10.31 Expectations for the child to take public examinations at school, by other disability, residual vision and type of school

'Do you expect that (child) will take any public examinations?' (S9Q48)

| | Other disability | | Residual vision | | Ordinary or special school | | Total |
| | NOD | OD | Hi | Lo | Ord | Spcl | |
	%	%	%	%	%	%	%
Yes, already taken	12	8	11	8	11	8	10
Yes, will take	81	35	66	45	78	29	56
No	4	49	18	40	5	50	29
Don't know	4	8	6	7	6	6	6
Total %	100	100	100	100	100	100	100
Base	121	150	136	135	126	145	271

(14 children were not at school)

Table 10.31 shows that nearly half (49%) of the children with another disability were not expected to take any examinations, compared with only 4% of those without another disability. Forty percent of children with low residual vision were not expected to take public examinations compared with 18% of those with high residual vision. This pattern was reflected between children in special and ordinary schools where 50 and 5 percent respectively were not expected to take examinations.

Where the child was expected to take some form of examination, a question was asked about the likelihood of going on to further education. Table 10.32 shows the results.

Table 10.32 Likelihood of the child going on to further education, by other disability, residual vision, and type of school

'Do you think he/she is likely to go on to further education?' (S9Q49)

	Other disability		Residual vision		Ordinary or special school		Total
	NOD	OD	Hi	Lo	Ord	Spcl	
	%	%	%	%	%	%	%
Yes	71	58	62	73	64	70	66
No	13	8	12	10	11	11	11
Don't know	16	34	27	17	25	19	23
Total	100	100	100	100	100	100	100
Base	111	64	104	71	112	63	175

(14 children were not at school, no public exams were expected for 95, 1 no information)

Overall, two-thirds were expected to go on to further education. The percentage differences in the tables were very much on the borderline of statistical significance (see section 20.5). The only thing that could be said with any degree of confidence was that there was a considerable amount of hope among parents. A large proportion simply said they didn't know (23%).

Where the child had another disability rather more doubt was expressed about the likelihood of further education. In contrast, children with low residual vision were thought equally able to go on to further education as their sub-group counterparts; similarly for children in ordinary and special schools.

For children with high and low residual vision, and those attending ordinary and special schools, the percentage differences (73 and 62, and 70 and 64 respectively), fall short of statistical significance. This suggests that there was no difference in the expectations of their going on to further education, given that they will have taken a public examination.

10.12.2 Careers advice and guidance

For children aged 11 years or over and considered able to work in the future, the informant was asked (at S9Q51) if they had seen a careers adviser. Table 10.33 shows the responses.

Table 10.33 Careers advice for children aged 11 and over who are expected to work, by other disability, residual vision and type of school

'Has he/she ever seen any careers advisers?' (S9Q51)

	Other disability		Residual vision		Ordinary or special school		Total
	NOD	OD	Hi	Lo	Ord	Spcl	
	%	%	%	%	%	%	%
Yes	34	19	24	28	29	24	26
No	63	36	58	39	66	36	48
Don't know	3	45	18	33	5	40	26
Total %	100	100	100	100	100	100	100
Base	64	78	67	75	56	86	142

(Only asked for children aged 11 years and over, and able to work)

Overall, nearly half of the children had not seen a careers adviser, a quarter had, and the remainder of the informants did not know. The lack of knowledge was greatest among those informants with children at special schools; 40% reported not knowing compared with only 5% for ordinary schools.

Children with no other disabilities were more likely to be reported as having seen a careers adviser than those with other disabilities (34 and 19 percent). The other sub-groups showed no statistically significant differences.

Of the 37 children who had seen a careers adviser, 17 (46%) had seen a specialist who dealt with people with disabilities. It seems that being in a special school increased the likelihood of seeing such a specialist. While 15 (71%) of the 21 in a special school had seen a specialist adviser, only 2 (13%) of the 16 in ordinary schools had seen one.

10.12.3   Future work prospects

Asked whether they considered the child able to work in a normal work-place or whether he/she would need to work in a sheltered scheme, just over half (54%) of informants felt the child would be able to work in a normal workplace. A large proportion, 37%, were not able to express an opinion one way or the other. Table 10.34 shows the data.

Children with no other disability were the ones thought most likely to be able to work in a 'normal' workplace (84%), compared with 28% for those with other disabilities. However, the largest uncertainty was expressed about those children with another disability; 59% of informants were recorded as 'don't know'.

Table 10.34 Work environment for children expected to work in the future, by other disability, residual vision and type of school

'Do you think he/she would be more suited to working in a sheltered place specially set up for people with handicaps, or in a place where most people do not have sight problems or other handicaps?' (S9Q54)

| | Other disability | | Residual vision | | Ordinary or special school | | Total |
| | NOD | OD | Hi | Lo | Ord | Spcl | |
	%	%	%	%	%	%	%
Sheltered	6	13	5	15	2	20	10
'Normal' workplace	84	28	66	43	84	34	54
Don't know	9	59	29	43	14	40	37
Total %	100	100	100	100	100	100	100
Base	64	78	67	75	56	86	142

(Only asked for children aged 11 years and over and able to work)

Overall, it was felt that 10% of children would need to work in a sheltered work place; again this was expressed most frequently for more severely disabled children (about 14 compared with 6 percent), and for those in special compared with ordinary schools (20 and 2 percent respectively).

10.13 Educational expectations

10.13.1 Important elements sought from education

We tried to gain some insight into parents' expectations from the education system in terms of what they considered important. We asked:

> Which one of the following do you think is/was the most important thing for (child) to get from his/her education?
> . . . the second most important
> . . . and the third
> . . . and which would you say was the least important thing?
> (S9Q72)

Table 10.35 summarises the prompted alternatives presented to the informants. (For the precise wording the show card T, in Appendix to Chapter 20, should be consulted.)

Three items stood out as the most important elements parents expected the child to get from his or her education. These were: 'class work suited to the child's pace of working' (27%); 'teachers who understand the child's visual handicap' (22%); and the 'chance to integrate into the local community on leaving school' (13%).

Table 10.35 The most important elements in the education of visually impaired children, by other disability, residual vision and type of school

'Which one of the following do you think is/was the most important thing for . . . (child) to get from his/her education . . .?' (S9Q72)

	Other disability		Residual vision		Ordinary or special school		Total
	NOD	OD	Hi	Lo	Ord	Spcl	
	%	%	%	%	%	%	%
Class work suited to the child's pace of working	29	25	35	19	36	40	27
Teachers who understand child's visual handicap	27	17	17	27	20	23	22
Chance to integrate into the local community on leaving school	14	13	17	9	17	9	13
Help from specialist	0	17	2	4	14	16	9
LVAs and braille or large print books	10	4	5	8	9	6	7
Good employment prospects	9	6	10	4	13	3	7
Chance to grow up with friends locally	6	4	6	4	7	3	5
Sheltered surroundings	0	7	2	6	0	7	4
Don't know	6	7	5	7	5	7	6
Total %	100	100	100	100	100	100	100
Base	126	158	145	139	129	154	284

(1 child had not yet been to school)

Areas where some clear differences appear are between children with and without another disability; specialist help such as physiotherapist and other therapist (17%), and sheltered surroundings (7%) were mentioned as needed for children with other disabilities, but not for children without additional disabilities.

The need to provide for the visual handicap itself was mentioned more often for children with no other disability than for children with another disability. For example, low vision aids or braille and large print books (10 and 4 percent), and teachers who understood visual handicap (27 and 17 percent) were cited, suggesting that where another disability is present the consideration given to the sight problem alone may be reduced. In Chapter 6 we see that where another disability is present only 38% of informants said that sight was the major concern.

Table 10.35 shows that class work at the child's pace was rated as more important for children with high than with low residual vision (35 and 19 percent). This was counterbalanced by informants who mentioned teachers who understood the child's visual handicap, where it was mentioned more frequently for children with low than with high residual vision (27 and 17 percent).

Two interesting items which emerge are that for children with high residual vision, integration into the community and employment prospects were rated more highly than for children with low residual vision (17 and 9 percent, and 10 and 4 percent respectively).

The school sub-groups showed no statistically significant differences on the two main items. The special education factors were the main concerns, particularly work suited to the child's pace (about 40% each), and teachers with an understanding of visual handicap (about 20% each).

Votes for social integration factors tended to run at a lower level, but did reveal statistically significant differences between the school sub-groups; e.g. 'chance to integrate into the local community on leaving school' (17% ordinary schools, 9% special schools); 'good employment prospects' (13 and 3 percent); and 'sheltered surroundings' (zero and 7%).

Question S9Q72 asked for the **single** most important expectation from education: the format of the question puts into competition the social integration and sheltered issues with those of special education. It seems that in this forced choice situation many with children in ordinary schools, in much the same proportion as those in special schools, will give greatest weight to educational factors. There is ample evidence from other sections (sections 10.11.2 to 10.11.4) that those with children in ordinary schools do attach importance to the social integration aspect. What the results in Table 10.35 seem to show is that, forced to choose, most parents will nevertheless give primacy to the need for special educational provision.

10.13.2 Summarising the important elements

Question S9Q72 also asked informants to list the three most important expectations for their children's education. Table 10.36 aggregates the three responses giving an overall percentage for each item. This gives a more general rating rather than a single forced choice measure. The same three items as in Table 10.35 remain the most frequently mentioned: class work suited to child's pace (55%), teachers who understand visual handicap (54%), and a chance to integrate into the community on leaving school (42%).

The split remained, with the integration/social elements predominating for the less severely disabled children, and the special provision elements for those more severely disabled. This overall tendency differed for specific items, for example: 'teachers who understand child's visual handicap'. Informants with children with high and low residual vision, 37 and 17 percent respectively, rated this element as important. This contrasted with the need for 'LVAs and braille or large print books' where the percentages were 19 and 27 respectively. This

Table 10.36 Summary of the elements considered important for the child to get from his/her education, by other disability, residual vision and type of school

'Which one of the following do you think is/was the most important thing for . . . (child) to get from his/her education . . .

. . . and which is/was the second most important

. . . and the third?' (S9Q72)

	Other disability		Residual vision		Ordinary or special school		Total
	NOD	OD	Hi	Lo	Ord	Spcl	
	%	%	%	%	%	%	%
Class work suited to the child's pace of working	57	53	57	52	54	56	55
Teachers who understand child's visual handicap	61	49	37	17	54	55	54
Chance to integrate into the local community on leaving school	43	42	46	38	45	40	42
Chance to grow up with friends locally	47	30	48	27	59	20	38
Good employment prospects	36	20	37	17	41	15	27
LVAs and braille or large print books	33	14	19	27	22	23	23
Help from specialist	3	37	18	26	7	34	22
Sheltered surroundings	1	25	7	22	2	25	14
Total %	100	100	100	100	100	100	100
Base	126	158	145	139	129	154	284

(1 child had not yet been to school)

suggests that for children with low residual vision who tend to be in special schools, it was the equipment that came to the fore: we may assume that this is because the specialist teachers were already there. Children with high residual vision tended to be in ordinary schools, and the parents therefore considered that getting a teacher who could understand the child's needs was more important, since the child often might not need 'special' equipment.

In Table 10.36 children in ordinary and special schools are now seen to differ sharply on the items 'chance to grow up with friends locally' (59 and 20 percent respectively) and 'help from specialist' (7 and 34 percent). The fact that these items now discriminated between the two groups, while failing to do so in Table 10.35 (which asked about their single most important item), suggests that though felt to be important, they were not most important when in competition with other elements.

10.13.3 The least important elements in the child's education

When further asked (at S9Q72) what were considered to be the least important elements in the child's education, 'sheltered surroundings'

(47%), 'good employment prospects' (14%), and 'LVAs and braille or large print books' (10%) were the only items mentioned with any notable frequency. Sheltered surroundings were considered least important; integration was mentioned as one of the most important elements in the previous section. The results are shown in Table 10.37.

Table 10.37 The least important elements in the education of visually impaired children, by other disability, residual vision and type of school

	Other disability		Residual vision		Ordinary or special school		Total
	NOD	OD	Hi	Lo	Ord	Spcl	
	%	%	%	%	%	%	%
Sheltered surroundings	65	32	54	39	66	31	47
Good employment prospects	5	21	6	22	3	23	14
LVAs and braille or large print books	7	11	11	7	8	11	10
Help from specialist	8	6	8	6	8	6	7
Chance to grow up with friends locally	2	9	5	7	2	8	6
Class work suited to the child's pace of working	1	4	2	3	1	4	3
Chance to integrate into the local community on leaving school	2	0	1	1	2	0	1
Teachers who understand child's visual handicap	0	0	0	0	0	0	0
Don't know	11	18	13	17	11	18	15
Total %	100	100	100	100	100	100	100
Base	126	158	145	139	129	154	284

(1 child had not yet been to school)

The main differences in the comparison between informants with children in ordinary and special schools were that more of the latter considered 'good employment prospects' as least important (23 and 3 percent). In contrast, twice as many informants with children in ordinary schools considered 'sheltered surroundings' as least important (66 and 31 percent). Parallel differences occurred on these items between the other disability and residual vision sub-groups.

11 Reading and Writing

11.1 The ability to read and write print

In our sample just 10% of children were reported as having no light perception (see Chapter 18). In fact 51% of children were reported as being able to see to pick up a coin without having to fumble for it, and a quarter (24%) were able to recognise a friend across a road. Therefore, it may be assumed that a large proportion of visually impaired children have a considerable amount of usable sight.

Table 11.1 shows that overall, just under two-thirds (60%) of children were reported as being able to read **or** write print. Fifty-six percent could both read and write print, with the other 4% split between those either reading or writing. Differences were evident between the other disability, residual vision and, to a lesser extent, the age sub-groups; these were then reflected in the differences seen between children in ordinary and special schools.

Table 11.1 Reading and writing print, by other disability, residual vision, age and type of school

'Can . . . (child) read or write print at all?' (S11Q1)

	Other disability		Residual vision		Age		Ordinary or special school*		Total
	NOD %	OD %	Hi %	Lo %	3–11 %	12+ %	Ord %	Spcl %	%
Yes, read print	2	3	3	3	3	2	2	3	3
Write print	1	2	0	3	1	2	0	3	1
Read **and** write print	79	38	75	37	50	63	82	35	56
Read or write print	**82**	**43**	**78**	**43**	**54**	**67**	**84**	**41**	**60**
Neither, mental handicap	0	18	6	14	9	11	1	18	10
Neither, no information	10	21	12	20	20	11	11	20	16
Don't know	3	3	4	2	5	2	3	3	3
No light perception	4	15	0	21	11	9	1	18	10
Total %	100	100	100	100	100	100	100	100	100
Base	126	159	145	140	152	133	129	155	285

(*1 child not at school)

11.1.1   Other disabilities

Eight in ten (82%) children with no other disability were able to read or write print, compared with 43% of children with other disabilities. A mental handicap was explicitly stated as the 'other disability' that prevented 18% of this sub-group from reading or writing print. 'Neither' reading nor writing, with no further information being sought by the interviewer, was recorded for an additional 21% of children with other disabilities. It is possible to surmise that age and some physical disability may be contributory factors. Fifteen percent had no light perception.

For children without other disabilities, 10% were unable to read or write print and 4% had no light perception. Three percent of informants were unable to say either way.

11.1.2   Residual vision

Seventy-eight and forty-three percent respectively of children with high and low residual vision could read print. Fourteen per cent of children with low residual vision could not read or write because of a mental handicap, 21% had no light perception and 20% were simply reported as unable to read or write print with no further information. Again one might surmise that the reasons for the failure were age and some physical disability.

Six percent of children with high residual vision had a mental handicap, with no information being recorded for 12%.

11.1.3   Age

Examined by age (3 – 11 and 12 +) smaller differences in print reading and writing were found, reflecting the greater influence of residual vision and other disabilities. A larger number of older than younger children were reported as reading or writing print (67 and 54 percent respectively).

The reasons for the inability to read print were similar for both older and younger children: mental handicap, 11 and 9 percent; no light perception, 9 and 11 percent; and 'neither' without any further information, 11 and 20 percent respectively.

A more detailed examination by age, however (not shown), reveals that where the child was aged 3 – 7 years, 27% of informants reported 'neither' without any further information, compared with 14% for children aged 8 – 11 years. This suggests that where a parent simply said that the child could not read or write print, with no further explanation, then the young age of the child might have been the reason for this failure.

11.1.4 Type of school

Eighty-four percent of visually impaired children in ordinary schools could read or write print, 82% reading <u>and</u> writing, 2% only reading print. For children in special schools the corresponding percentages were 41, 35 and 6.

Eighteen percent of children in special schools were reported as having a mental handicap which prevented them from reading or writing, and 20% had no light perception. 'Neither', with no further information, was offered for 20 and 11 percent respectively of children in special and ordinary schools.

11.1.5 Future prospects

11.1.5.1 Children unable to read or write print

Where a 'mental handicap' was given as the reason for the child not reading or writing print, informants were not questioned further.

Where no reason was given, or a response of 'don't know' was recorded, informants were asked about the future prospects of the child reading and writing (55 children). Eighteen children were in ordinary schools, 36 in special schools and 1 was not at school; 38 had another disability; and 31 had low residual vision.

A third reported that they expected the child to read or write in the future, a third did not expect the child to read or write, and a third did not know. Of those who were uncertain, or did not expect the child to read or write print when older (37 informants), the reasons given for doubting the child's future ability to read or write varied: 'sight was too poor' (11 informants); 'other disability' (9 informants); 5 gave a variety of other reasons and 12 gave no reason.

11.1.5.2 Children either currently, or previously, able to read or write print

Where the child was currently able to read or write print the possibility existed that there might come a time when he/she could not. Asked (at S11Q3) about the likelihood of the child not reading print in the future, 44% of informants expressed doubt; 13% emphatically stated the child would not be able to read print, and 31% were unsure about future prospects. Two-thirds of children who were considered unlikely to be able to read print in the future had low residual vision.

Some children had regressed from being able to read print. In those cases where the child's sight had been reported as becoming worse since onset, and he or she was not able to read print, informants were asked about the child's past ability to read it. Of the 16 children to whom this applied, four read print in the past and were now unable to do so. Three of these four children had other disabilities.

Where the child was not able to write print (and did not have a mental handicap) the ability to sign his/her own name was investigated. Of the 92 children involved, only 14% could sign their name. Residual vision and other disability made no difference, but age did; all those who could sign their name were aged eight or more.

11.1.6 Print size

Table 11.2 shows that 41% of children were able to read both ordinary and large print; 16% reading only ordinary print, and 25% reading both. Three-fifths (63%) of children with high residual vision read ordinary print, compared with one-fifth (18%) of those with low residual vision.

Table 11.2 The reading of ordinary and large print, by residual vision

'Does he/she read ordinary size print, or large print, or both?' (S11Q2)					
	Residual vision		Ordinary or special school*		Total
	Hi %	Lo %	Ord %	Spcl %	%
Ordinary print only	26	6	28	6	16
Both, ordinary and large print	37	12	40	12	25
All reading ordinary print	**63**	**18**	**68**	**18**	**41**
Large print only	15	21	16	19	41
Don't know which reads	1	1	0	2	1
Not read print	22	57	16	59	40
Write print only at S11Q1	0	3	0	3	1
Total %	100	100	100	100	100
Base	145	140	129	155	285

(*1 child was not at school)

Sixty-eight percent of children in ordinary schools read ordinary print, with an additional 16% only able to read large print. In contrast to those in ordinary schools, just 18% in special schools were reading ordinary print, with an additional 19% only reading large print.

A point to note is that 40% of children in ordinary schools read both large print and ordinary print, giving an overall demand for large print of 56% in ordinary schools.

If one had based the percentages only on those children who were able to read print, then overall 69% read ordinary print, and 31% read only large print.

11.2   Braille reading and writing

Table 11.3 shows that overall 14% of visually impaired children were reported as being able to read braille; 8% 'didn't know' whether the child could read braille.

Table 11.3 Braille reading, by age, residual vision and type of school

'Can . . . (child) read braille at all?' (S11Q8)

	Age		Residual vision		Ordinary or special school*		Total
	3 –11 %	12 + %	Hi %	Lo %	Ord %	Spcl %	%
Yes	11	18	3	26	5	22	14
No	70	68	84	49	91	47	67
Don't know	11	6	6	11	4	12	8
Don't know what braille is	0	1	1	0	0	1	#
Mental handicap	9	11	6	14	1	18	10
Total	100	100	100	100	100	100	100
Base	152	133	145	140	129	155	285

(*1 child was not at school)

Residual vision and type of school showed large differences in the number of braille and non-braille readers. Age, as expected, also showed some difference, but this was relatively small, with younger children slightly less likely to be braille readers than older children.

Twenty-six percent of children with low residual vision were reported as reading braille, compared with 3% of those with high residual vision. Eighty-four percent of those with high residual vision were reported as not reading braille, reflecting the large number of print readers among this group.

Of the 40 children able to read braille, 5 had started reading it when they were less than 5 years old; 23 between the ages of 5 and 11 years, 11 between 9 and 15 years and 1 informant could not say. Thirty-six of the forty children could also write braille. Three of the four who could not write braille had other disabilities.

11.2.1   Type of school

Twenty-two percent of children in special schools could read braille, compared with the 5% in ordinary schools. It should be noted that nearly a fifth (18%) of children in special schools had a mental handicap and so questions were not asked about braille reading. Possibly of more interest is the 12% in special schools whose parents reported not knowing about their child's ability to read braille.

Of the 40 children (6 in ordinary, and 34 in special schools) able to read braille, 36 could also write in braille (4 in ordinary and 32 in special schools).

11.2.2 Future prospects of learning braille

Table11.4 shows the results of enquires into the future likelihood of learning braille for those children reported as not being able to read braille at question S11Q8. Overall 17% were considered as likely to learn braille in the future and 63% were not; future braille reading was uncertain for 20%.

Table 11.4 Likelihood of learning braille, by residual vision, age and type of school

'Do you think he/she will learn to read or write braille when he/she is older?' (S11Q11)

	Residual vision		Ordinary or special school		Total
	Hi %	Lo %	Ord %	Spcl %	%
Yes	10	29	13	23	17
No	72	46	66	59	63
Don't know/depends	18	25	21	18	20
Total %	100	100	100	100	100
Base	122	69	117	73	191

(29 were mentally handicapped, 40 read braille; 25 replied don't know at S11Q8)

More children with low residual vision were reported as likely to learn braille than those with high residual vision (29 and 10 percent). Just under half (46%) of the children with low residual vision were reported as unlikely to learn braille, compared with just under three-quarters (72%) of those with high residual vision.

More children were considered likely to learn braille in special schools than in ordinary schools (23 and 13 percent).

11.2.3 Reasons for not learning braille

Table 11.5 shows the reasons reported for the children not learning braille in the future. 'Good sight/won't need' (57%) and 'reads print at the moment' (20%) were the main reasons given. Adding together the two previous responses, and those children who 'manage without' (3%), suggested that print was or would be the reading and writing medium used for 80% of children unlikely to learn braille in the future. 'Other disability prevents' the learning of braille was reported for 12% of children.

Table 11.5 Reasons for not learning braille in future, by residual vision, age and type of school

	Residual vision		Ordinary or special school		Total
	Hi %	Lo† %	Ord %	Spcl† %	%
Good sight/won't need	66	34	64	45	57
Reads print at the moment	23	13	27	7	20
Other disability prevents	2	34	1	31	12
Manages without	3	3	3	5	3
Not taught at school	2	3	1	5	3
Other	5	9	4	10	6
Total %	100	100	100	100	100
Base	87	32	77	42	119

(†Low base percentage to be treated with caution)

Two-thirds of children with high residual vision were reported as having sight good enough not to need braille, and a further 23% read print. For nearly 90% of children with high residual vision who did not read braille at the time of the survey, print was or would be the reading and writing medium used.

For children with low residual vision, nearly half (15 of the 32 children) were reported as either having 'good sight/won't need' or as 'reading print at the moment'. However, for just over a third (12 of 32 children) it was reported that the presence of other disabilities would prevent the learning of braille.

For children in ordinary schools, 91% were reported as not needing to use braille, 27% 'read print at the moment' and 64% had 'good sight/won't need'. For those in special schools, 7% reported they 'read print at the moment', and 45% reported 'good sight/won't need'. Other disability prevented as many as 31% of children in special schools from learning braille compared with only 1% of those in ordinary schools. Just 3% said that braille was not being taught at the school: a tentative indication of an unmet, albeit small, need.

11.3   The teaching of braille in school

Table 11.6 gives the results of asking about the opportunity to learn braille through its teaching at the child's school. Twenty-eight percent of informants reported that braille was taught at the school, 46% said it was not, and 31% did not know.

Braille was reported as being taught to 5% of children in ordinary schools. The tentative conclusion is that braille is being provided in ordinary schools for those for whom it is required (also see Table 11.3).

Table 11.6 The teaching of braille in ordinary and special schools

'Can I just check, is braille taught at . . . (child's) school?' (S11Q13)

	Ordinary or special school		Total†
	Ord %	Spcl %	%
Yes	5	47	28
No	84	14	46
Don't know	6	15	31
Don't know what braille is‡	0	1	#
Child has a mental handicap‡	1	18	10
Not currently at school‡	3	6	5
Total %	100	100	100
Base	129	155	285

(†Total 285 although 1 child was not at school)

‡These categories are from previous questions, but have been added back into the table to allow a direct comparison with earlier tables on the same base numbers

For children in special schools, 47% of informants reported the school as teaching braille, but only 22% of children in special schools were reported as actually reading it (see Table 11.3). We have also seen that 17% of children who did not read braille might learn in the future (Table 11.4); and that 41% of those in special schools were able to read ordinary or large print (Table 11.1). Thus, braille may not be needed, or may be of little use, to a large number of children in special schools who do not know braille, but where there are opportunities for learning it.

11.3.1 The opportunity to learn braille in school

Table 11.7 shows that in schools where braille is taught (mostly special schools) 45% of the children were reported as being able to read braille. Two percent of those in non-braille teaching schools were reported as reading braille. If we then go on to look at those children reported as not reading braille at question S11Q8 (section 11.2), we see an indication of a wider interest in or demand for braille. Table 11.8 shows this.

Table 11.8 shows that for those children in schools where braille was taught, who did not know braille at the time of the survey, 41% (15 of 37 children) were reported as likely to learn braille in the future, 49% (18 children) were reported as unlikely to learn, and 11% of informants could not say.

In those schools where braille was not taught, 11% were reported as likely to learn braille in the future. Two-thirds (67%) were reported as unlikely to learn, and 22% of informants could not say.

Table 11.7 Ability to read braille by whether braille is taught in the child's school

S11Q8 Can the child read braille?	S11Q13 Is braille taught in the child's school	
	Yes %	No %
Yes	45	2
No	46	97
Don't know	9	1
Total %	100	100
Base	80	130

(Analysis of informants answering 'yes' or 'no' at S11Q13; also excludes the two braille readers who were not at school)

Table 11.8 Likelihood of learning braille in the future, by whether braille is taught in the child's school

S11Q11 Will the child learn braille in future	S11Q13 Is braille taught in the child's school	
	Yes %	No %
Yes	41	11
No	49	67
Don't know/depends	11	22
Total %	100	100
Base	37	127

(Analysis includes only those who said no at S11Q8)

For children considered as unlikely to learn braille, Table 11.9 looks at the reasons why and the teaching of braille in the school. For the relatively few children (18) in schools where braille was taught, 'good sight/won't need' and 'reads print' were the main reasons given. These were again the overwhelming reasons reported (by 84%) for children in schools where braille was taught. 'Not taught at school' was mentioned for only 1%.

The overall conclusion, therefore, is that those capable of learning braille will go on to do so. Even in schools were braille is not taught, the child's future needs are given due consideration. For those children reported as unlikely to learn braille, it is either a matter of the child not being capable of learning braille, or that the child has sufficient sight for print to be the chosen reading and writing medium.

Table 11.9 Reasons for not learning braille in the future among non-braille readers, by whether braille is taught in the child's school

	S11Q13 Is braille taught in the child's school	
S11Q12	Yes†	No
Reason child won't learn braille in the future	%	%
Good sight/won't need	56	60
Reads print at the moment	22	24
Other disability prevents	6	8
Manages without	0	4
Not taught at school	6	1
Other	6	3
Don't know	6	0
Total %	100	100
Base	18	85

(Only those who said no at S11Q11, see Table 11.8)
†Small base, % are only for guidance

11.4 Reading and writing of braille among other people in the household

Table 11.10 shows that overall, 14% of households had someone other than the visually impaired child who was able to read or write braille – 9% both read and wrote it; 5% only read it.

The majority of these, presumably non-visually impaired braillists, were to be found where the child was in a special school rather than an ordinary school (20 and 8 percent respectively), or had low rather than high residual vision (27 and 3 percent respectively). The other disability sub-groups showed no difference (14% each).

Overall, 15% of informants felt that there was no need to learn braille, which was expressed more for those whose children had high rather than low residual vision (24 and 5 percent).

Two-thirds (66%) of informants reported never having tried to learn braille and 4% had tried but given up. Where the child had another disability a larger number of informants simply reported never having tried (73 and 60 percent).

The learning of braille for non-visually impaired parents is really only relevant if the child is able, or is likely, to learn braille. Among the 40 children able to read braille, 25 (63%) had other people in the house who were able to either read or write it.

Table 11.10 Reading and writing of braille among other people in the house, by type of school, residual vision and other disability

'Can you or anyone else in the household read or write braille?' (S11Q19)

'Have you or anyone else in the household tried to learn braille but given up?' (S11Q21)

	Ordinary or special school		Residual vision		Other disability		Total
	Ord %	Spcl %	Hi %	Lo %	NOD %	OD %	%
Read or write braille							
Read braille	2	7	1	9	4	5	5
Write Braille	1	0	0	1	0	1	#
Read and write braille	5	13	2	17	10	8	9
Reading or writing	8	20	3	27	14	14	14
Non-braillist							
Tried to learn	3	6	2	8	6	3	4
Never tried to learn	70	63	71	62	60	73	66
Not needed	19	11	24	5	21	10	15
Total %	100	100	100	100	100	100	100
Base	128	127	136	120	126	130	256

(29 children with a mental handicap were not included)

There were nine further households in which the child was unable to read braille but another member of the household could do so; in six of these households there were other people with sight problems.

11.5 The use of reading and writing aids and equipment

11.5.1 Use in the home

Asked (at S11Q14) about the use of aids for reading and writing at home, 63% of children were reported as not using any of the listed aids. Table 11.11 shows the responses. (Note that this and the subsequent analysis excludes, unless stated, the 10% of children whom informants reported as having a mental handicap and thus unable to read or write at S11Q1, see Table 11.1.)

Overall, a typewriter (21%) was the most frequently used aid followed by a braille machine (11%), word processor (4%), and closed-circuit television (4%). None of the others was reported as being used by more than 1% of children, including: Optacon, braille writing frame and microwriter.

Even when examined from within the sub-groups, few of the items were used widely. Only age showed any marked difference, with 38 and 6 percent respectively of older and younger children using a typewriter. 'Word processor' and 'closed-circuit television' were each used by

Table 11.11 Reading and writing aids used in the home, by other disability,residual vision, age

'Does . . . (child) use any of these for reading or writing at home?' (S11Q14)

	Other disability		Residual vision		Age		Total
	NOD %	OD %	Hi %	Lo %	3 –11 %	12 + %	%
Typewriter	25	17	20	22	6	38	21
Braille writing machine	9	12	1	22	10	11	11
Word processor	6	2	4	3	1	7	4
Closed-circuit television	6	2	4	5	2	7	4
Optacon	0	2	0	3	0	3	1
Braille writing frame	1	2	0	3	0	3	1
Microwriter	2	0	1	2	1	2	1
Versabraille	0	0	0	0	0	0	0
Don't know	2	12	4	12	9	6	7
None of these reported	62	64	72	53	73	51	63
Base = 100%	126	130	136	120	138	118	256

(29 children with a mental handicap were not included)

about 7 and 1 percent and 7 and 2 percent of older and younger children respectively. Braille writing machines, e.g. a Perkins, were used more by children with low residual vision (22%) than those with high residual vision (1%).

Non-use of these reading and writing aids was reported more among younger children (73%) and children with high residual vision (72%) than among older children and those with low residual vision (51 and 53 percent respectively).

School type displayed similar percentage differences as above. Only the use of braille machines showed any large differences, with 18% of children in special schools reported as using one compared with 3% in ordinary schools. Non-use of any of the aids was reported for 73 and 53 percent respectively of children in ordinary and special schools.

11.5.2 Use in school

The use of aids for reading and writing was far more extensive in schools than in the home. About half (47%) of the children were reported not to use any of these aids at school, compared with the 63% who did not do so at home. The most widely-used items were: 'typewriter', 23%; 'braille machines', 16%; 'word processor', 14%; and 'closed-circuit television', 13%. Also mentioned were 'braille writing frames', 'Versabraille' and 'Optacon'. Table 11.12 shows the data.

Table 11.12 shows that the use of reading and writing aids at school was greater among older than younger children (51 and 30 percent respectively).

Table 11.12 Reading and writing aids used in school, by other disability, residual vision, age and type of school

'And does he/she use any of these at school?' (S11Q15)

	Other disability		Residual vision		Age		Ordinary or special school†		Total
	NOD %	OD %	Hi %	Lo %	3–11 %	12+ %	Ord %	Spcl %	%
Typewriter	25	20	15	31	10	39	9	36	23
Word processor	17	11	11	18	8	22	9	20	14
Closed-circuit television	15	11	9	18	10	18	7	19	13
Optacon	1	2	0	3	0	4	0	3	2
Braille machine	14	17	2	30	13	19	4	28	16
Braille writing frame	1	2	0	3	0	3	0	3	1
Versabraille	1	0	0	1	1	0	0	1	#
Microwriter	6	1	3	3	3	4	5	2	3
All using a reading or writing aid	**43**	**36**	**29**	**51**	**30**	**51**	**25**	**54**	**39**
None of these	50	43	59	33	55	36	66	27	47
Don't know	7	21	12	16	15	13	9	19	14
Base	121	123	128	116	136	108	125	119	244

(29 children had a mental handicap, 14 were not at school)
†Only those attending school were asked S11Q15

We have seen in section 11.1 that a large proportion of visually impaired children, especially those in ordinary schools or with high residual vision, were able to use ordinary print. This use of ordinary print was reflected in the use and non-use of reading and writing aids in the school setting. Children in special schools were twice as likely as those in ordinary schools to be making use of one or more of these aids (54 and 25 percent respectively), and more children with low than high residual vision used them (51 and 29 percent).

11.5.2.1 Other disabilities

None of the more stark differences noted between the other sub-groups was exhibited between children with or without another disability. There was a tendency for marginally more of the children without other disabilities to be reported as using the individual pieces of equipment, but the differences were not statistically significant. However, there was a much higher reporting of 'don't know' for children with other disabilities (21 and 7 per cent).

11.5.2.2 Residual vision

The fact that the use of aids was more extensive among children with lower residual vision may be explained by more of these children attending special schools, where more use was made of such equipment. Use of typewriters was greater among children with low than high residual vision (31 and 15 percent); braille writing machines showed the largest difference in use betweeen the same two sub-groups (30 and 2 percent respectively). Non-use of these aids was 33 and 59 percent for children with low and high residual vision respectively.

11.5.2.3 Age

Age also exhibited notable differences. Children aged 12 or over were reported as using the aids more than younger children; the respective percentages using the various aids were: typewriter, 39 and 10; word processor, 22 and 8; closed-circuit television, 18 and 10; braille writing machine, 19 and 13. Those reported as not using any of them were 36 and 55 percent respectively for the same two age groups.

11.5.2.4 School

The use of reading and writing aids was greater among children in special than in ordinary schools: typewriters were used by 36 and 9 percent; word processors, 20 and 9 percent; closed-ciruit television, 19 and 7 percent; and braille writing machines, 28 and 4 percent. Nineteen percent of informants with children in special schools said that they did not know about the use of such aids compared with 9% of informants with children in ordinary schools.

The overall picture is of children in special schools making greater use of equipment and aids for reading and writing compared with those in ordinary schools. As shown in Chapter 10, special schools have a larger proportion of more severely disabled children. It therefore seems logical that children who attend special schools do so because they are more severely disabled and require the use of special equipment. As the equipment listed was to aid reading and writing for those with poor sight, it was those children with lower residual vision who made the most use of such equipment.

11.6 The use of computers

11.6.1 Use of computers in the home

The use of equipment for reading and writing was quite specific, so a more general enquiry was made about the possession and use of computers. Table 11.13 shows that 42% of homes with visually impaired children had a computer; 36% of children were reported as using it and 6% did not.

The overall level of possession of computers in the home (42%) was comparable with the 44% for households with children in the general population (British Market Research Bureau, Target Group Survey).

Table 11.13 Possession and use of computers at home, by type of school, residual and other disability

'Do you have a computer at home?'(S11Q16)
'Does . . . (child) use a computer at home?' (S11Q17)

| | Ordinary or special school | | Residual vision | | Other disability | | Total |
	Ord %	Spcl %	Hi %	Lo %	NOD %	OD %	%
Have a computer							
Use the computer	43	28	43	28	44	28	36
Do not use	4	9	3	10	4	8	6
All having a computer	47	37	46	38	48	36	42
Do not have a computer	53	63	54	62	52	64	58
Total %	100	100	100	100	100	100	100
Base	128	127	136	120	126	130	256

(29 children with a mental handicap were not included)

Differences in the use and possession of a computer in the home were remarkably similar within the sub-groups. Twenty-eight percent of children in special schools, with low residual vision, or with other disabilities were each reported as using the computer. A much higher usage was recorded for children in ordinary schools, with high residual vision or with no other disabilities (about 43%). Non-use was greater among more severely disabled children than those with less severe disabilities (about 8 and 4 percent respectively).

Age showed a smaller difference with 40 and 32 percent respectively of older and younger children reported as having and using a computer. Six percent for both age groups had, but did not use, a computer.

11.6.2 Use of computers in school

Table 11.14 shows that the reported use of computers at school was relatively high at 68%, with 11% reporting 'don't know/depends'.

Table 11.14 Use of computers in school, by type of school, residual vision and other disabilities

'Does . . . (child) use a computer at school?' (S11Q18)

| | Ordinary or special school | | Residual vision | | Other disability | | Total |
	Ord %	Spcl %	Hi %	Lo %	NOD %	OD %	%
Yes	66	68	70	65	70	65	68
No	28	14	23	20	26	16	21
Don't know/depends	6	17	7	16	3	19	11
Total	100	100	100	100	100	100	100
Base	125	119	128	116	121	123	244

(29 children had a mental handicap and 12 were not at school)

More informants with children in special schools than in ordinary schools exhibited a lack of knowledge about the use of computers in the school (17 and 6 percent respectively). This pattern of less knowledge or awareness among parents of children in special schools also emerged in section 11.5.2.4 concerning the use of aids for reading and writing.

The larger number of informants who answered 'don't know' among those with children in special schools suggests that these parents may be less informed about what goes on within special schools. There may be a number of reasons for this, not least being that some of those children in special schools were away from home. Even when the child did not board, the special school tended to be some distance from his/ her home, providing less opportunity for contact with school and staff.

Part F

Leisure

12 Leisure and Holidays

12.1 Leisure interests outside school

12.1.1 Sports activities outside school

Table 12.1 shows that just under half (48%) of children were reported as being involved in some sporting activity outside their schools; this compared with 83% who did some form of sporting activity in school (see Chapter 10). Swimming (31%) was the most frequently mentioned activity followed by 'rugby/soccer' (16%). 'Walking/cycling' was reported for 4%; the other sports mentioned by 3% or less included athletics, cricket, racquet sports and snooker/pool.

Table 12.1   Sports activities outside school, by other disability, residual vision, and type of school

'What sports, if any, does . . . (child) take part in outside school/nursery?' (S14Q1)

	Other disability		Residual vision		Ordinary or special school*		Total
	NOD	OD	Hi	Lo	Ord	Spcl	
	%	%	%	%	%	%	%
Swimming	33	30	33	29	29	34	31
Rugby/soccer	22	11	22	10	21	12	16
Walking/cycling	4	3	6	1	5	3	4
Athletics	4	2	3	2	3	3	3
Cricket	5	2	4	2	3	3	3
Horse riding	4	3	3	3	2	4	3
Racquet sports	4	1	4	1	5	0	3
Snooker/pool	4	2	4	1	4	2	3
Other ball games	2	1	1	3	2	2	2
Skating/skiing	2	1	1	2	0	3	2
Rounders	1	1	1	1	2	0	1
Martial arts	2	1	1	2	2	1	1
Gymnastics	2	1	2	0	2	1	1
Dancing	1	1	1	1	2	0	1
Other physical activity	1	1	1	1	1	1	1
One or more sporting activity	58	40	52	43	52	45	48
No sport activity	42	60	48	57	48	55	52
Base = 100%	126	159	145	140	129	155	285

(* 1 child was not at school)

The sub-groups showed no real difference in the numbers reporting any one activity except for 'rugby/soccer', where children with 'no other disability' and 'high residual vision' (each 22%) were reported as doing these sports more than those with 'other disabilities' (11%), and 'low residual vision' (10%). This difference was also present between children in ordinary and special schools (21 and 12 percent respectively).

Although few of the individual sports showed a statistically significant difference in the level of participation between the sub-groups, marginally more children without other disabilities, with higher residual vision and those in ordinary rather than in special schools were reported as taking part in some form of sport outside school. This difference is illustrated by the summary totals and is most clearly seen in connection with the other disability sub-groups; 58 and 40 percent respectively of children without and with other disabilities taking part in one or more sport.

12.1.2   Hobbies and interests outside school

Table 12.2 shows that general hobbies and interests were pursued by a larger number of children than those taking part in sports (68 and 48 percent respectively). The range of activities listed illustrates the broad range of leisure activities that visually impaired children are able to do. Listening to music was the most frequently mentioned leisure pursuit (15%), followed by 'cubs and scouts' (8%); and 'computing games', 'reading', 'watching television' and 'cycling/riding bike/ (6% each). Children were reported as having numerous other hobbies and interests ranging from 'singing' and 'cooking' to 'helping round the house' reported for between 1 and 4 percent of children. Within the sub-groups the percentages varied between 1 and 5, but few individual interests showed statistically significant differences between the sub-groups.

We see, however, a larger number of less severely disabled children reported as having a hobby or leisure interest. More children without other disabilities (80%), and with high residual vision (72%) were reported as having a hobby or interest than children with other disabilities (58%) and low residual vision (63%). This difference is reflected between children in ordinary and special schools who have hobbies (74 and 63 percent respectively).

12.1.3   The effect of age on participation

It would be surprising if age were not associated with some difference in the level of leisure activities, but it is expected that any such difference would also be equally evident among children in the general population. Fewer younger children were reported as participating in some form of sport, compared with the older children. Sixty-six percent of those aged 3 – 7 were reported as not taking part in any sporting

Table 12.2 Hobbies and interests outside school, by other disability, residual vision and type of school

'What (other) hobbies and interests does . . . (child) have outside school/nursery?' (S11Q2)

	Other disability		Residual vision		Ordinary or special school*		Total
	NOD %	OD %	Hi %	Lo %	Ord %	Spcl %	%
Listening to music	14	16	12	19	10	19	15
Cubs/guides/scouts	12	6	10	6	11	7	8
Reading	7	5	8	4	7	5	6
Computing games	7	5	6	6	9	4	6
Cycling/riding bike	8	4	9	3	10	3	6
Watching television	5	7	7	5	5	7	6
Playing music	4	2	5	4	6	3	5
Painting/drawing/art	5	3	7	1	8	1	4
Pets/animals	4	3	3	4	5	3	4
Walking	5	3	6	2	4	4	4
Playing with friends	4	4	4	4	5	3	4
Collecting things	4	3	5	2	4	3	4
Religious activities	4	2	4	1	3	3	3
Indoor games	3	3	3	2	4	2	3
Cooking	1	3	1	2	3	1	2
Disco/dancing	3	1	3	1	5	0	2
Sport/physical activity	3	1	1	2	2	1	2
Spectator sports	3	1	3	1	2	1	2
Singing	2	1	1	2	1	2	1
Listening to stories	2	1	1	1	0	2	1
Writing stories	3	0	2	1	3	0	1
Acting/drama	1	1	1	0	1	1	1
Pottery/basket work	1	1	1	0	2	0	1
Knitting/sewing	1	1	1	0	2	0	1
Meeting friends/people	2	0	0	2	2	1	1
Helping round the house	1	1	1	1	1	1	1
Outings/visit places	1	1	2	1	1	1	1
Club for disabled people	1	1	1	1	1	1	1
Non-disabled club	2	1	1	1	0	2	1
Making things by hand	2	0	1	0	2	0	1
Models/trains etc.	2	1	1	1	2	0	1
Has hobby or interest	**80**	**58**	**72**	**63**	**74**	**63**	**68**
No hobbies or interests	**20**	**42**	**28**	**37**	**26**	**37**	**32**
Base = 100%	126	159	145	140	129	155	285

(* 1 child was not at school)

activity, compared with 43 and 49 percent for those aged 8 – 11 and 12 or over respectively.

Numbers of children without hobbies and interests decreased from 52 to 25 percent respectively for children aged 3 – 7 years, and 8 years and over. Younger children, as well as participating less, did not take part in the wider range of sports and activities reported for older children.

12.2   Friends living locally

Table 12.3 shows that overall, over a third (37%) of children were reported as having no friends living locally. This overall figure, however, masks large differences between the sub-groups. The picture is one of greater isolation for children who are more severely disabled, with fewer friends reported as living locally than for less severely disabled children.

Children with no other disability (81%), or with high residual vision (78%) are reported as having more local friends than children with other disabilities (49%), or with low residual vision (46%). We noted in Chapter 10 the lower number of more severely disabled children reported as playing with school friends during the school holidays; the reason for this is seen here with a larger number of children in ordinary schools reported as having friends who live locally compared with children in special schools (85 and 44 percent respectively) (Table 12.3). The reason for this pattern is the larger number of more severely disabled children to be found in special compared with ordinary schools (section 10.1.1).

Table 12.3   Friends living locally, by age, other disability, residual vision and type of school

'Does . . . (child) have friends who live locally?' (S14Q3)

	Age		Other disability		Residual vision		Ordinary or special school*		Total
	3 – 11	12 +	NOD	OD	Hi	Lo	Ord	Spcl	
	%	%	%	%	%	%	%	%	%
Yes	63	47	81	49	78	46	85	44	63
No	37	53	19	51	22	54	15	56	37
Total %	100	100	100	100	100	100	100	100	100
Base	152	133	126	159	145	140	129	155	285

(* 1 child was not at school)

We also noted, in Chapter 10, that more severely disabled children attend special schools, and that they do so when they are older. Table 12.3 shows that this pattern of attendance results in older children having fewer friends who live locally than younger children (47 and 63 percent respectively).

Table 12.4 tries to provide some insight into the difference between those children who have friends living locally and those who do not. By looking at the attendance at special and ordinary schools separately for those children with high and low residual vision, we can try to see whether it is the sight level that makes the difference, or whether it is the type of school attended. Within both the residual vision sub-groups (high or low), a statistically significant difference (see section 20.5) is still present between children in ordinary and special schools who have friends living locally. One can therefore be confident in concluding that the attendance at special schools – or factors related to attending special schools – has the effect of hindering the fostering of local friendships for disabled children.

Table 12.4   Children with friends living locally, by type of school attended within residual vision levels

'Does . . . (child) have friends who live locally?' (S14Q3)

	Type of school within residual vision levels				Total
	High residual vision		Low residual vision		
	Ord	Spcl	Ord	Spcl	
	%	%	%	%	%
Yes	88	59	77	37	63
No	12	41	23	63	37
Total %	100	100	100	100	100
Base	95	49	34	106	284

(1 child was not at school)

12.2.1   Characteristics of friends

Looking further at the possible isolation of the child from other children without disabilities, informants were asked (at S14Q4) whether those friends who lived locally had sight problems or were sighted. Eighty-eight percent of informants reported that all the friends were sighted, 10% reported a mixture of sighted and visually impaired. Just 2% reported that all the child's friends had a visual impairment.

Asked (at S14Q5) about the age range of these friends, overall about half (48%) had friends of the same age; for children in ordinary schools this was 56%, decreasing to 37% for those in special schools. Table 12.5 shows the data.

12.3   Outings and other leisure visits

Table 12.6 shows that overall only 2% of children were reported as not being taken out at some time. The most frequently mentioned outing was 'shopping', where 88% of children accompanied their parents. The

Table 12.5   The age of friends living locally, by type of school

Of children with friends living locally

'. . . how old are these children? Are they younger than . . . (child), older, or about the same age or a whole mixture of ages?' (S14Q5)

	Ordinary or special school		Total
	Ord	Spcl	
	%	%	%
Younger	4	10	6
Older	5	8	6
A mixture of ages	36	43	38
Mixed age range	44	61	50
About the same age	56	37	48
Don't know	1	2	1
Total %	100	100	100
Base	110	68	178

(107 children had no friends living locally)

Table 12.6   Places that child was taken to or visited with his/her family, by other disability, residual vision and type of school

'I have a list of various places you might visit, or things you might do – which, if any, of these do you go to with . . . (child)?' (S14Q6)

	Other disability		Residual vision		Ordinary or special school*		Total
	NOD	OD	Hi	Lo	Ord	Spcl	
	%	%	%	%	%	%	%
Shopping	91	86	90	86	91	85	88
Beaches	75	69	77	66	78	66	72
Play grounds/parks	58	64	61	62	66	58	61
Swimming pools	68	56	63	56	70	54	61
Walking	61	58	66	53	67	53	59
Zoos/nature reserves	56	47	54	48	50	52	51
Leisure parks e.g. Alton Towers	41	30	39	31	38	33	35
Museums	44	19	36	24	34	26	30
Historical homes/gardens	33	16	28	19	26	21	24
Sports centres	24	17	21	19	20	20	20
Sports events	22	15	21	16	20	17	18
Plays	14	10	15	9	16	8	12
Art galleries	12	10	15	7	12	10	11
Classical concerts	6	3	4	5	5	4	5
Pop concerts	4	3	2	5	4	3	4
Cinema	42	27	43	24	47	23	3
Other shows	22	13	20	14	22	14	17
No/none/don't know	2	2	1	3	1	3	2
Base = 100%	126	159	145	140	129	155	285

* 1 child was not at school

other most frequently mentioned places were: 'beaches' (72%), 'playgrounds', 'swimming pools' (each 61%), 'walking' (59%), 'zoos' (51%), 'leisure parks' (35%), 'cinemas' (34%) and 'museums' (30%); other places mentioned were 'sporting events', 'plays', and 'art galleries'. The list shows that visually impaired children are exposed to a wide range of places of interest and entertainment.

Although nearly all the children were taken out by the informants the sub-groups do show some differences.

12.3.1 Places of interest visited without adult supervision

Table 12.7 shows the places the child was reported as visiting with friends but without adult supervision; overall 35% of children were reported as visiting these places without supervision. Age is an important factor, with unsupervised visits increasing across the three age groups, 3 – 7, 8 – 11 and 12 +, from 18 and 33 to 52 percent (Table 12.8).

A comparison of the data in Tables 12.6 and 12.7 reveals that while a large number of visually impaired children were taken to a wide range of places (Table 12.6), going out without other adults was more restricted (Table 12.7). If one considers that only 54% of children aged 12 or over with high residual vision were going out alone, when one may expect a far greater proportion of children in the general population to be doing so, it may be surmised that the child's impairment is a clear constraint (Table 12.9).

12.3.2 The effect of age on going out

From Table 12.7 one can see that while about half of less severely disabled children were reported as going out with friends and no adults, the corresponding figure for more severely disabled children was about 20%.

Older children are of course more independent than younger children, but the data in Table 12.8 indicate that for children of the same age the level of residual vision still has a marked affect. Whether one looks at younger or older children, more children with high residual vision were reported as going out than those with low residual vision; for those aged 12 and over the totals were 74 and 33 percent, and for those aged 3 – 11 years, 29 and 9 percent.

Informants were asked (at S14Q10) about the places the child visited on their own. The most frequently mentioned places were: shopping (17%), walking (8%), playgrounds/parks (7%) and swimming pools (5%). No table is shown.

Table 12.7 Places that child was taken to or visits with friends but no adults, by other disability, residual vision and type of school

'Can I just check, apart from visits with the family that we've just talked about, does . . . (child) visit any of these places with friends and no adults?' (S14Q9)

	Other disability		Residual vision		Ordinary or special school*		Total
	NOD	OD	Hi	Lo	Ord	Spcl	
	%	%	%	%	%	%	%
Shopping	35	10	28	14	30	14	21
Swimming pools	25	11	23	11	24	12	17
Play grounds/parks	24	9	23	7	22	10	15
Walking	22	9	21	9	17	13	15
Sports centres	16	5	15	5	17	4	10
Cinema	15	3	12	4	13	5	8
Beaches	8	1	7	2	9	1	5
Sports events	6	2	6	1	6	1	4
Zoos/nature reserves	6	1	5	1	5	1	3
Leisure parks e.g. Alton Towers	5	1	3	3	4	2	3
Museums	4	1	3	1	3	1	2
Plays	3	1	3	1	2	1	2
Pop concerts	4	1	2	2	2	2	2
Art galleries	1	1	1	0	1	1	1
Classical concerts	0	1	0	1	1	0	#
Historical homes/gardens	1	0	7	0	1	0	#
Other shows	3	0	2	1	3	0	1
Visits one or more place	52	20	48	21	47	24	35
No/none visited	44	76	48	75	49	72	61
Don't know	4	4	4	4	4	4	4
Base = 100%	126	159	145	140	129	155	285

* 1 child was not at school

Table 12.8 Children visiting places with friends and no adults by residual vision within two age groups

'Can I just check, apart from visits with the family that we have just talked about, does . . . (child) visit any of these places with friends and no adults?' (S14Q9)

	Residual vision within age				Total
	3 – 11		12 +		
	Residual vision		Residual vision		
	Hi	Lo	Hi	Lo	
	%	%	%	%	%
Visits places with friends	29	9	74	33	35
No/none	65	88	25	63	61
Don't know	6	3	1	4	4
Total %	100	100	100	100	100
Base	85	67	60	73	285

Table 12.9 shows that 22% of children were reported as going out unaccompanied. Age is again an important factor; the overall total of 22% is made up of 35% for children aged 12 and over, and 11% for younger children. The data in Table 12.9 show that the most restricted children were those who are more severely disabled.

Among children aged 12 and over, 54% of those with high residual vision were reported as going out alone compared with only 19% of those with low residual vision. Younger children showed a similar pattern, with corresponding totals of 18 and 1 percent respectively.

Table 12.9   Children visiting places by themselves, by residual vision within two age groups (S14Q10)

	Residual vision within age				Total
	3 – 11		12 +		
	Residual vision		Residual vision		
	Hi	Lo	Hi	Lo	
	%	%	%	%	%
Visits places by self	18	1	54	19	22
No/none	82	99	43	78	77
Don't know	0	0	3	3	1
Total %	100	100	100	100	100
Base	85	67	60	73	285

Because of the strong association of other disabilities with more severe sight loss (see Chapter 6), if Table 12.9 were reconstructed using the other disability sub-groups within the two age groups, the percentages found would be similar to those for residual vision within age groups.

12.3.3   Problems or difficulties experienced when visiting places

Fifty-eight percent of informants experienced problems or difficulties in the places that they visited with the child. Table 12.10 shows the data.

Marginally more informants reported difficulties for children with other disabilities than for those without other disabilities (62 and 54 percent). Residual vision showed the largest difference; 71% of children with low residual vision were reported as having difficulties compared with 46% with high residual vision. Children going to ordinary (51%) and special (65%) schools also showed a difference, but this was very much a consequence of more children with other disabilities or lower residual vision level attending special schools. Age showed no statistically significant difference (see section 20.5) between those who did and did not report problems.

Table 12.10 Children who experience problems when visiting places, by other disability, residual vision and type of school

'When you visit . . . (place) do you find that there are any problems caused by your child's disabilities?' (S14Q8)

	Other disability		Residual vision		Ordinary or special school*		Total
	NOD %	OD %	Hi %	Lo %	Ord %	Spcl %	%
Yes (has problems)	54	62	46	71	51	65	58
No (problems reported)	46	38	54	29	49	35	42
Total %	100	100	100	100	100	100	100
Base	123	156	143	136	128	150	279

(6 children were reported as not being taken out)

* 1 child was not at school

A wide range of problems was reported when informants were asked (at S14Q11) about the two biggest problems encountered when taking the child out. Table 12.11 shows the responses. The problems most mentioned were: 'unfamiliar surroundings' (14%), 'having to watch the child' (10%), 'getting close to see', 'steps and stairs' (8% each), 'people's behaviour', 'wheelchair access' (7% each), 'lighting conditions', 'access to toilets', 'behaviour/tantrums', 'problems wearing glasses' (6% each). A range of other difficulties was mentioned by 3 or 4 percent including, 'feeding/special food' and 'noise frightens child'. Sixteen percent said they had no problems when visiting places with the child.

More children without other disabilities or with high residual vision were reported as not experiencing any problems (24 and 28 percent respectively), compared with children with other disabilities and low residual vision (10 and 4 percent respectively).

When looked at within the comparative sub-groups, most of the individual problems were reported with only one or two showing notable differences. Problems reported more for children with other disabilities than those without were: 'wheelchair access' (13 and 0 percent); 'behaviour/tantrums' (11% and none); 'feeding/special food' (6% and none); and 'difficulty walking/tires' (7 and 1 percent).

Problems reported more for children without other disabilities than children with other disabilities were 'getting close to see' (15 and 3 percent) and 'lighting conditions' (10 and 2 percent). The extra emphasis on the visual aspect of difficulties, among children without other disabilities, implied that where the child was multiply disabled the additional disabilities interact with the sight difficulties to exacerbate the difficulties parents experience.

Table 12.11 Problems experienced when taking children to visit places by other disability, residual vision and type of school

'When . . . (child) does things or visits places, which are the two biggest problems caused by child's disabilities?' (S14Q11)

	Other disability		Residual vision level		Ordinary or special school*		Total
	NOD	OD	Hi	Lo	Ord	Spcl	
	%	%	%	%	%	%	%
Unfamiliar surroundings	14	14	10	19	16	12	14
Have to watch	8	11	8	11	10	9	10
Steps and stairs	6	9	7	9	8	8	8
Getting close to see	15	3	10	6	12	6	8
Wheelchair access	0	13	3	12	1	13	7
People's behaviour	4	9	5	9	3	10	7
Lighting conditions	10	2	5	6	6	5	6
Access to toilets	2	9	3	9	3	8	6
Problem wearing glasses	7	6	9	4	9	4	6
Behaviour/tantrums	0	11	4	9	1	11	6
Difficulty walking/tires	1	7	3	5	2	7	4
Mid/long distance	8	1	6	2	8	1	4
Unhappy in crowds	3	3	3	4	2	5	3
Feeding/special food	0	6	0	6	0	6	3
Generally can't see	2	4	3	3	5	2	3
Traffic safety	2	2	2	2	2	2	2
Noise frightens	2	1	1	1	1	2	1
All experiencing one or more problems	76	90	72	96	77	90	84
No problems	24	10	28	4	23	10	16
Base = 100%	123	159	145	140	129	155	285

* 1 child was not at school

A comparison of children with high and low residual vision levels showed little real difference between them for most of the individual difficulties. Slightly more low residual vision children reported difficulties due to 'unfamiliar surroundings' (10 and 19 percent) and 'wheelchair access' (3 and 12 percent). These results reflected the association between the presence of additional disabilities and low residual vision. A further illustration of this is the fact that all those children for whom 'feeding/special food' (6%) was reported as a difficulty were also children with low residual vision.

The results above are paralleled in the differences between children in ordinary and special schools; those in special schools experience more problems, reflecting the fact that more severely disabled children attend special than ordinary schools (see Chapters 6 and 10).

12.4 Clubs and associations outside school

Table 12.12 shows that nearly 4 in 10 children (37%) belonged to clubs or associations outside school. Residual vision level displayed no difference; the main difference found is that between children with and without another disability (31 and 44 percent respectively).

Table 12.12 Membership of clubs or associations outside school, by other disability and type of school

'Does . . . (child) belong to any clubs, groups, societies, or associations (outside school)?' (S14Q12)

	Other disability		Ordinary or special school*		Total
	NOD	OD	Ord	Spcl	
	%	%	%	%	%
Yes	44	31	40	34	37
No/don't know	56	69	59	66	63
Total %	100	100	100	100	100
Base	126	159	129	155	285

* 1 child was not at school

Table 12.13 Clubs or associations attended, by other disability, residual vision and type of school (S14Q13)

	Other disability		Residual vision		Ordinary or special school*		Total
	NOD	OD	Hi	Lo	Ord	Spcl	
	%	%	%	%	%	%	%
Brownies/cubs etc.	18	8	15	9	15	10	12
Religious group	8	6	9	5	5	8	7
Other leisure club – unspecified	6	2	7	4	9	3	6
Specified sport or activity club	8	4	6	5	7	5	6
PHAB club	1	6	1	6	0	7	4
Youth club	6	2	3	4	3	5	4
Other sports club – unspecified	6	2	3	4	5	3	4
Specified leisure club	3	2	3	2	5	1	3
Leisure centre	2	1	2	1	2	2	2
Ballet/dance group	2	1	3	1	4	0	2
Club/society for blind people	2	1	1	2	0	3	1
Unidentified club for disabled people	0	2	1	1	0	2	1
All belonging to one or more club	44	31	38	36	40	34	37
No clubs attended	56	69	62	64	60	66	63
Base = 100%	126	159	145	140	129	155	285

* 1 child was not at school

The data in Table 12.13 show the variety of clubs and associations visually impaired children belong to. Most frequently mentioned were:

'brownies or cubs' (12%), 'religious group' (7%), 'specified sport or activity club' and 'other leisure club – unspecified' (6% each). No other club or association was reported by more than four percent, including: 'PHAB club', 'youth club' and 'ballet/dance group'.

Brownies or cubs were attended more by less severely disabled children (18 and 8 percent respectively for those without and with other disabilities). Attendance at a physically handicapped and able bodied (PHAB) club was greater among children with other disabilities (6 and 1 percent).

A comparison of club attendance by age showed some difference, but this might simply be a reflection of a generally expected age difference rather than anything to do with disability (no table shown). Thirty-one per cent of children aged 3 – 11 attended a club or association compared with 44% of those aged 12 or over. The type of clubs showed little difference, other than 'youth club' and 'sport/activity' clubs where attendance was greater among older children; this lends credence to the fact that any difference may be as much to do with age as disability.

12.4.1 Attendance at clubs for people with disabilities or at general clubs

Asked specifically (at S14Q14) about the type of club children attended, just under a third (30%) were reported as attending a club 'for everybody', 5% went to clubs 'for people with different disabilities' and 4% to a 'club for people with sight problems'. That is, 80% of children who belong to a club or association were members or participants in clubs described as for 'everybody' not just for people with disabilities. Table 12.14 shows the data.

Table 12.14 Types of club or association children attended, by other disability, residual vision and type of school

'Is . . . [club at S14Q13] mainly for people with sight problems, or mainly for people with a different disability, or is it for everybody?' (S14Q14)

	Other disability		Residual vision		Ordinary or special school*		Total
	NOD %	OD %	Hi %	Lo %	Ord %	Spcl %	%
Club for:							
– people with sight problems	6	3	1	8	0	7	4
– people with different disabilities	1	8	1	9	1	8	5
– everybody	40	22	37	23	40	21	30
No clubs at all	56	69	62	64	60	66	63
Base = 100%	126	159	145	140	129	155	285

(* 1 child was not at school)

The more disabled the child, the greater the likelihood that he/she would be attending a club catering for children with some form of disability. Thus, about 40% of less severely disabled children were reported as attending a 'club for everybody'; the corresponding total for those more severely disabled was just over 20%.

A larger number of children with low rather than high residual vision attended clubs for people with sight problems (8 and 1 percent). Similarly, more children with an additional disability than without attended clubs for 'people with different disabilities' (8 and 1 percent).

12.4.2 Problems joining clubs

Joining a club may present problems, due to either the perceived or real needs of children with disabilities. Informants were asked (at S14Q15) whether they had encountered any problems in joining clubs. The interviewers recorded the replies to distinguish between those who answered 'no' without any further comment and those who said that they had not tried to get into clubs (see Table 12.15). Overall, 6% of informants said that they had encountered problems.

Table 12.15 Problems encountered in joining clubs due to the child's disability, by age, other disability, residual vision and type of school

'Some clubs or societies are reluctant to have handicapped members. Have you ever had any problems getting . . . (child) into any club or society?' (S14Q15)

	Age		Other disability		Residual vision		Ordinary or special school*		Total
	3 – 11 %	12 + %	NOD %	OD %	Hi %	Lo %	Ord %	Spcl %	%
Yes	3	8	5	6	2	9	3	8	6
No, no comment	41	48	56	35	54	34	58	33	44
No, haven't tried	56	42	40	57	43	56	39	58	50
Don't know	0	1	0	1	1	0	0	1	1
Total %	100	100	100	100	100	100	100	100	100
Base	152	133	126	159	145	140	129	155	285

(* 1 child was not at school)

Disregarding the age and school sub-groups for the moment, about 55% of informants with less severely disabled children reported that they had not encountered any problems, compared with about 34% with more severely disabled children.

Where additional information was recorded of not having tried to get the child into a club, the proportions were reversed. Among those with more severely disabled children, about 56% reported not having tried, compared with about 42% among those with less severely disabled children. The data suggest that parents were not trying to get children who were more severely disabled into 'ordinary' clubs based on a self-assessment of either the child's disability, or the ability of clubs to provide for the child's needs. Although tentative, this hypothesis is supported by our qualitative interviews at the development stage of the study.

Table 12.15 shows that among informants with children in ordinary schools more parents reported that they had not faced any problems, without further comment, than those who said 'no' and commented that they had not tried (58 and 39 percent respectively). These figures were reversed for those with children in special schools (33 and 58 percent). The figures parallel the difference between more and less severely disabled children, reflecting the larger number of more severely disabled children in special schools.

More informants with younger children (56%) said that they had not tried to get the child into a club than those with older children (42%): possibly a reflection of a lesser interest in joining clubs among younger children.

The 16 informants who had experienced problems joining clubs were asked what sort of problems had been encountered. Eight informants reported that the club organisers did not want the responsibility of a child with a disability; two that the club felt they would not be able to cope; a variety of other reasons were reported by the other six informants.

12.5 Holidays

Table 12.16 shows that just over 80% of children had been taken on holiday at some time. A larger number of children without other disabilities had been taken on holiday than children with other disabilities (91 and 76 percent respectively). In fact, among children who had **not** been on holiday with informants, three-quarters had another disability, that is to say, it is more severely disabled children who are not being taken on holiday.

Table 12.16 Holidays, by other disability

'Do you ever go away on holidays with . . . (child)?' (S14Q17)

	Other disability		Total
	NOD	OD	
	%	%	%
Yes	91	76	82
No	9	24	18
Total %	100	100	100
Base	126	159	285

Further questioning established that of the 51 children who had not been on holiday, just under half (24) had been on holiday at some time without the informant. The other sub-groups did not show any clear differences.

12.5.1 Holiday accommodation

Table 12.17 shows that the most popular holiday accommodation reported was 'self-catering' (44%), followed by 'caravan' (36%) and 'guest house/hotel' (26%).

Table 12.17 Holiday accommodation, by other disability, residual vision and age

'What sort of accommodation do you usually stay in when you go on holiday with him/her?' (S14Q18)

	Other disability		Residual vision		Age		Total
	NOD	OD	Hi	Lo	3 – 11	12 +	
	%	%	%	%	%	%	%
Self catering	42	48	40	51	39	51	44
Caravan	38	33	39	32	37	34	36
Guest house/hotel	34	18	27	24	23	28	26
Holiday camp	6	8	7	7	7	7	7
Camping/tent	9	5	7	7	6	8	7
Friends' house	9	7	6	10	10	6	7
Relatives' house	7	7	7	6	7	6	7
Specially adapted bungalow	0	1	1	0	1	0	#
Other	1	0	1	0	0	1	#
Base = 100%	114	120	124	110	125	109	234

(51 children had not been on holiday)

Those using guest houses or hotels and self-catering provided the most notable differences between the sub-groups. The severity of the disability provided the main area of difference. Where the child had no other disability, informants were almost twice as likely to have used a guest house or hotel compared with those whose children had another disability (34 and 18 percent respectively). The self-catering accommodation was used more by informants whose children had low residual vision compared with high residual vision (51 and 40 percent respectively). These figures suggest that the severity of the child's disability influences the type of accommodation used.

More use was made of self-catering accommodation among informants with older than younger children (51 and 39 percent).

12.5.2   Children holidaying without parents

Table 12.18 shows that nearly 6 in 10 children (57%) were reported as having been on holiday without the informant. More children with low residual vision (64%) were reported as having been on such a holiday than children with high residual vision (50%): likewise, more children in special than those in ordinary schools (66 and 46 percent). Age showed the largest difference, with older children more than twice as likely to have been on separate holidays (83 and 34 percent). The presence or absence of other disabilities showed no statistically significant difference (see section 20.5).

Table 12.18   Children holidaying without parents, by age, residual vision and type of school

'Has . . . (child) ever been away on holiday without you?' (S14Q19)

| | Age | | Residual vision | | Ordinary or special school* | | Total |
| | 3 – 11 | 12 + | Hi | Lo | Ord | Spcl | |
	%	%	%	%	%	%	%
Yes	34	83	50	64	46	66	57
No	66	17	50	36	54	34	43
Total %	100	100	100	100	100	100	100
Base	152	133	145	140	129	155	285

(* 1 child was not at school)

Table 12.19 shows that the child's school was by far the most frequently mentioned organisation or person with whom the child had had a separate holiday. Fifty-seven percent reported the school, followed by 'relatives' (17%). Others mentioned were 'scouts' (8%), 'hospital or residential home' (6%); no more than 4% mentioned 'friends/other family', 'organisations for blind people', 'other disability organisations' and 'religious groups'.

Among older children the school was by far the major source for separate holidays, 68% having been with the school. Among younger children the school (35%) and relatives (37%) together provided the bulk of separate holidays.

An interesting difference can be seen between more and less severely disabled children. More severely disabled children exclusively were taken on holiday by the 'hospital or residential home', 10% each for those with other disabilities or low residual vision. The 'scouts' and other such organisations provided almost exclusively for less severely disabled children: 14 and 16 percent respectively for children without other disabilities and high residual vision.

Table 12.19   Holidays without parents, by age, other disability, residual vision and type of school

'Thinking about his/her last holiday without you, who did he/she go with?' (S14Q20)

	Age		Other disability		Residual vision		Ordinary or special school		Total
	3 – 11	12 +	NOD	OD	Hi	Lo	Ord	Spcl	
	%	%	%	%	%	%	%	%	%
School	35	68	51	62	55	59	42	66	57
Relatives	37	7	22	13	17	17	31	9	17
Scouts etc.	12	6	14	2	16	1	15	3	8
Hospital or residential home	4	7	0	10	0	10	0	9	6
Friend/other family	2	6	6	2	4	3	7	2	4
Organisations for blind people	2	3	3	2	1	3	0	4	3
Other disability organisations	2	3	1	3	0	5	0	4	3
Religious group	0	3	1	2	3	1	2	2	2
Other	6	4	6	3	6	3	7	3	4
Base = 100%	51	108	72	87	71	88	59	100	159

(124 had not been on a separate holiday: no information for 2)

Table 12.19 shows that the type of school attended determined even more with whom the child spent a separate holiday, emphasising the association between the severity of the disability and the type of school attended. Sixty-six percent of children attending special schools were reported as being taken by the school, compared with 42% of those in ordinary schools. The extra-curricular role of the school is being illustrated here, and no doubt both kinds of school are using these holidays to develop self-help, daily living and mobility skills among visually impaired children. The significantly greater provision by the special schools probably reflects their longer history of involvement in the education of the 'whole' child.

Thus, the more frequent mention of the school as a source of separate holidays among older and more severely disabled children was a possible reflection of the greater placement of such children in special compared with ordinary schools.

Relatives were reported as taking 9% of those in special schools on holiday, compared with 31% in ordinary schools. Those taken by the 'scouts' were 15 and 3 percent for those in ordinary and special schools respectively.

None of the children in ordinary schools was reported as being taken on holiday by organisations for blind or other disabled people, compared with 4% among those in special schools. Hospitals or residential homes were only reported for children in special schools (9%).

12.5.3 Holidays specially for disabled children

Table 12.20 shows that 38% of informants were aware of special holidays for handicapped children. A higher level of awareness was found among informants with more severely disabled children; about 43% where the child had low residual vision or other disability compared with about 33% for less severely disabled children.

Table 12.20 Awareness of holidays for children with disabilities, by other disability, residual vision and type of school

'Do you know of any special holidays provided for children with handicaps?' (S14Q21)

	Other disability		Residual vision		Ordinary or special school*		Total
	NOD	OD	Hi	Lo	Ord	Spcl	
	%	%	%	%	%	%	%
Yes	33	42	32	44	32	43	38
No/don't know†	67	58	67	56	68	57	62
Total %	100	100	100	100	100	100	100
Base	126	159	145	140	129	155	285

* 1 child was not at school

† single informant reported 'don't know'

Asked if they knew who provided such holidays, the informants mostly mentioned 'social services' and 'school/education authority' (19% each). Local societies for the blind, societies for those with other disabilities and RNIB were each mentioned by 10% of informants. Other national charities and local groups of parents were also mentioned by small numbers of informants. Informants with less severely disabled children, or those in ordinary schools, were almost twice as likely to be recorded as 'don't knows', suggesting less knowledge about who may provide such a service.

12.5.4 Use of special holidays

Among informants who reported knowing about special holidays, 28% (30 children) were said to have been on one of these holidays. Of these children, 26 were in special schools, 22 had low residual vision and 23 had additional disabilities.

Table 12.21 shows the responses to the following questions based on the full sample: 'Has . . . (child) ever been on one of these holidays?' and 'Do you think such a holiday would be suitable for . . . (child)?'

Overall 11% of children had been on a special holiday for disabled children; 31% of informants thought such holidays might be suitable for

Table 12.21   Suitability of special holidays, by other disability, residual vision and type of school

'Has . . . (child) ever been on one of these holidays?' (S14Q23)

'Do you think such a holiday would be suitable for . . . (child)?' (S14Q24)

	Other disability		Residual vision		Ordinary or special school*		Total
	NOD	OD	Hi	Lo	Ord	Spcl	
	%	%	%	%	%	%	%
Been on special holiday	6	15	6	16	3	17	11
Think suitable	25	36	27	36	24	37	31
Not suitable	52	37	55	33	59	32	44
Don't know/depends	17	12	13	16	14	14	14
Total %	100	100	100	100	100	100	100
Base	126	159	145	140	129	155	285

(* 1 child was not at school)

the child; 44% felt that special holidays would not be suitable; and a further 14% could not say.

The severity of the child's disabilities clearly determined the use of special holidays and how suitable they were thought to be. Children with low residual vision (16%) were more likely to have been on such holidays compared with children with high residual vision (6%); they were also thought to be more suitable for children with low residual vision by 36 and 27 percent respectively. The figures in the residual vision sub-groups were closely paralleled by the other disability and type of school sub-groups. Well over half of informants with less severely disabled children considered such holidays as 'not suitable' for the child compared with about a third of those with more severely disabled children.

12.5.5   Holiday activities and play schemes

Table 12.22 shows that, overall, 28% of children were reported as attending a play scheme, or taking part in a holiday activity during the school holidays. A larger proportion of children with other disabilities were reported as taking part in such schemes compared with those without other disabilities (33 and 21 percent respectively). The proportions were similar for those in special (31%) and ordinary (24%) schools (these differences are not statistically significant: see section 20.5).

Asked who provided these holiday play schemes, a variety of sources were mentioned. The 'school/LEA' (40%) and 'social services/local authority' (31%) were most frequently mentioned, followed by 'local voluntary society for handicapped' (8%) and 'local group of parents'

(7%). Unspecified other local groups (11%), and the local voluntary society for the blind (1%) were also mentioned. Table 12.23 shows the data.

Of the 40% (30 informants) who mentioned 'school/LEA', 23 children were at special schools and 22 had another disability. Of the 7% (5 informants) who reported 'local group of parents', all five had children in ordinary schools.

Table 12.22 Use of play schemes during the school holidays, by other disability and type of school

'During school holidays, are there any play schemes or holiday activities that . . . (child) goes to?' (S14Q25)

	Other disability		Ordinary or special school		Total
	NOD	OD	Ord	Spcl	
	%	%	%	%	%
Yes	21	33	24	31	28
No	79	67	76	69	72
Total %	100	100	100	100	100
Base	121	150	126	145	271

(14 children were not at school)

Table 12.23 Providers of play schemes and holiday activities

'Who offers play schemes or holiday activities?' (S14Q26)

	All who have used a holiday play scheme
	%
School/LEA	40
Social services/local authority	31
Local voluntary society for handicapped	8
Local group of parents	7
MENCAP	5
Local voluntary society for the blind	1
Other local group	11
Other	5
Base = 100%	75

(210 had not used holiday play schemes)

The main activities on these holiday schemes were 'sports' (47%), 'day outings' (37%), 'play schemes' (26%), 'arts and crafts' (25%), 'drama and music' (4%), and 'additional care for the child' (2%).

177

12.6 Respite care

Caring for a child with a disability can place a tremendous strain upon parents, no matter how loving they may be. The opportunity to have time to oneself can provide the chance to re-charge one's batteries. Table 12.24 shows that half (49%) of informants said that they got the opportunity to take a break from caring for the child.

On average 55% of informants with more severely disabled children reported getting a chance for a break compared with just over 40% of those with less severely disabled children. These percentages also applied to those in special and ordinary schools.

More informants with younger children reported getting the chance for a break than those with older children (56 and 41 percent). After looking within the age groups, we still found that it was the informants with more severely disabled children who reported getting such a break, confirming that such breaks were being provided for those with more severely disabled children (no table shown).

Table 12.24 Respite care for parents, by age, other disability, residual vision and type of school

'Do you ever have an opportunity to take a break from caring for your child while someone else looks after him/her?' (S14Q28)

	Age		Other disability		Residual vision		Ordinary or special school*		Total
	3 – 11	12 +	NOD	OD	Hi	Lo	Ord	Spcl	
	%	%	%	%	%	%	%	%	%
Yes	56	41	40	56	43	54	42	55	49
No	44	59	60	44	57	46	58	45	51
Total %	100	100	100	100	100	100	100	100	100
Base	152	133	126	159	145	140	129	155	285

* 1 child was not at school

12.6.1 Source of respite care

Table 12.25 shows that for a quarter of informants who received respite care the social or welfare services provided this help. Such help was clearly being delivered to those with more severely disabled children. Overall, 38% of those with more severely disabled children reported receiving such help. For children without additional disabilities or with high residual vision, the totals were 2 and 10 percent respectively. Similarly, where the child was in a special or ordinary school the totals reported as receiving help from the social or welfare services were 40 and 2 percent respectively.

Informants with older children were more likely to report receiving help from this source than those with younger children (35 and 19 per cent respectively).

Table 12.25 Respite care from social and welfare services, by other disability, residual vision and type of school

'Did you get any help from the welfare or social services to find someone to take care of . . . (child) while you took a break?' (S14Q29)

	Other disability		Residual vision		Ordinary or special school		Total
	NOD	OD	Hi	Lo	Ord	Spcl	
	%	%	%	%	%	%	%
Yes	2	38	10	38	2	40	25
No/don't know	98	62	90	52	98	60	75
Total %	100	100	100	100	100	100	100
Base	50	89	63	76	54	85	139

(146 received no respite care)

Those who received no help from the welfare services were asked who looked after the child to give them a break. Table 12.26 shows the responses. Three-quarters (76%) reported that relatives were the main respite carers, far exceeding the next group which was friends (11%), with school based carers being reported by 7% of informants. Other carers reported were 'neighbours' and 'child minder/baby sitter'. 'Hospital/social services/residential home' were still mentioned by 5%

Table 12.26 Respite care from non-welfare services, by other disability and type of school

Informants who did not receive help from welfare services were asked: 'Who looks after him/her on those occasions?' (S14Q30)

	Other disability		Ordinary or special school		Total
	NOD	OD	Ord	Spcl	
	%	%	%	%	%
Relatives	86	68	83	69	76
Friends	18	4	17	4	11
School based carer	6	7	2	12	7
Hospital/social services/residential home	0	9	0	10	5
Neighbours	2	4	2	4	3
Child minder/baby sitter	2	0	0	2	1
Other	2	4	2	4	3
Base = 100%	49	56	53	52	105

(35 received help from social services, 146 received no break)

of informants although the question concerned non-welfare service carers. It should be noted that these carers were only mentioned by informants with children who had other disabilities and children in special schools.

For children without other disabilities (86%), or those in ordinary schools (83%), relatives were more likely to provide the respite care than for children with other disabilities (68%), or in special schools (69%). Although this was on the borderline of statistical significance (see section 20.5), friends were also reported more frequently as the main respite carers among these sub-groups.

12.6.2 Demand for respite care from the welfare services

Table 12.27 shows that among informants who had not received respite care help from the welfare or social services, three-quarters (76%) said that they did not want it. Eighty-three percent of informants whose children had no other disabilities said that they would not like such help. But even among those whose children had other disabilities a large majority, 68%, did not want help. Among this group 16% expressed a desire for such help, with an equal number recorded as 'don't knows', showing some uncertainty.

More informants with children in ordinary schools than in special schools reported not wanting respite care help from the welfare services (81 and 71 percent).

Table 12.27   Demand for respite care help from the welfare services, by other disability and type of school

'Would you like help from the welfare or social services to help you take a break?' (S14Q31)

	Other disability		Ordinary or special school		Total
	NOD	OD	Ord	Spcl	
	%	%	%	%	%
Yes	6	16	8	14	11
No	83	68	81	71	76
Don't know	10	16	12	15	13
Total %	100	100	100	100	100
Base	125	125	128	121	250

(35 received help from social services)

* 1 child was not at school

Table 12.28 summarises the receipt of, and desire for respite care help. Overall, 12% of informants reported receiving help with respite care from the welfare services, and a slightly smaller number (10%) would like such help: two-thirds (66%) did not want any help.

The analysis shows that those most interested in help from the social services were parents with more severely disabled children.

Table 12.28 Receipt of and demand for respite care help from the welfare services, by other disability, residual vision level and type of school (S14 Q29 & 31)

	Other disability		Residual vision		Ordinary or special school*		Total
	NOD	OD	Hi	Lo	Ord	Spcl	
	%	%	%	%	%	%	%
Gets help from the SSD	1	21	4	21	1	22	12
Would like SSD help	6	13	8	12	8	11	10
Does not want any help	83	54	76	56	80	56	66
Don't know	10	13	12	11	12	12	12
Total %	100	100	100	100	100	100	100
Base = 100%	126	159	145	140	129	155	285

(* 1 child was not at school)

13 Special Toys and Games

13.1 Advice about suitable toys and games

The provision of toys that will help the visually impaired child learn about the world is arguably more important than the provision of stimulating toys for the sighted child. Special effort is required to encourage the child to explore its world, and toys are one means by which this is done. Informants were asked (at S13Q1) whether they had received any guidance in finding suitable toys and games. Table 13.1 shows the responses.

Table 13.1   Help and advice about suitable toys and games for visually impaired children, by type of school, residual vision and other disability

'Has anyone ever given you any help or advice about finding suitable toys and games for . . . (child)?' (S13Q1)

| | Ordinary or special school* | | Residual vision | | Other Disability | | Total |
| | Ord | Spcl | Hi | Lo | NOD | OD | |
	%	%	%	%	%	%	%
Yes	33	47	34	48	26	52	41
No	67	53	66	52	74	48	59
Total %	100	100	100	100	100	100	100
Base	129	155	145	140	126	159	285

(*1 child was not at school)

Overall 41% of informants said that they had received advice about suitable toys and games for their child. More of those with children in special schools (47%), with low residual vision (48%), and with other disabilities (52%) reported receiving such advice compared with those in ordinary schools (33%), with high residual vision (34%) and with no other disabilities (26%).

The larger percentage difference between those with and without other disabilities suggests that some informants in the former sub-group might be receiving such advice to do with the child's other disabilities as well as his/her sight problem. The data in Table 13.2 confirm this.

Looking at children with and without other disabilities within the two residual vision sub-groups, we find that in both sub-groups, where the child has another disability those parents are more likely to have received this advice.

Table 13.2 Help and advice about suitable toys and games for visually impaired children, by other disability within residual vision levels

'Has anyone ever given you any help or advice about finding suitable toys and games for . . . (child)?' (S13Q1)

	Residual vision and other disability				Total
	High residual vision		Low residual vision		
	NOD	OD	NOD	OD	
	%	%	%	%	%
Yes	26	44	27	57	41
No	74	56	72	43	59
Total %	100	100	100	100	100
Base	82	63	44	96	285

For children with high residual vision and no other disabiity, 26% of informants had received advice and help about toys and games. This compares with 44% of those with other disabilities within this high residual vision group. This difference is maintained among children with low residual vision where the corresponding percentages were 27 and 57 respectively.

13.1.1 Sources of advice

Informants had received advice from a wide variety of individuals and other sources. Table 13.3 shows the main sources reported.

The most frequently mentioned sources of advice were: peripatetic teacher (21%); child's school (20%); toy libraries (16%); physio- or occupational therapist (13%); RNIB (general mention) (10%); and RNIB special education adviser (9%). Others mentioned included social or welfare workers, educational psychologists, parents of other handicapped children and hospital assessment units.

The various sub-groups showed no clear differences. However, there was some indication that the peripatetic teacher was reported more frequently by informants with children in ordinary than special schools, and among informants whose children had other disabilities marginally more mentioned a physio-/occupational therapist. For children in

Table 13.3 Sources of advice and information on toys suitable for visually impaired children

'Who has given you advice?' (S13Q2)

	%
Peripatetic teacher	21
Child's school	20
Toy library	16
Physio/occupational therapist	13
RNIB (general mention)	10
RNIB education adviser	9
Other teacher/adviser	7
Social/welfare worker	6
Health visitor/clinic	5
Blind/mobility officer	5
Educational psychologist	3
Other medical specialist	3
Paediatrician	3
Base = 100%	116

(169 had not received any advice)

special schools the 'child's school' and the 'toy library' tended to receive more frequent mentions.

13.2 Use of special toys and games

While 41% of parents had received advice or help in finding suitable toys and games for visually impaired children, Table 13.4 shows that a similar number (42%) reported that the child had at some time played with such toys and games.

More of the children reported as not having played with such toys and games were in ordinary schools (70%), had high residual vision (66%), or had no other disabilities (61%), compared with children in special schools (42%), with low residual vision (43%) or with other disabilities (50%).

'Puzzles and jig-saws' (25%), were the most frequently mentioned item, and 'push-pull toys' (15%) the least, with most of the items reported as having been played with by about 20% of children.

Among children who had played with special toys and games, the mean number used was four; 12% were reported to have played with all 8 toys and games listed.

13.2.1 Source of toys and games

Informants were asked (at S13Q4) about the source of these toys and games. There was little real difference between the comparative sub-groups.

Table 13.4 Special toys and games used, by type of school, residual vision and other disability

'There are various toys and games which are sold specially for children with sight problems. Has ... (child) ever played with any of these toys and the games that are specially sold for children with sight problems?' (S13Q3)

	Ordinary or special school*		Residual vision		Other disability		Total
	Ord	Spcl	Hi	Lo	NOD	OD	
	%	%	%	%	%	%	%
Puzzles and jig-saws	19	30	21	29	21	28	25
Dominoes	17	25	16	26	21	21	21
Games that make noises	9	27	13	25	13	24	19
Audible balls	10	27	11	28	18	21	19
Tactile toys and games	10	24	9	26	16	19	18
Cards	12	24	12	25	18	19	18
Board games	12	24	10	26	19	18	18
Push-pull toys	9	21	9	22	14	17	15
All playing with one or more	**28**	**53**	**31**	**53**	**36**	**47**	**42**
None	70	42	66	43	61	50	55
Don't know	2	5	3	4	3	3	3
Base = 100%	129	155	145	140	126	159	285

(* 1 child was not at school)

Table 13.5 Source of special toys and games

'Where did you mostly get these special toys or playthings from? (S13Q4)

	%
Toy shops	32
RNIB	25
Educational toy supplier	18
Education authority/school	16
Toy library	15
Social services	4
Local society for the blind	3
Make them	2
Health service	2
Base = 100%	120

(165 had not used special toys and games)

Table 13.5 shows that the main source was ordinary toy shops (32%), followed by RNIB (25%). Other main sources include: 'educational toy suppliers' (18%), 'education authority/school' (16%) and 'toy library' (15%). Of the 30 informants who mentioned RNIB, 28 had children with low residual vision and 24 children were in special schools.

Of those who had used special toys and games just over two-thirds (68%) had bought them and the remainder had borrowed them.

Table 13.6 shows the pattern of use and buying, based on all visually impaired children, not just those who had used the special toys. More informants reported having used and bought special toys for children with low residual vision (39%), or in special schools (38%), than for children with high residual vision (18%), or in ordinary schools (17%). This pattern was repeated between children with and without another disability, though the percentage difference was smaller (32 and 24 per cent respectively). Children who had played with such toys, but for whom they had not been bought, averaged 14% across all the sub-groups.

Table 13.6 Purchase and use of special toys for children with sight problems, by other disability, residual vision and type of school

'There are various toys and games which are sold specially for children with sight problems. Has . . . (child) ever played with any of these toys and games that are specially sold for children with sight problems?' (S13Q3)

'Have you ever bought any of these special toys or games?' (S13Q5)

	Other disability		Residual vision		Ordinary or special school*		Total
	NOD	OD	Hi	Lo	Ord	Spcl	
	%	%	%	%	%	%	%
Bought and used	24	32	18	39	17	38	28
Used, but not bought	12	15	13	14	12	15	14
Not used any	61	50	66	43	70	42	55
Don't know at S13Q1	3	3	3	3	1	5	3
Total	100	100	100	100	100	100	100
Base	126	159	145	140	129	155	285

(*1 child was not at school)

Informants who had bought these toys and games were asked (at S13Q6) if they had experienced any difficulty getting them: just over a third (35%) said that they had. No further enquiry was made into the difficulties encountered.

14 Radio, Television, Tape Players and Telephones

14.1 Radio

Table 14.1 shows that nearly 9 in 10 children were reported as listening to the radio. A clear majority are reported as preferring music to talk shows (68 to 5 percent). No notable difference in radio listening was evident between any of the sub-groups.

Table 14.1 Radio listening, by other disability and residual vision

'Does . . . (child) listen to the radio at all?' (S12Q1)

'Would you say that he/she mostly prefers music programmes, or programmes with a lot of talking on the radio?' (S12Q2)

	Other disabilities		Residual vision		Total
	NOD	OD	Hi	Lo	
	%	%	%	%	%
Prefers music	71	65	72	64	68
Prefers talking	6	4	3	7	5
Both equally	15	15	12	18	15
Don't know preference	0	1	0	1	#
All listening to the radio	**93**	**85**	**88**	**89**	**88**
No radio listening	**7**	**15**	**12**	**11**	**12**
Total %	100	100	100	100	100
Base	126	159	145	140	285

Table 14.1 shows that there are no statistically significant differences in the type of programme listened to between the sub-groups. However, not unexpectedly, there is some indication that younger children did not listen to the radio as much as older children; 18% of those aged 3 –7 did not listen decreasing to 7% among those aged 12 and over.

14.2 Television

Table 14.2 shows that overall 92% of children were reported as watching or listening to television. Those with other disabilities, low residual vision or in special schools were reported as watching television less than their sub-group counterparts, averaging 86 and 98 percent respectively.

Table 14.2 Watching and listening to television, by other disability, residual vision and type of school

'Does . . . (child) watch or listen to TV at all?' (S12Q3)

	Other disability		Residual vision		Ordinary or special school*		Total
	NOD	OD	Hi	Lo	Ord	Spcl	
	%	%	%	%	%	%	%
Yes	98	87	99	86	99	86	92
No/don't know	2	13	2	14	1	15	8
Total %	100	100	100	100	100	100	100
Base	126	159	145	140	129	155	285

*1 child was not at school

14.3   Tape players

The use of audio equipment among young children may be dependent on age. Table 14.3 confirms that there is some age effect, with older children generally making more use of the individual tape players than younger children; for example, 'Talking Book machine' (9 and 3 percent), 'cassette player' (64 and 43 percent) and 'music centre' (47 and 26 percent).

Table 14.3 Use of tape players among visually impaired children, by age

'Does . . . (child) use any of these at home for playing or recording tapes?' (S12Q4)

	Age		Total
	3 – 11	12 +	
	%	%	%
Cassette with radio	43	64	53
Cassette player	42	35	39
Walkman or similar	33	39	36
Music centre	26	47	36
Talking Book machine	3	9	6
Dictaphone	1	2	1
Other	3	4	3
All using a tape player	81	86	83
None used	19	14	17
Base = 100%	152	133	285

Table 14.4 shows the use of tape players within the other disability, residual vision and school sub-groups. More children with other disabilities were reported as not using any of the listed items than children without other disabilities (23 and 8 percent respectively). The

individual items that showed the largest difference in the level of use between children without and with other disabilities respectively were: a 'cassette with radio' (68 and 41 percent), and 'music centre' (46 and 28 percent). The absence of large differences in use between the other sub-groups suggests that it was the presence or absence of other disabilities that is the main influence on use.

Table 14.4   Tape players used, by other disability, residual vision and age

'Does . . . (child) use any of these at home for playing or recording tapes?' (S12Q4)

	Other disability		Residual vision		Ordinary or special school*		Total
	NOD	OD	Hi	Lo	Ord	Spcl	
	%	%	%	%	%	%	%
Cassette with radio	68	41	54	52	60	48	53
Cassette player	40	38	39	39	43	36	39
Walkman or similar	38	34	36	36	36	35	36
Music centre	46	28	38	34	36	36	36
Talking Book machine	8	4	1	11	4	8	6
Dictaphone	2	1	0	3	1	2	1
Other	2	4	3	3	3	3	3
All using a tape player	92	77	87	80	91	78	83
None used	8	23	13	20	9	22	17
Base = 100%	126	159	145	140	129	155	285

(*1 child was not at school)

Among children with low and high residual vision, only the use of a Talking Book machine showed a statistically significant difference; more children with low residual vision (11%) used one than those with high residual vision (1%). The 3% (4 children) who used a 'dictaphone' were all children with low residual vision.

Fewer children in special schools (78%) made use of a tape player compared with those in ordinary schools (91%). This difference is probably a reflection of the fact that special schools have a larger proportion of more severely disabled children than ordinary schools.

When looked at within the two broad age groups, a tendency was found for a larger number of younger children in ordinary schools to use the various tape players than those in special schools. Among older children no clear difference was found (no table shown).

14.3.1   Frequency of tape player use

For children with a tape player two-thirds were reported as listening to it on 'most days', and a further 21% listened to it 'at least once a week'.

189

Greater daily use was made of their tape player by older children (77 and 56 percent), children in special schools (77 and 56 percent) and children with low residual vision (78 and 56 percent) compared with their sub-group counterparts. The presence or absence of another disability among children had no effect on the level of usage.

14.3.2 Subjects or items listened to on tape

Table 14.5 shows that 88% of children were reported as listening to 'music' and 57% to 'stories'. 'Talking Books (RNIB mentioned)' (5%) and 'talking books (no further comment)' (8%) were the only other items mentioned by more than three per cent of informants.

Table 14.5   Subjects or items listened to on tape by residual vision

'What sort of things does your child listen to on tape?' (S12Q6)

	Residual vision		Total
	Hi	Lo	
	%	%	%
Music	90	87	88
Stories	52	63	57
Talking books (no further comment)	5	9	8
Talking Books (RNIB mentioned)	1	9	5
Personal use, recording sounds	1	5	3
Television/radio/films	1	4	2
School lessons/educational use	3	1	2
Letters from friends	1	2	1
Base = 100%	126	112	238

(238 children: 47 did not have a tape player)

Table 14.5 gives the responses by residual vision, the sub-group comparison where one might have expected the largest difference in tape listening to be present. 'Stories' showed a difference between those with high and low residual vision (52 and 63 per cent respectively), as did 'Talking Books (RNIB mentioned)', 1 and 9 percent. The other items listened to did not show any statistically significant differences, but were consistent in that more children with low residual vision tended to be reported as listening to these items than children with high residual vision.

'Stories' was the only item that consistently showed a difference in listening between the sub-groups. Story listening was reported more for children attending special schools than ordinary schools (64 and 53 percent) and among younger than older children (77 and 35 percent).

Table 14.6 looks at what was listened to on tape by the frequency with which the tape player was used. The frequency of use is divided between those children who used the tape on a daily basis, and those using it less frequently. If listening to music is disregarded in this analysis – as it is not necessarily influenced by any disabilities that the child may have – and the other items are looked at, a pattern emerges.

Table 14.6 Subjects or items listened to on tape, by the frequency of tape usage

'What sort of things does your child listen to on tape?' (S12Q6)

	Frequency of tape usage		Total
	Daily	Less than daily	
	%	%	%
Music	92	81	88
Stories	53	64	57
Talking books (no further comment)	10	3	8
Talking Books (RNIB mentioned)	7	0	5
Personal use, recording sounds	3	3	3
Television/radio/films	3	1	2
School lessons/educational use	3	0	2
Letters from friends	2	0	1
Base = 100%	158	80	238

(238 children: 47 did not have a tape player)

We noted above that children in special schools seemed to listen to stories more than those in ordinary schools, and that those with low residual vision also listened to stories more than those with high residual vision, thus implying that the tape may be replacing 'print books' as a source of stories or 'reading'. The results in Table 14.6 suggest that, in fact, this may not be the case; fewer children who make daily use of the tape player listen to stories than those who make less frequent use of it (53 and 64 percent respectively).

Among the other items, although none showed statistically significant percentage differences (see section 20.5), the pattern seems to be that children who used the tape player more frequently employed it for purposes one would have expected among visually impaired people compared with sighted people; for such uses as 'letters from friends', talking books (both categories) and 'school lessons/educational use'.

14.3.3 Subjects or items recorded on tape

Table 14.7 shows the sort of things that visually impaired children have recorded for them on audio tape. Overall, 71% of children had nothing recorded; only the residual vision sub-groups showed any clear differences. Sixty-two percent of children with low residual vision had nothing recorded compared with 79% of those with high residual vision. In other words, more children with low residual vision (38%) had something recorded for them than children with high residual vision (21%).

Table 14.7   Items or subjects recorded on audio tape, by residual vision and frequency of use of the tape player

	Residual vision		Frequency of tape player usage		Total
				Less than	
	Hi	Lo	Daily	daily	
	%	%	%	%	%
Television programmes	12	21	22	4	16
Radio programmes	6	13	12	3	9
People	4	10	7	6	7
School lessons	2	5	4	0	3
House/garden sounds	1	5	4	0	3
Music	2	2	3	0	2
Stories/readings	1	1	0	2	1
Letters	0	1	1	0	#
Lists/reminders	0	1	1	0	#
One or more item recorded	21	38	37	15	29
None	79	62	63	85	71
Base = 100%	126	112	158	80	238

(238 children: 47 did not have a tape player)

Table 14.7 shows that when examined by residual vision, the items clearly recorded for low but not high residual vision children were 'television programmes' (21 and 12 percent) and 'radio programmes' (13 and 6 percent). The other items did not have large percentage differences, but were consistent in that more children with low residual vision had the items recorded for them than those with high residual vision.

More children who made daily use of a tape player had things recorded for them than those who used it less frequently (37 and 15 percent); 'television programmes' (22 and 4 percent) and 'radio programmes' (12 and 3 percent) showed the clearest differences. Items such as 'school lessons', 'house/garden sounds', 4% each; 'letters' and 'lists/reminders', 1% each, were only reported as being recorded for children who used the tape player daily.

14.3.4 Source of tape cassettes

Table 14.8 shows that tape cassettes were obtained from a wide variety of sources, the overwhelming majority (86%) getting commercially recorded tapes from shops. Other sources were: 'family and friends' (34%), 'local library' (15%), and 'RNIB Talking Book Service' (8%), with none of the others mentioned by more than 3% of informants.

Table 14.8 Source of recorded tapes, by the frequency of tape player usage

'Does . . . (child) get his/her tapes from any of these places?' (S12Q7)

	Frequency of tape player usage		Total
	Daily	Less than daily	
	%	%	%
Commercially recorded tapes from shops	88	81	86
Family and friends	37	28	34
Local library	17	11	15
RNIB Talking Book Service	12	0	8
Calibre	3	3	3
Tapes from local society	4	0	3
Talking magazines	3	0	2
Records own/not commercial	1	0	1
Book club/other tape service	1	0	1
RNIB Student Tape Library	1	0	#
National talking newspapers	1	0	#
Base = 100%	158	80	238

(238 children; 47 did not have a tape player)

The residual vision sub-group comparison was the only one that showed any real differences in the source of tapes. Thirteen percent of children with low residual vision were reported as getting their tapes from 'RNIB Talking Book Service' compared with 3% of those with high residual vision.

Comparison of the frequency of use suggests that children who made most use of the tape player were more likely to obtain their tapes from sources specifically for visually impaired people.

Thirteen percent (30) of informants reported (at S12Q7) difficulties experienced in getting tape cassettes.

14.4 Telephones

Eighty-seven percent of informants reported having a telephone in the home. Table 14.9 shows that of those homes with a telephone, 74% of children were reported as being able to use it. Among those who could not use the telephone (26%), 2% were reported as being too young.

A larger number of younger compared with older children were only able to answer the telephone, while older children were capable of both answering and making calls. Across the three age groups 3 – 7, 8 – 11 and 12 +, those able to do both increased from 35 and 53 to 68 percent respectively.

Among children aged 12 and over, 25% were reported as not being able to use the telephone. Twenty-three percent of those aged under 12 were not able to use the telephone – this excludes the 6% of the 3 – 7 year olds who were reported as being 'too young'.

Table 14.9 Use of the telephone by age

'Does . . . (child) use the telephone, either to ring people up, or to answer when people call, or both?' (S12Q11)

	Age			Total
	3 – 7	8 – 11	12 +	
	%	%	%	%
Rings people up	2	3	1	2
Answers the telephone	41	13	6	17
Both	35	53	68	55
Neither, too young	6	0	0	2
Neither	15	31	25	24
Don't know	2	0	1	1
Total %	100	100	100	100
Base	66	61	120	247

(247 children: 38 did not have a telephone)

Looking at those children both able to make and answer calls, we see that they were less severely disabled. More children without other disabilities (80%), with high residual vision (67%) and in ordinary schools (73%) were able to both make and answer calls; the corresponding totals for their comparative sub-groups were 36, 43 and 41 percent respectively. Table 14.10 shows the data.

In contrast the children reported as neither able to make or answer calls were more severely disabled. Within the comparative sub-groups the percentages are: other disability, 39 and 5 percent; and residual vision, 31 and 17 percent. This pattern is reflected in the fact that there were more children in special than ordinary schools who were unable to use the telephone (41 and 3 percent).

Table 14.10 Use of the telephone, by other disability, residual vision and type of school

'Does . . . (child) use the telephone, either to ring people up, or to answer when people call, or both?' (S12Q11)

	Other disability		Residual vision		Ordinary or special school		Total
	NOD	OD	Hi	Lo	Ord	Spcl	
	%	%	%	%	%	%	%
Rings people up	2	1	2	2	2	1	2
Answers the phone	13	20	14	21	19	15	17
Both	80	36	67	43	73	41	55
Neither, too young	0	3	1	3	2	1	2
Neither	5	39	17	31	3	41	24
Don't know	1	1	1	1	1	1	1
Total %	100	100	100	100	100	100	100
Base	108	139	126	121	109	138	247

(247 informants: 38 did not have a telephone)

Part G

Information, Accommodation and Finance

15 Information

15.1 General sources of information

'We are interested in how parents with children with sight problems find out about things they need to know about. How do you find out about things you want to know?' (S15Q1) was the first question asked to find out about sources of information used. Table 15.1 shows the results.

'School/LEA' (46%) was the most frequently mentioned source of information, followed by 'social services' (22%), 'ophthalmologist/ optician' (17%), 'other parents/relatives' (15%), and 'NHS therapist/ specialist' (14%); the 'GP' (12%) and 'NHS counsellor or health visitor' (9%) were also mentioned.

The broad groups above were broken down in more detail, but were too numerous to show here. However, one or two individual areas of service stood out. In the broad group of 'LEA/school', 27% specifically mentioned the child's school and 11% the peripatetic teacher. Ophthalmologist (14%) was the main eye specialist mentioned, and parents of other handicapped children (10%) predominated among the 'other parents/relatives' group.

Overall, the social services were reported most frequently as a source of information by a larger number of those with more severely disabled children, while the health services formed a greater source of information for informants with less severely disabled children.

For only one or two sources of information could significant differences be seen between the sub-groups. 'Social services' was twice as likely to be mentioned where the child had other disabilities, lower residual vision, or attended a special rather than an ordinary school (about 28 and 14 percent respectively). Among parents with less severely disabled children 'ophthalmologist/optician' was mentioned far more than among parents of more severely disabled children (about 26 and 9 percent).

Informants with children in special schools were nearly three times as likely to mention the school as a source of information (39 and 14 percent); the peripatetic teacher was singled out as a more important information source in ordinary than in special schools (17 and 7

Table 15.1 Sources of information used, by other disability, residual vision, type of school and registration status

'We are interested in how parents with children with sight problems find out about things they need to know about. How do you find out about things you want to know? (S15Q1)

	Other disability		Residual vision		Ordinary or special school*		Registration status		Total
	NOD	OD	Hi	Lo	Ord	Spcl	R	NR	
	%	%	%	%	%	%	%	%	%
LEA/school	51	43	45	48	43	49	37	52	46
Social services	14	28	16	29	14	29	28	19	22
Ophthalmologist/optician	25	11	23	10	29	7	13	19	17
Other parents/relatives	13	18	14	17	12	18	15	15	15
NHS therapist/specialist	11	16	15	13	12	16	13	15	14
GP	13	11	14	9	10	13	8	14	12
Hospital counsellor/health visitor	11	8	11	7	9	9	9	9	9
Other voluntary organisations	6	9	5	10	5	10	8	7	7
Library/CAB	6	6	7	5	7	5	8	5	6
RNIB	4	6	3	6	3	7	7	3	5
Television/print media	2	7	4	6	4	6	6	4	5
Talking media/braille	1	0	0	1	1	0	0	1	#
Base = 100%	126	159	145	140	129	155	104	181	285

(*1 child was not at school)

percent) (details not shown in the table). For children with and without other disabilities 'school' was mentioned by 31 and 23 percent of informants; the peripatetic teacher was more frequently mentioned for children without other disabilities than for those with other disabilities (17 and 7 percent respectively). This suggests that, while within a special school setting the school may be quoted as a general source of information within the ordinary school the specialist role of the peripatetic teacher is highlighted.

A larger number of informants with children with low than high residual vision reported the social services as a source of information (29 compared with 16 percent). For children with higher residual vision, health service sources were reported more, including 'ophthalmologist/optician' (23 and 10 percent) and 'GP' (14 and 9 percent).

Voluntary organisations, including RNIB, were more likely to be mentioned by informants with more severely disabled children, those with other disabilities or low residual vision, or with children in special rather than ordinary schools. Those mentioning 'other voluntary organisations' averaged 10 and 5 percent between the sub-groups. Mention of RNIB averaged 6 and 3 percent between the same groups.

15.1.1 Registration status and sources of information

Registration as blind or partially sighted is generally considered less important for people of school age than for adults. This is because of the mandatory duty of the education authority to provide for children with special needs, compared with the more discretionary provision by social services. Only 'LEA/school', as a source of information, showed a statistically significant difference based on registration status; fewer informants with registered than non-registered children mentioned this source (37 and 52 percent respectively). There was a tendency for the registered sub-group to mention 'social services' more (28 and 19 percent), and 'GP' less (8 and 14 percent) than the non-registered: these were on the borderline of statistical significance.

15.1.2 The most important sources of information

When people are asked generally about their sources of information they will produce an unlimited list of sources. To gain a more meaningful catalogue of items, people have to be encouraged to make a judgement about the items that they can name. Table 15.2 shows the results of doing this by getting informants to say which were the three most important sources of information from a limited list; these were then summarised into a single table.

Table 15.2 The most important† sources of information, by other disability, residual vision, type of school and registration status

'Overall, which of these ways would you say is the most important way for you to find out about things?' (S15Q2)
'And which would you say is the second most important?' (S15Q3)
'And which would you say is the third most important?' (S15Q4)

	Other disability		Residual vision		Ordinary or special school*		Registration status		Total
	NOD %	OD %	Hi %	Lo %	Ord %	Spcl %	R %	NR %	%
Talking to teachers	64	59	60	62	53	68	58	63	61
Talking to medical experts	70	54	71	51	78	47	50	67	61
Meeting parents of other handicapped children	42	54	40	58	36	59	53	46	49
Reading books and leaflets	44	45	48	41	46	44	33	51	45
Social services/worker	29	37	30	36	35	31	41	28	33
RNIB	16	16	10	21	14	17	25	10	16
Television/radio	10	9	8	11	9	11	13	8	10
Base = 100%	126	159	145	140	129	155	104	181	285

(*1 child was not at school)
† Although three questions were asked the responses have been aggregated

Table 15.2 shows that overall, the two information sources rated as most important were 'talking to teachers' and 'talking to medical experts' (61% each). 'Meeting parents of other handicapped children' (49%) and 'reading books and leaflets' (45%) also scored highly, followed by 'social services/worker' (33%); well behind were 'RNIB' (16%) and 'television/radio' (10%).

The pattern of response to this question within the sub-groups supports the results from question S15Q1. 'Talking to teachers' shows relatively little difference between the sub-groups, except that between ordinary and special schools (53 and 68 percent respectively). This result suggested rather more confidence in the knowledge of teachers in special schools.

'Talking to medical experts' shows a clear pattern, with a larger number of informants with less severely disabled children citing this group as an important information source than informants with more severely disabled children (about 70 and 50 percent respectively). The 20 point percentage difference between children with high and low residual vision, and children without and with other disabilities, increased to 31 points between children at ordinary and special schools (78 compared with 47 percent).

'Meeting parents of other handicapped children' was mentioned more frequently as an important source of information by informants with children in special than in ordinary schools (59 and 36 percent respectively). As we have seen in Chapter 10, the school provides the opportunity to meet other parents; in ordinary schools where there were fewer children with disabilities, this opportunity was more limited. It is through these meetings, formal or informal, that experiences and information can be shared.

'Reading books and leaflets', and 'social services/workers' showed comparatively little difference between the sub-groups, registration status being the notable exception. Informants with non-registered as opposed to registered children were more likely to read books and leaflets (51 and 33 percent respectively). A larger number of informants with registered children rated 'social services/workers' as important compared with informants with non-registered children (41 and 28 percent respectively). The pattern of these two sources suggested that informants with non-registered children had to seek out their own information more than the registered, and that the registered made use of the social services to which they have access. An important point here is that even among the non-registered, 28 percent of informants still considered social services an important information source. This indicates that official registration as blind or partially sighted does not affect contact with social services for a substantial proportion of visually impaired children.

Although only 16 percent overall rated RNIB as important, it was mentioned more where the child had low residual vision (21 and 10 percent), or where the child was registered (25 and 10 percent) compared with children with high residual vision and non-registered respectively.

When examined by age, only 'meeting parents of other handicapped children' showed any difference in importance as an information source. Sixty-one per cent of informants with children aged 3 – 7 years considered this important, compared with 48 and 42 percent respectively for children aged 8 – 11 and 12 and over.

15.2 Information provision

Although parents may have access to various sources of information, the desire for more information at times can seem insatiable. The provision of printed material is one way of meeting this information need. As shown in Table 15.3, only a quarter of informants felt that there was enough printed material available.

Table 15.3 The need for printed information for parents by age and type of school

'Some parents say that there is a need for more printed publications to help parents of children with sight problems. Others say that there is already enough printed material. Do you think there is a need for more publications, or do you think there is enough already?' (S15Q5)

	Age		Ordinary or special school*		Total
	3–7	8 +	Ord	Spcl	
	%	%	%	%	%
Need for more	74	51	60	54	57
Enough already	15	29	16	34	25
Don't know	11	20	25	12	18
Total %	100	100	100	100	100
Base	79	206	129	155	285

(* 1 child was not at school)

The age sub-group in Table 15.3 was divided differently from that normally used in this report, because it was obviously informants with children aged from 3 to 7 years who felt a greater need for printed material; nearly three-quarters (74%) said there was a need for more printed information, compared with a half of those with children aged 8 years and over. The corollary of this is that nearly twice as many of those with children aged 8 years and over felt that there was enough information (29 and 15 percent).

Well over half of informants with children in ordinary and special schools felt that there was a need for more information (60 and 54 percent respectively). However, twice as many with children in special schools than in ordinary schools felt that there was already enough information (34 and 16 percent).

The results in Table 15.3 suggest that parents with younger children were still searching for information or had not had all their information needs satisfied. Those with children in special schools might have had more access to printed material which met their information needs. The outcome, however, was still a desire for more information.

15.2.1 Difficulties experienced in gaining information about the child's disabilities

Our develpment work in the early stages of the research revealed that many parents felt that they had to search very hard for information on the child's condition(s). Informants were asked to express their level of agreement with the statement: 'Some parents say that everything they have found out they have had to go out and search for themselves. In your case would you say you agree a lot, a little, or disagree that you had to go out and search for everything yourself?' (S15Q6).

Seventy-six percent of informants agreed with the statement. Thus, not only did informants feel that not enough information was available, but that what was available had to be sought out by themselves.

Forty-three percent of all informants said that from birth to two years was the most difficult period for obtaining information, with a further 23 percent reporting the period when the child was three to five years old; effectively the pre-school years.

Asked specifically about the difficulty of getting information about the child's sight problems, informants were fairly evenly split between those who thought it 'very' or 'fairly' difficult and those who though it 'not very' or 'not at all' difficult (53 and 45 percent respectively); the remaining 2% could not say.

15.2.2 Information sought

Informants who said that they had to search out information for themselves were asked what sort of information. Most frequently mentioned were: 'medical advice' (26%), 'specialist education' (24%) and 'entitlements to benefits' (23%). Table 15.4 shows the results.

Informants also had to seek information on 'toys/games available' (15%), 'aids and equipment' (13%) and 'how to care for the child' (8%); 18% simply said 'everything'.

Table 15.4   Information parents had to search out for themselves, by other disability, residual vision, type of school and registration status

'What sort of things have you had to search out for yourself? (S15Q71)'

	Other disability		Residual vision		Ordinary or special school*		Registration status		Total
	NOD	OD	Hi	Lo	Ord	Spcl	R	NR	
	%	%	%	%	%	%	%	%	%
Medical advice	35	20	33	20	35	19	20	29	26
Specialist education	29	21	25	23	26	22	25	23	24
Entitlement to benefits	11	31	17	27	11	30	22	23	23
Toys/games available	16	14	12	17	14	16	21	11	15
Aids and equipment	14	13	10	16	16	12	19	10	13
How to care for the child	4	11	5	10	3	11	9	7	8
Information on holidays	1	2	2	2	2	2	1	2	2
Everything	17	18	20	16	17	19	19	18	18
Base = 100%	86	132	101	117	80	129	81	137	218

(67 had not had to search out information)

(*1 child was not at school)

It was difficult to find a clear pattern between the sub-groups about the information sought. 'Medical advice' was more frequently mentioned by informants with children without other disabilities or high residual vision (35 and 33 percent respectively), than among those with children with other disabilities or low residual vision (20% each). These figures were reflected in the school type sub-groups because of the larger numbers of more severely disabled children to be found in special than in ordinary schools. We found that more informants with children in ordinary schools said that they had to seek out 'medical advice' than those with children in special schools. It may be that parents with children in special schools – who were more severely disabled – had the medical advice more readily available via the school or other sources.

About 30% of informants with more severely disabled children (with other disabilities, lower residual vision, or in special schools) mentioned searching out information on 'entitlement to benefits' compared with about 11% for their sub-group counterparts.

Information on 'how to care for the child', though only reported by 8% overall, showed a similar pattern with the more severely disabled groups about twice as likely to say that they had to seek out this information (about 11 and 4 percent respectively). Registration status did not show a statistically significant difference.

'Toys and games' and 'aids and equipment' did not show any clear pattern between the sub-groups. However, registration status showed some tendency for more informants with registered than non-registered children to say that they had to search out such information; possibly because they were made more aware of the availability of such items.

15.3 Sources of information

15.3.1 Organisations mentioned spontaneously

There are many organisations, both statutory and voluntary, which provide advice and help to people with disabled children. Asked (at S15Q10) whether there were any particular organisations that they had found helpful in finding out about the child's problems, fewer than a fifth (17%) said that there were. Only school type showed any statistically significant difference, with informants with children in special schools being twice as likely to report having used a particular organisation than those with children in ordinary schools (22 and 11 percent respectively).

Informants who had found specific organisations useful were then asked (at S15Q11) which ones, and their spontaneous replies noted – no prompting or lists of possible organisations were offered. Of the 48 informants who had named organisations, 16 (33%) mentioned RNIB; no other organisation was mentioned by more than 4. Other organisations mentioned included: 'local association for the blind', 'social services', 'LEA', 'MENCAP', 'SENSE', 'MIND', 'retinitis pigmentosa society' and the 'albino society'. Some note of caution should be inserted here that the much larger total who mentioned RNIB might have been influenced by the fact that informants were aware that the survey was being conducted on behalf of RNIB (even though interviewers were careful to restrict naming RNIB as much as possible before and during the interview).

15.3.2 Suggested sources of information

Informants were asked directly whether they had used any of a number of suggested ways of getting information (S15Q12). The results are shown in Table 15.5.

Overall 86% of informants had used at least one of the suggested ways of getting information. Sixty-seven percent of informants had used the 'hospital', 50% had talked to experts, 14% had seen special films or videos, and 8% had visited an 'RNIB centre'; there was little variation between the sub-groups.

Visiting schools for handicapped children (44%), visiting an assessment centre (29%), and talking to families with similar children (36%), though mentioned less than visits to hospitals and talking to experts, were much more likely to be used as a means of information-gathering by informants with more severely disabled children.

Table 15.5 Suggested ways of getting information, by other disability, residual vision and type of school

'Have you ever used any of these ways of getting information about ... (child's) problems?' (S15Q12)

	Other disability		Residual vision		Ordinary or special school*		Total
	NOD	OD	Hi	Lo	Ord	Spcl	
	%	%	%	%	%	%	%
Visit to a:							
Hospital	71	65	68	66	68	66	67
School for handicapped children	33	53	32	56	20	64	44
Assessment centre	22	35	24	35	21	37	29
RNIB centre	8	9	8	9	8	9	8
Talking to:							
Experts	54	47	51	49	52	49	50
Families with similar children	30	43	30	45	26	47	36
Seeing special films	11	17	15	14	14	15	14
All using one or more	**88**	**84**	**84**	**88**	**83**	**88**	**86**
Not used any	11	15	15	11	16	10	13
Don't know	1	1	1	1	1	1	1
Base = 100%	126	159	145	140	129	155	285

(* 1 child was not at school)

Where the child had high residual vision or no other disability, about a third of informants reported visiting a school for handicapped children, compared with about a half for children with low residual vision or with other disabilities. The percentage difference widened between those who had used this means with children in special schools (64%) and ordinary schools (20%).

Visiting an 'assessment centre' was reported more for informants with children who had lower residual vision, other disabilities or were in special schools than among their sub-group counterparts – about 35 as compared with 20 percent.

Talking to 'families with similar children' again was mentioned by about 30% of informants with less severely disabled children or children in ordinary schools, compared with about 45% of those with more severely disabled children or children in special schools.

So while the 'hospital' and 'experts' were widely used, not surprisingly more specialised sources of information were used by those with more severely disabled children.

15.3.3 Useful sources of information

Overall 93% of those who had used one or more of the information sources specified in question S15Q12 had found them useful. Table 15.6 shows how this is broken down for each of the individual sources of information.

Visiting an RNIB centre and seeing special films or videos were the sources least used and also the sources found to be least useful among those who had used them. Only 8 of the 24 informants who had visited an RNIB centre found it useful, and 20 of the 41 who had seen special films found them useful.

Eighty-five percent of those who had talked to 'families with similar children' found it useful. Also highly rated was visiting schools for handicapped children (82%), talking to experts (79%) and visiting a hospital (74%).

Table 15.6 Proportion of informants who found a suggested source of information useful (percentage across rows)

'Did you find . . . (way used at S15Q12) . . . useful or not?' (S15Q13)

		Yes, useful	No, not useful	Total %	Base: All used
Visit to a:					
School for handicapped children	%	82	18	100	125
Hospital	%	74	26	100	192
Assessment centre	%	68	32	100	84
RNIB centre	%	33	67	100	24
Talking to:					
Experts	%	79	21	100	143
Families with similar children	%	85	15	100	106
Seeing special films	%	49	51	100	41

15.4 Royal National Institute for the Blind

Seventy-four percent of informants said that they had heard of RNIB before being asked to take part in the survey, replying 'yes' to the question: 'Had you heard of the RNIB before being asked to take part in this survey?' (S15Q15). Only the residual vision sub-groups showed any difference, with 80% of informants with children with low residual vision reporting pre-survey awareness of RNIB compared with 68% where the children had high residual vision.

To check the reliability of the claim of awareness, those who said that they were aware of RNIB before the survey were asked if they knew what the initials RNIB stood for; 90% answered correctly; an additional 6% got some of the words correct, and 4% got them wrong or said that they did not know.

15.4.1 Unprompted awareness of RNIB services

To be aware of RNIB may be one thing, to know what services are provided shows more detailed knowledge. Respondents were asked (at question S15Q17) what sort of things they knew that RNIB provided, and no prompting was given at this stage. Table 15.7 shows the results.

Table 15.7 Spontaneous mention of services RNIB is thought to provide, by residual vision, type of school and registration status

'What sort of things do you know that RNIB does?' (S15Q17)

	Residual vision level		Ordinary or special school		Registration status		Total
	Hi	Lo	Ord	Spcl	R	NR	
	%	%	%	%	%	%	%
Gadgets and aids	23	37	24	35	40	24	30
Schools/training centres	22	31	22	31	31	24	27
General help/advice	14	23	18	19	14	22	19
Talking Books	21	16	22	16	17	20	18
Braille books/services	19	11	14	15	14	15	15
Guide dogs	16	9	14	11	14	11	12
Training for blind or partially sighted people	4	17	8	13	20	23	11
Arrange holidays/trips	8	8	12	5	8	8	8
Homes for blind or partially sighted people	5	5	1	8	6	4	5
Counselling services	3	6	7	4	4	6	5
Fundraising	7	3	8	3	5	5	5
Sunshine schools/homes	3	5	2	6	5	4	4
Holiday places/hotels	3	5	4	3	7	2	4
Tape machines/cassettes	2	5	3	4	5	3	4
Blind centres/clubs	3	3	0	5	2	3	3
Talking newspapers/magazines	4	2	2	3	2	3	3
Publish print books	2	4	2	3	1	4	3
Toys and games	3	2	2	3	1	3	2
Books (unspecified)	0	5	1	3	4	2	2
Radios	0	1	0	1	1	0	1
Rehabilitation centres	1	1	0	2	1	1	1
Do not know	25	13	23	16	12	23	19
Base = 100%	99	112	92	119	83	128	211

(74 were not aware of RNIB before the survey)

Over 20 individual services were spontaneously mentioned by informants as being provided by RNIB: only seven exceeded 10% including 'guide dogs' which is not an RNIB service. Informants with children with low residual vision, in special schools, or registered tended to be more knowledgeable about RNIB services than their sub-group counterparts; a smaller proportion of the former sub-groups were also recorded as 'don't knows'.

The services mentioned correctly as being provided by RNIB included: 'gadgets and aids' (30%), 'schools/training centres' (27%), 'general help/advice' (19%), 'Talking Books' (18%), 'braille books/services' (15%), and 'training for blind or partially sighted people' (11%).

Two services mentioned that RNIB does not provided were 'arrange holidays/trips' (8%) and 'talking newspapers/magazines' (3%). (Note that since the survey fieldwork RNIB does arrange holidays and trips for children during the school holidays.)

There was some indication that registration may not be as important for children as for adults, in that those informants with registered children were not considerably better informed about RNIB services than informants with non-registered children. A separate survey of adults showed that registered adults were more aware of available services than non-registered adults (Bruce, McKennell and Walker, 1991).

15.4.2 Prompted awareness of RNIB services

After asking informants to recall spontaneously any RNIB services, informants were then shown a list of services and asked which ones they thought RNIB provided. The results are in Table 15.8.

Table 15.8 Services informants thought RNIB provided

'Here are some services provided for children with eyesight problems – some are provided by RNIB and some are not. Which ones do you think RNIB provides?' (S15Q18)

	All aware of RNIB before the survey
	%
Braille books for children	85
Special toys and aids	76
Schools for the visually handicapped	68
Guide dogs for children	55
Colleges for further education and training	51
Careers advisers	49
Pre-school education advisers	45
Education advisers for older children	44
Schools for children with multiple handicaps	25
Don't know	6
Base = 100%	211

(74 were not aware of RNIB before the survey)

The association of RNIB with braille is clearly seen. Eighty-five percent of informants said that they thought RNIB provided braille books for children; this was followed by 'special toys and aids' (76%) and 'schools for visually handicapped children' (68%). Fifty-one percent thought RNIB provided 'colleges for further education and training', 49% 'careers advisers', 45% 'pre-school education advisers', 44% 'education advisers for older children' and 25% 'schools for children with multiple handicaps'.

Fifty-five percent also thought RNIB provided guide dogs for children, which is not so. This figure indicates that all the percentages have to be treated with caution, and rather than being a measure of what people think RNIB provides, may be more a measure of what people think RNIB should or could provide.

The sub-group analyses showed no clear statistically significant differences in the responses, though there was some indication that informants with children in special schools might be marginally better informed, similarly among those whose children had lower residual vision.

15.4.3 Usage of RNIB services

Awareness of RNIB services is one measure; the other is the actual usage of RNIB services. Table 15.9 shows that among those aware of RNIB, 37% reported having made use of one or more of the services listed. Residual vision and the type of school sub-groups showed the largest difference in the use of RNIB services. Reported use of RNIB services for children with high and low residual vision was 19 and 51 percent respectively; the corresponding totals for those in ordinary and special schools was 24 and 46 percent.

Only children with other disabilities were said to use schools for multiply handicapped children (5%), and 11% of this group were reported to use schools for visually handicapped children, compared with 3% of those with no other disabilities.

More children with low than high residual vision were reported to use special toys and aids (38 and 8 percent respectively), and braille books (18 and 2 percent respectively). Only these two services clearly showed statistically significant differences. Although not statistically significant, the number reported to use the other services was consistently larger for children with low than high residual vision.

School type showed a similar pattern to the residual vision analysis, with more children in special than ordinary schools reported to use special toys and aids (35 and 10 percent), and braille books (17 and 2 percent). Twelve percent of children in special schools were reported to have made use of an RNIB school for the visually handicapped, and 1% of children in an ordinary school.

Table 15.9   RNIB services used, by other disability, residual vision, type of school and registration status

'Can I just check, have you or your child ever made use of . . . (service at S15Q18) provided by RNIB?' (S15Q19)†

	Other disability		Residual vision		Ordinary or special school		Registration status		Total
	NOD	OD	Hi	Lo	Ord	Spcl	R	NR	
	%	%	%	%	%	%	%	%	%
Special toys and aids	22	26	8	38	10	35	39	14	24
Pre-school advisers	17	14	10	19	13	17	18	13	15
Braille books for children	12	10	2	18	2	17	21	4	11
Education advisers for older children	6	9	5	10	6	9	6	9	8
Schools for visually handicapped children	3	11	5	10	1	12	11	5	8
Schools for children with multiple handicaps	0	5	2	3	0	4	4	2	3
Guide dogs for children	2	1	1	2	0	3	2	1	2
Careers advisers	5	2	1	5	0	5	5	2	3
Colleges for further education and training	2	3	2	3	0	4	2	3	3
All using RNIB services	36	38	19	51	24	46	49	28	37
None of the services used	64	62	81	49	76	54	51	72	63
Base = 100%	89	109	89	109	83	115	82	116	198

(74 were not aware of RNIB, 13 answered don't know at S15Q18)

† The percentage for this question was based on informants who were aware of RNIB

The registered children made more use of RNIB services than the non-registered (49 and 28 percent respectively). The use of special toys and aids (39 and 14 percent) and braille books (21 and 4 percent) showed the largest difference between registered and non-registered children. Age showed no differences across any of the services.

15.4.4   Awareness and use of RNIB services

Table 15.10 shows the overall awareness and use of RNIB services for the full sample. In terms of the overall level of awareness, only between the residual vision sub-groups is there a clear statistically significant difference; it is in the actual use of services that differences can most be seen.

About 1 in 2 of the low residual vision, special school, and registered sub-groups who were aware of RNIB services made use of them, compared with 1 in 4 or less of their sub-group counterparts. That is to say, while almost as aware of services, those with high residual vision, in ordinary schools or not registered made less use of RNIB services. In

Table 15.10 Awareness and use of RNIB services, by residual vision, type of school and registration status

	Residual vision		Ordinary or special school*		Registration status		Total
	Hi	Lo	Ord	Spcl	R	NR	
	%	%	%	%	%	%	%
Aware of RNIB:							
but does not use	56	40	56	43	41	53	48
and uses	12	40	16	34	39	18	26
All aware of RNIB	68	80	72	77	80	71	74
Not aware of RNIB	32	20	29	23	20	29	26
Total %	100	100	100	100	100	100	100
Base	145	140	129	155	104	181	285

(* 1 child was not at school)

summary, about 3 in 4 informants with visually impaired children reported being aware of RNIB services, but only 1 in 4 reported using any of them.

We only asked informants about the use of services that they were aware of. RNIB provides many support services to schools, some of which informants might not have been aware of.

15.4.5   Sources of information about RNIB services

Table 15.11 shows that informants found out about RNIB services from an extensive range of sources. The most frequently mentioned was the general media i.e. radio, television, papers and leaflets (21%), followed by 'social worker/welfare officer' (12%), and those who had 'always known about RNIB' (11%).

Seven percent reported that RNIB had contacted them, and 5% that a sighted 'friend or relative' told them about RNIB. No other source of information was mentioned by more than 3% of informants including through RNIB fundraising, the health service, advertisements, looking RNIB up in the telephone directory and through the local association for the blind.

There was no clear difference or pattern in the source of information about RNIB, except that marginally more informants with registered than with non-registered children mentioned social workers, and more informants with children in special rather than ordinary schools said 'through the school or teacher'.

It is worth noting from Table 15.11 that when asked question S15Q20, 15% said they did not know about any RNIB services. These informants would have been among those hazarding a guess at question S15Q18 as to the services that they thought RNIB provided.

Table 15.11   Sources of information about RNIB services

'How did you find out about the services RNIB provides?' (S15Q20)

	Informants aware of RNIB services %
General media (radio/television/papers/leaflets)	21
Social worker/welfare officer	12
Through school or teacher	12
Always known about RNIB	11
Contacted by RNIB	7
Sighted friend or relative	5
Through their fundraising	3
Health service/visitor	3
Visually handicapped person	2
Telephone directory	2
Advertisements	2
Peripatetic teacher	2
Local association for the blind	1
Contacted by RNIB adviser/peripatetic teacher	1
Don't know	7
Don't know at S15Q18	14
Don't know about any services	15
Base = 100%	193

(74 were not aware of RNIB before the survey, 18 had no information)

Table 15.12   Expectation of help and advice from RNIB, by residual vision, type of school and registration status

'Did you expect RNIB to contact you to offer help and advice about . . . (child)?' (S15Q21)

	Residual vision		Ordinary or special school		Registration status		Total
	Hi %	Lo %	Ord %	Spcl %	R %	NR %	%
Yes	15	25	13	26	33	13	20
No	79	71	80	71	64	82	75
Don't know/depends	6	4	7	3	4	6	5
Total %	100	100	100	100	100	100	100
Base	99	112	92	119	83	121	211

(74 were not aware of RNIB)

15.4.6   Expectation of help and advice from RNIB

Some people may have expectations from RNIB, as a large national organisation for blind people, which it is not able to meet. Informants were asked whether they expected RNIB to contact them to offer help and advice. Table 15.12 shows the results.

Twenty percent of respondents expected RNIB to contact them; expectation was greater among informants with children in special compared with ordinary schools (26 and 13 percent respectively), among those with registered than non-registered children (33 and 13 percent), and with children with low compared with high residual vision (25 and 15 percent).

16 Accommodation

16.1 Length of time at present address

Table 16.1 shows that 51% of informants had lived in their present dwelling for up to six years, 18% for 7–10 years and 30% for 11 years or more. The age of the visually impaired child showed some relationship with the length of residence. While 51% of informants had been in residence for 6 years or less, this ranged from 77% where the child was aged 3 – 7 years, to 39% where the child was aged 12 or over. This simply says that the parents of younger children had moved more recently.

Table 16.1   Number of years lived at present address, by age of visually impaired child

'. . . how long have you lived at this address?' (S10Q1)

	Age			Total
	3 – 7	8 – 11	12 +	
	%	%	%	%
3 years or less	36	25	26	28
4 – 6 years	41	22	13	23
7 – 10 years	8	27	19	18
11 –19 years	14	19	35	25
20 – 49 years	1	7	7	5
No data	1	0	1	1
Total %	100	100	100	100
Base	79	73	133	285

16.2 House moving

The important issue is whether informants had moved because of the child's disabilities or simply as part of the normal pattern of house moving. Table 16.2 shows that two-thirds of informants said that they had moved **after** they first realised the child had problems.

To assess the role the child's disabilities played in any house move, informants were asked two questions. The first allowed a spontaneous response while the second was more direct, asking informants if they had moved for any of the child-related reasons offered from a prepared list.

Table 16.2 Moving home before or after child's problems were realised, by other disability and residual vision

'So can I just check did you move here before or after you first realised that (child) had problems?' (S10Q2)

	Other disability		Residual vision		Total
	NOD	OD	Hi	Lo	
	%	%	%	%	%
Before	40	29	35	32	34
After	60	70	65	67	66
Don't know	0	1	0	1	#
Total	100	100	100	100	100
Base	126	159	145	140	285

Informants who said that they had moved after the realisation of the child's problems were first asked: 'What was your main reason for moving on this occasion?' (S10Q3) and allowed to provide their own answers: these are shown in Table 16.3.

The more direct question linking the move and the child's problems was then asked: 'Thinking of (child), did you move here for any of these reasons?' (S10Q4). A list of reasons related to services or advantages to the child was then given, designed to gauge whether consideration of the child's needs may have influenced the decision to move house. The responses are shown in Table 16.4.

16.2.1 Spontaneous reasons given for moving house

Table 16.3 shows the spontaneous reasons informants gave for moving. Altogether just over half (51%) of informants gave one of several reasons that were child-related: closer to family/friends; wanted (larger) garden; child's benefit e.g. adaptations to the house; child's education; convenient facilities; and those wanting a larger house or more space.

The most frequently mentioned reason was that of wanting a larger house, or more space (29%). This reason, however, could apply to most people, as could the other two main reasons given: a dislike for the neighbourhood lived in (13%), and changing or losing a job (11%). Though given by 51% of the informants in total, most of the child-related reasons – apart from a larger house (29%) – were mentioned by relatively few informants, 7% or less.

Although not statistically significant, there was a tendency for more informants of children with additional disabilities, or lower residual vision, to have given one of the child-related reasons; 56% for both sub-

Table 16.3 Spontaneous reasons given for moving house, by other disabilities and residual vision

	Other disability		Residual vision		Total
	NOD	OD	Hi	Lo	
	%	%	%	%	%
Larger house/more space†	32	27	28	30	29
Disliked neighbourhood	12	13	15	11	13
Changed job/lost job	13	10	13	10	11
Closer to family/friends†	11	5	10	5	7
Wanted (larger) garden†	3	9	4	9	6
Child's benefit e.g. adaptation to the house†	1	9	3	9	6
Child's education e.g. near school†	7	5	5	5	5
Convenient facilities†	3	5	4	3	4
Semi-forced move	4	5	5	3	4
Marital breakdown	4	3	2	4	3
All giving a child-related reason	**43**	**56**	**46**	**56**	**51**
Non-child-related reason	**57**	**44**	**54**	**44**	**49**
Base = 100%	76	112	94	94	188

(188 children: those moving after onset of child's problems)
† Child-related reasons

groups, compared with 43 and 46 percent respectively for those with children without other disabilities, or with high residual vision. The individual reasons showed no differences between the sub-groups.

16.2.2 Child-related reasons for moving house

Table 16.4 shows the replies to the prompted reasons for moving house. Overall, 41% of informants said that they had moved because of one of these child-related reasons, and 59% that they had not. A larger number of informants with more severely disabled children said that they had moved for one of these reasons than informants with less severely disabled children (about 50 and 30 percent).

'Features of the house/flat which make it easier for your child' was the most frequently mentioned reason for moving (29%). This was the predominant item on which residual vision and the other disability sub-groups differed. Where the child had low residual vision or other disabilities 39% gave this reason compared with 18 and 13 percent for their sub-group counterparts. Comparatively few informants gave the following reasons for moving: to be near a particular school (12%); local facilities, such as shops (7%); or local services, e.g. social services (2%).

Table 16.4 Prompted child-related reasons for moving house, by other disability, residual vision and type of school

'Thinking of . . . (child), did you move here for any of these reasons?' (S10Q4)

	Other disability		Residual vision		Ordinary or special school		Total
	NOD	OD	Hi	Lo	Ord	Spcl	
	%	%	%	%	%	%	%
Features of the house/flat which make it easier for your child	13	39	18	39	17	37	29
Local school nearby	12	12	13	11	16	8	12
Local facilities e.g. shops	5	9	6	9	7	7	7
Local services available	1	3	3	1	4	1	2
All moving for one of the child-related reasons	**25**	**53**	**30**	**53**	**31**	**50**	**41**
None of these	**75**	**47**	**70**	**47**	**69**	**50**	**59**
Base = 100%	76	112	94	94	81	107	188

(188 children: those moving after onset of child's problems)

The results for those in ordinary and special schools largely paralleled the differences between the residual vision and other disability sub-groups. However, more informants with children in ordinary schools than in special schools said that they had moved because of a 'local school nearby' which they wanted their child to attend (16 and 8 percent).

16.3 Financial help in moving home

Asked (at S10Q5) whether they had applied for any financial help for their move, 11% of informants said that they had. This 11% amounted to 20 informants, 14 of whom had been successful in their application.

Eight of the informants had applied to the local authority or social services for this financial help, 11 to the (then) DHSS, and one to a housing association. None of the factors, such as other disability or level of residual vision, made any difference to whom they applied for financial help.

16.4 Changes and adaptations made to the home

Table 16.5 shows that 24% of informants had made some form of change to their home to make things easier for the child. Not unexpectedly, more informants of children with other disabilities (34%) or low residual vision (35%) had made such changes, compared with 12 and 14 percent for their respective sub-group counterparts.

Table 16.5 Changes or adaptations to the home, by other disability and residual vision

'Have you made any changes, or adapted your home in any way, to make it easier for . . . (child) to cope?' (S10Q8)

	Other disability		Residual vision		Total
	NOD %	OD %	Hi %	Lo %	%
Yes	12	34	14	35	24
No/don't know	88	66	86	65	76
Total	100	100	100	100	100
Base	126	159	145	140	285

Table 16.6 shows that the most common changes made to the house were the building of an extension and adaptations to the toilet or bathroom (29 and 26 percent respectively). The installation of handrails, making more space in the house and changing the lighting were each mentioned by 17% of informants; other adaptations included the installation of ramps (9%) and stairlifts (7%).

The base of 70 informants is too small to break down further and maintain confidence in any differences which may occur. However, it is worthwhile noting that in those cases where changes had been made, 71% of the children had low residual vision and 79% had another disability. Further, only 17% mentioned an adaptation which was clearly linked to sight, that is, change of lighting.

Table 16.6 Type of changes and adaptations made to the home

	All who made adaptations to the house
	%
Built extension	29
Adapted bathroom/toilet	26
Installed handrail	17
Made more space	17
Changed lighting	17
Made path/garden safer	14
Installed ramps	9
Installed stairlift	7
Safety features	6
Changed heating method	4
Other work involving little building work	4
Rearranged home	3
Base = 100%	70

(70 children: where changes had been made to the home)

16.4.1 Financial help to make changes or adaptations to the home

Fifty-one percent of those who had made changes to the home had applied for financial help towards this, and 82% had received it. The vast majority (94%) had applied to the local authority or social services. The 'family fund' or some other trust were the other sources of funds applied to.

Thirty-eight percent (26 informants) of those who had made changes said that they had received help, other than financial, mainly in the form of advice. The main sources of advice mentioned were: 'social or welfare worker', by 6 informants; 'social worker for the blind/mobility officer', 5 informants. The 'physio/occupational therapist' was mentioned by 9 informants.

16.5 Future likelihood of moving because of the child's sight problem

The subject of interest in our survey is visually impaired children, therefore the question asked about moving in the future specified moving because of the child's sight problem. Informants were asked: 'Do you think that you will have to move in the future because of (child's) eyesight problems?' (S10Q15). Eight percent of parents said that they might have to move. The number of respondents was evenly divided between the following reasons: 'need stair-less house'; 'need larger garden'; 'to be near school'; 'better house generally'; and 'quieter/safer roads'. If one were to exclude all those parents who had moved since the child's onset and had made changes to the house, there would be a marginal increase from 8 to 11 percent. This suggests that for many parents moving house because of the child's disability is not an option open to them.

17 Demographics, Social Security Benefits and Income

17.1 The household

17.1.1 Tenure

Table 17.1 shows a comparison of the pattern of housing tenure found in the RNIB survey with that in the general population. The overall percentages are very similar, suggesting that in terms of housing tenure parents of children with disabilities are little different from the general population.

Table 17.1 Housing tenure

	RNIB survey	Great Britain (GHS 1987)
	%	%
Owner occupiers		
Own outright	8	24
Buying on a mortgage	54	39
All owner occupiers	**62**	**63**
Tenants		
Local authority	33	26
Housing association	3	2
Private	3	6
All tenants	**39**	**34**
Other	1	3
Total %	100	100
Base	285	10,367

Source: General Household Survey 1987 (OPCS 1989)

Fifty-four percent of informants in the RNIB survey were still buying their property on a mortgage and 8% were outright owners; this compared with 39 and 24 percent respectively in the general population. This difference may be explained by the fact that informants in the RNIB survey were all parents of children who had either not started or were still at school and, therefore, younger than people in the general population where many older people would have completed the mortgage payments on their property.

17.1.2 Marital status

No discernible difference in the marital status recorded for the informants could be found between the analysis sub-groups. Those recorded were: single 3%, married 81%, widowed 4% and separated or divorced 13%.

17.1.3 Ethnic composition

Detailed information on ethnic origins was not collected; the data are therefore very general and are based on the informant's ethnicity, not the child's. Ninety-three percent of informants were recorded as 'white', 1% 'black, Afro-Caribbean', 4% 'Asian, Indian/Pakistani', and 1% as 'other'. The 1988 General Household Survey (OPCS 1990) gives the percentage of the ethnic groups in Great Britain as: white, 95%, Indian and Pakistani/Bangladeshi, 1% each; West Indian, 1%; and remaining groups, 2%.

17.1.4 Age and sex

Table 17.2 gives an age and sex breakdown among visually impaired children. Sixty-four percent were boys and 36% girls. These totals were not very different from those reported in the OPCS disability survey, Report 6 (Meltzer, Smyth and Robus, 1989) where the percentages of disabled boys and girls were 60 and 40 respectively. Though an age and sex breakdown is shown for the three age groups, this is more for information as the percentage differences of boys and girls are not statistically significant (see section 20.5).

Sex differences among the sub-groups used for analysis were similar to those for the sample as a whole.

Table 17.2 Age and sex of visually impaired children

	Age			Total
	3 – 7	8 – 11	12 +	
Sex	%	%	%	%
Boys	56	60	70	64
Girls	44	40	30	36
Total %	100	100	100	100
Base	79	73	133	285

17.1.5 Other people with disabilities in the house

Table 17.3 shows that a quarter (26%) of households had another person who had either a sight problem or other disability. The analysis sub-groups showed no differences.

Table 17.3   Other people with disabilities in the household

'Do any other people in the household have eyesight problems? By that I mean sight problems which cannot be corrected by ordinary glasses or contact lenses?' (S17Q4)

'And does anyone else (other than the child) have any other permanent handicaps or disabilities?' (S17Q6)

	%
Sight problem only	16
Other disability only	6
Sight and other disability	4
All with a disability or sight problem	26
None with a disability or sight problem	74
Total %	100
Base	285

17.2   Social security benefits and allowances

To keep the questionnaire at a reasonable length, the assessment of social security benefits and allowances was one of the areas that was drastically curtailed. This topic was therefore reduced to a single question: 'Do you or anyone else in the household receive any of these allowances or benefits?' (S16Q9).

Tables 17.4.a. and 17.4.b. give breakdowns for age and registration status, and other disability, residual vision and type of school respectively. It should be noted that the questions (at S16Q9) relate to the household, not just the informants or the visually impaired child.

A quarter of the households had another person with disabilities so we cannot be certain that the disabled child was the recipient of the benefits mentioned: in some cases they clearly would not be, e.g. unemployment benefit. However, as the proportion of households with another disabled person did not vary between the analysis sub-groups, and differences are found in the receipt of benefits between them, we can be fairly confident that the differences observed are due to factors related to the children who form the subject of the study.

Ninety-one percent of households were in receipt of child benefit. Nineteen percent had someone in receipt of supplementary benefit.

Seventeen percent of households had someone in receipt of the Invalid Care Allowance given to a household member not working because they look after someone who needs care, and who gets the Attendance Allowance. Nineteen percent of households received housing benefit, a recognition of low household income.

The summary category, 'income maintenance, excluding housing benefit but including pension', shows that 40% of households were in receipt of some form of income maintenance benefit. If housing benefit and retirement pensions are excluded, the total hardly changes (from 40 to 39 percent).

Table 17.4.a   Allowances and benefits received, by age and registration status

'Do you or anyone else in the household receive any of these allowances or benefits?' (S16Q9)

	Age		Registration status		Total
	3 – 11	12 +	R	NR	
	%	%	%	%	%
Child benefit	98	84	86	93	91
Family Income Supplement	3	5	6	3	4
Supplementary benefit	19	18	16	20	19
Retirement pension	2	2	1	2	2
Unemployment benefit (UB)	4	8	4	7	6
Invalid Care Allowance	22	11	24	13	17
Income maintenance excluding HB, including pension	**43**	**37**	**44**	**38**	**40**
Housing benefit (HB)	23	15	26	16	19
All income maintenance benefits including HB and pension	**48**	**41**	**52**	**40**	**45**
Income maintenance benefits excluding HB and pension	**42**	**35**	**43**	**37**	**39**
Income maintenance benefit ISB, SDA, UB	10	24	17	16	17
Invalidity or sickness benefit (ISB)	5	8	7	6	6
Severe disablement allowance (SDA)	2	12	11	4	7
Disablement benefits ISB, SDA	**6**	**18**	**14**	**10**	**12**
Attendance Allowance	55	37	61	38	46
Mobility Allowance	23	20	23	20	21
Attendance and mobility allowances	**55**	**40**	**61**	**41**	**48**
Attendance Allowance and Invalid Care Allowance	**22**	**11**	**24**	**13**	**17**
All in receipt of one or more benefits (excluding child benefit)	67	64	76	60	66
No benefits (excluding child benefit)	33	36	24	40	34
Base = 100%	152	133	104	181	285

Table 17.4.b Allowances and benefits received, by other disability, residual vision and type of school

'Do you or anyone else in the household receive any of these allowances or benefits?' (S16Q9)

	Other disability		Residual vision		Ordinary or special school		Total
	NOD	OD	Hi	Lo	Ord	Spcl	
	%	%	%	%	%	%	%
Child benefit	95	88	93	89	96	87	91
Family Income Supplement	5	4	2	6	3	5	4
Supplementary benefit	15	21	15	22	16	20	19
Retirement pension	3	1	1	2	3	1	2
Unemployment benefit (UB)	8	4	4	7	5	7	6
Invalid Care Allowance	6	25	8	26	7	25	17
General income maintenance excluding HB, including pension	**33**	**45**	**28**	**53**	**30**	**48**	**40**
Housing benefit (HB)	18	20	16	23	19	19	19
All maintenance benefits including HB and pension	**37**	**50**	**32**	**58**	**35**	**52**	**45**
Maintenance benefits excluding HB and pension	**31**	**45**	**27**	**51**	**28**	**48**	**39**
Income maintenance benefit, ISB, SDA, UB	14	18	13	20	11	21	17
Invalidity or sickness benefit (ISB)	4	8	7	5	5	6	6
Severe disablement allowance (SDA)	5	8	3	10	2	10	7
Disablement benefits ISB, SDA	**8**	**15**	**10**	**13**	**6**	**16**	**12**
Attendance Allowance	20	67	26	68	23	66	46
Mobility Allowance	4	35	11	32	4	36	21
Disablement allowances AA, MA	**21**	**69**	**27**	**69**	**24**	**68**	**48**
Attendance Allowance and Invalid Care Allowance	**6**	**25**	**8**	**26**	**7**	**25**	**17**
All in receipt of one or more benefits (excluding child benefit)	48	80	47	85	46	82	66
No benefits (excluding child benefit)	52	20	53	15	54	18	34
Base = 100%	126	159	145	140	129	155	285

Invalidity or sickness benefit (ISB) and Severe Disablement Allowance (SDA) are paid to those unable to work because of illness or disability; 12% were in receipt of one of these disablement benefits.

Attendance Allowance is paid to people who need someone to look after them because of their disability; 46% of households have someone in receipt of this benefit. The reciprocal of this benefit is the Invalid Care Allowance. Twenty-one percent received Mobility Allowance, given to people unable or virtually unable to walk. Overall, 48% of households had someone in receipt of one or other of these allowances.

Seventeen percent of households had one person receiving Attendance Allowance and another getting the Invalid Care Allowance, which means that 29% of households had someone only getting the Attendance Allowance.

17.2.1 Age

More households with younger children (22%) had someone in receipt of the Invalid Care Allowance than those with older children (11%). The same percentages were found among households with younger and older children where both the Attendance Allowance and Invalid Care Allowance were received.

The Attendance Allowance alone was received by 55 and 37 percent respectively of households with younger and older children. The receipt of Mobility Allowance showed no age difference. All households with younger children with someone in receipt of Mobility Allowance also received Attendance Allowance . For households with older children, 3% received Mobility Allowance but not Attendance Allowance.

Doctors are advised that the entitlement to Attendance Allowance should be reviewed for children between the ages of 12 and 16 years. This can result in entitlement being withdrawn if the child is deemed to have adapted to his or her disability, and might explain why fewer older children received Attendance Allowance.

Households with younger children were as likely to have someone in receipt of some form of social security benefit or allowance (excluding child benefit) as households with older children (67 and 64 percent respectively).

17.2.2 Registration status

More households with registered children (76%) than non-registered children (60%) had someone in receipt of a social security benefit or allowance (excluding child benefit). This was also true for receipt of: the Invalid Care Allowance (24 and 13 percent); Severe Disablement Allowance (11 and 4 percent); and Attendance Allowance (61 and 38 percent). This suggests a greater degree of disability among registered children.

17.2.3 Other disabilities

As one might have expected, where the child had another disability someone in that household was more likely to be in receipt of one of the disability-based benefits, compared with households where the child only had a visual impairment. These benefits were Invalid Care Allowance (25 and 6 percent); Attendance Allowance (67 and 20 percent); and Mobility Allowance (35 and 4 percent). The overall receipt of any benefit, excluding the child benefit, was much greater among households where the child had another disability (80 and 48 percent).

Among households with children who had other disabilities, 25% had individuals where both the Attendance Allowance and Invalid Care Allowance were received. However, 42% of such households were in receipt only of Attendance Allowance.

17.2.4 Residual vision

The residual vision sub-groups reflected a similar pattern in the receipt of benefits to that among children with and without other disabilities. Eighty-five percent of households with children with low residual vision had someone in receipt of one or more benefit compared with 47% of households with children with high residual vision.

17.2.5 Type of school

A larger number of households with more severely disabled children were likely to receive social security benefits and allowances; more severely disabled children were to be found in special schools. These two factors produced the difference in the receipt of benefits between households with children in special and ordinary schools. The percentage differences paralleled those based on more and less severely disabled children. Eighty-two percent of households with children in special schools had someone in receipt of one or more of the benefits, compared with 46% where the child was in an ordinary school.

17.2.6 Residual vision and other disability

While Tables 17.4.a and 17.4.b allow us to look at whether households with children with differing residual vision and those with and without other disabilities received the disability-based benefits, it was not possible to say whether the determining factor was the presence of another disability or the residual vision. By statistically accounting for these factors it is possible to make some judgement as to which was the determining one. Table 17.5 shows the results of doing this.

Looking separately at households where the child had high and low residual vision, among those where the child had another disability a larger number were in receipt of one of the disability-based benefits than among households where the child had no other disability. The totals for Invalid Care Allowance, for example, are 16 and 2, and 31 and 14 percent respectively.

When households with children with low residual vision and other disabilities, and those with children with high residual vision and other disabilities are compared, a larger number of households with children with low residual vision were in receipt of the various benefits. For example, 80 and 49 percent respectively received the Attendance Allowance. It is clear, therefore, that the receipt of one of the disability-based benefits is determined by the presence of another disability. A similar pattern existed for those children with low residual vision, with and without other disabilities.

If another table were constructed, dividing children into high and low residual vision levels within the other disability sub-groups, one would also see that households with children with low residual vision tended to receive the disability-based benefits more often than those with high residual vision. The exception to this was Mobility Allowance, where in households with children without other disabilities a similar proportion received this allowance, irrespective of residual vision level, because the receipt of the Mobility Allowance is based on the physical ability to walk.

What can be seen, therefore, is that the presence of an additional disability increased the likelihood of obtaining a disability-based benefit, but there was also a combination effect with the level of residual vision.

Table 17.5 Allowances and benefits received by household members, by other disability within residual vision levels

'Do you or anyone else in the household receive any of these allowances or benefits?' (S16Q9)

	Other disability within residual vision levels				Total
	(High) Other disability		(Low) Other disability		
	NOD	OD	NOD	OD	
	%	%	%	%	%
Invalid Care Allowance	2	16	14	31	17
Attendance Allowance	11	49	41	80	46
Mobility Allowance	5	19	2	46	21
Attendance and Mobility allowance	11	41	41	82	48
Attendance Allowance and Invalid Care Allowance	2	14	14	31	17
Base = 100%	82	63	44	96	285

17.3   Income

Table 17.6 gives the net weekly income of households. At the time of our survey (1988) the average household disposable income for the UK was £233 per week. Fifty-nine percent of households in our survey had incomes below this level.

Table 17.6   Net weekly household income

'How much money do you have altogether coming into the house normally, after tax . . . please include any allowances or benefits you receive?' (S16Q11)

Net weekly income	%
£31 – £75	8
£76 – £100	14
£101 – £150	18
£151 – £200	19
£201 – £300	20
£301 or more	6
Don't know or refused	15
Total %	100
Base	285

Table 17.7 compares the income of households in receipt of one or more social security benefit with the income of those that were not. Nearly one-third (32%) of households with someone in receipt of social security benefits had an income of £100 or less per week, compared

Table 17.7   Comparison of net weekly income of households receiving social security allowances or benefits and those which were not

'Do you or anyone else in the household receive any of these allowances or benefits?' (S16Q9)

'How much money do you have altogether coming into the house normally, after tax . . . please include any allowances or benefits you receive?' (S16Q11)

	Receipt of one or more benefit or allowance excluding child benefit		
	None	Benefit	Total
	%	%	%
Net Weekly income			
£31 – £100	4	32	22
£101 – £200	40	36	37
£201 – £300	31	14	20
£301 or more	9	5	6
Don't know or refused	16	14	15
Total %	100	100	100
Base	98	187	285

with only 4% of households without someone on benefits. In contrast, 40% of households without anyone in receipt of benefits had a household income of over £200 per week compared with 19% of households with someone in receipt of benefits.

It was also possible to examine the data by those on benefits within the income groups (no table shown). This revealed that 75% of households with an income of £200 or less received allowances or benefits, compared with 47% of households with an income of over £200 per week. In fact, 94% of households with an income of £100 or less per week had someone in receipt of social security benefits.

As shown in section 17.2.3, 80% of households with more severely disabled children received social security benefits or allowances. It can be assumed, therefore, that these households had the lowest income.

17.4 Savings

Table 17.8 shows the level of savings. Over a third (35%) of households had no savings at all; 9% had savings of over £3,000.

A much clearer relationship existed between households on benefits and the level of household income than between benefits and the level of household savings. This may be for two reasons; firstly, most households had savings below the threshold which would debar them from the receipt of social security benefits. Secondly, eligibility for social security benefits and allowances is assessed mainly on income. Further, allowances such as the Attendance Allowance are received on medical, not income, grounds. This said, since the ability to save is related to the level of disposable income, 82% of households with no savings received benefits or allowances compared with 59% of households with some savings.

Table 17.8   Household savings

'. . . how much money do you have in savings?' (S16Q12)

	%
Household savings	
None	35
£500 or less	18
£501 – £1,000	11
£1,001 – £3,000	13
£3,001 – £6,000	4
£6,001 or more	5
Don't know or refused	13
Total %	100
Base	285

Part H

Method and Population Estimates

18 Method

18.1 Piloting and questionnaire development

The starting point of this research was a document commissioned from two very experienced workers with visually impaired children. This document reviewed the topic areas, and the kind of detail in each area which they thought should be covered by the survey. The document was circulated internally within RNIB and, to a limited extent, externally.

On the basis of the document, reactions to it, other advice and a review of the literature, a schedule of topics was prepared for qualitative interviewing (without a standardised questionnaire). Two of us (ACMcK and EW) carried out nine conversational interviews with parents in early 1987. After studying the transcripts of these interviews the initial draft questionnaire for the first pilot was drawn up in collaboration with the British Market Research Bureau (BMRB), the fieldwork agency.

An early decision was that the interview itself would be conducted with the parents or guardians of the child, rather than the child him/herself. This was for two main reasons:

- Younger children, or children with learning difficulties may not have been able to cope with the interviews.

- Much of the questionnaire concerned itself with the history of the child's sight problem, how the parents coped and how they were still coping. Obviously only the parents themselves could answer these questions.

It was also felt that the parents were the effective decision-makers for the child until he or she became economically independent.

Such was the length and scope of the questionnaire, that three pilot exercises were carried out – in June (12 interviews), July (12 interviews) and August (8 interviews) of 1987, in seven different areas in England, Scotland and Wales. Since the objective was to achieve a standardised questionnaire, the procedure adopted was for either a BMRB executive or an RNIB researcher to sit in on the interviews conducted by the interviewer at the pilot stages. (Each interview was also tape recorded.)

The questionnaire was revised extensively after each of the first two pilot exercises. Detailed comments on the first pilot questionnaire were received from members of staff in RNIB's Education and Leisure Division and also from external advisers. On the basis of these comments and suggestions and our own experience a second questionnaire was constructed and piloted.

However, the second pilot schedule took an average of two-and-a-half hours to administer. It was therefore vigorously cut so that an interview would ideally last no more than one-and-three-quarter hours. In the event, the third pilot questionnaire took an average of one-and-a-half hours to administer. With minor amendments this questionnaire was reproduced for the main fieldwork.

Our experience is that the interviewer gets tired in these long interviews before the informant! The extremely good response rate obtained in this survey (see 20.1.6) is testimony to the interest and cooperation we received from the parents.

18.2   The sample

18.2.1   Design

A two-stage stratified sample design was employed. (Full details are given in Chapter 20.) The first stage units were the local education authorities. These were stratified before selection by region, metropolitan or county area, education policy and population density. (The education policy stratification variable – related to integration of visually impaired children within schools – was devised by RNIB: see section 20.1.1.)

Selection of LEAs was made independently within eight regions with a probability proportional to size (PPS), size being taken as the total number of school children in the area. The eight regions were as follows.

1.   Scotland and Northern England

2.   Yorkshire and Humberside

3.   North West

4.   West Midlands

5.   East Midlands and East Anglia

6.   Wales and South West

7.   South East

8.   ILEA and London Boroughs

Thirty seven LEAs were selected, 4 or 5 from each of the 8 regions; 4 LEAs did not cooperate.

The second stage sample was therefore based on a sample frame of 33 LEAs. The second stage units were the visually impaired children. The PPS sample at the first stage meant that a fixed number of visually impaired children could be selected from within each LEA in a region, thereby giving each visually impaired child a chance of selection proportionate to the total number of school children in the area. Prior to selection the children were stratified by sight level from the pro formas (see section 20.2), and those aged 2 years or less or 19 years and over were excluded. Because of the elapsed time between the sample selection and interview, the final sample held a number of children who had by then reached the age of 19.

Although our sample was drawn on a different basis from the OPCS (Bone and Meltzer, 1989), we maintained consistency on two points. We did not include Northern Ireland and we sampled only children in private households. Children who attended establishments outside the LEA area in which they were resident were eligible for inclusion if they spent weekends or holidays at what would otherwise be their normal home. (OPCS found from its separate survey of communal establishments that less than 2% of disabled children were permanently institutionalised.)

18.2.2   The sampling operation

The first stage of the sampling operation, the selection of LEAs, was a simple matter of desk work. The selection of visually impaired children, which formed the second stage, took nearly a year to complete, and raised several problems. Contact was made initially with the Chief Education Officer of the LEA, and cooperating LEAs usually appointed a contact person who then completed a pro forma prepared by RNIB giving details of each child identified as visually impaired by the authorities. Over 4,000 pro formas were returned. (A copy of the pro forma and the distribution of replies is shown in the appendix to Chapter 20. The data collected here would repay secondary analysis.)

LEAs were asked to provide the names and addresses of the children whose serial numbers were selected by RNIB to form the sample. Most LEAs wrote to the parents of the children to obtain their consent before supplying names and addresses. (For the letters to Chief Education Officers, the contacts within LEAs, and to parents, see appendix to Chapter 20.)

Pilot work with 10 LEAs revealed two main problems.

A.   LEAs varied widely in the numbers of children listed.

B.   The quality of information provided on each child was variable and often lacking in detail, particularly with respect to ophthalmic information.

On point A it was concluded that this variability was a fact about the recording practices of LEAs and was something that would have to be accepted. Therefore a sample was arrived at that is representative of the population of children that are on record with LEAs as visually impaired. This is not quite the same as a national sample of visually impaired children. Independent evidence from the OPCS children's survey, discussed in Chapter 19, indicates that overall the LEAs under-record the numbers of visually impaired children.

While, on part B, it would have been preferable to have drawn the sample on the basis of ophthalmic information, it was concluded that it was not possible to obtain this information from the LEA records, and any other route to this information would not have been practical. The main step taken therefore was to tighten up the wording on the pro forma to maximise the information that could be gained on sight levels that the LEAs did have on record. Section 20.2 describes how the information on the pro forma was used to stratify the sampling frame by sight level. From the sample data obtained it has been possible to compare the stratification used on the pro forma with more detailed questions on residual vision obtained during the interview. This comparison shows that the initial stratification by sight level on the basis of the pro forma information was very effective (see section 20.2).

18.3   The main fieldwork

The British Market Research Bureau (BMRB) carried out the fieldwork. All BMRB interviewers working on the main fieldwork attended a half-day briefing session, chaired by a BMRB executive. The briefings covered background to the survey, terminology, interviewing style, contacting procedure and a series of dummy interviews to familiarise interviewers with the questionnaire.

Interviews took place in the home of the parents. Interviewers were instructed to make at least four attempts to contact parents. Appointments were made by telephone where possible; otherwise interviewers called on parents personally to make appointments.

All work carried out by BMRB's field force undergoes a strict quality control procedure. Five percent of all informants were re-contacted (either by post or telephone), to check the accuracy of the information collected. Additionally, the first day's work that each interviewer completed was thoroughly checked in the area office.

All main stage interviews took place in April or May 1988. The fieldwork was very successful – there was a near perfect match between the target numbers to be achieved within each region and the actual numbers (see section 20.1.6). BMRB issued 422 addresses in total to their interviewers, of which 357 were used in reaching the 300 achieved interviews. Interviews were therefore achieved with 84% of informants contacted.

18.4 Analysis

Most tables show the precise question wording that generated the data. The question number quoted refers to the questionnaire sections noted in section 20.4. In order to complete the analysis within a finite time scale, breakdown of the data has generally been confined to a limited number of classificatory variables or 'standard heads', namely: age, residual vision, type of school attended, other disability and, where relevant, registration status. In a number of cases these have been combined, for example age and other disability.

Each standard head is split into two levels, except age where a three level split is also used. The splits are as follows:

> Age: 3 – 7, 8 – 11 and 12 + ; 3 – 11 and 12 +
> Registration status: registered and non-registered
> Type of school: ordinary and special
> Other disability: other disability and no other disability
> Residual vision: high and low

Unless otherwise noted, it can be taken that differences between percentages singled out for comment are statistically significant (see section 20.5).

Although the target sample was set at 300 children, this report is based on a sample of 285. This is because we drew disproportionately on and included an extra 15 of those children found to be registered blind in ordinary schools, as these children were of special interest. However, to have included them in the analysis at this stage would have meant weighting back the data to obtain a balanced sample. We decided therefore to exclude this supplementary sample for the purposes of the present report in order to avoid the additional complexity of weighting. This has the advantage that the percentages quoted in the report are not only based on the numbers actually interviewed but reflect directly the percentages in the population from which the sample was drawn. (For the same reason we avoided weighting by levels of residual vision – see section 20.2.)

The population sampled is that of children aged between 3 and 18 living in private households in Britain who are identified as visually impaired by the local education authorities.

We estimate that there are 10,000 such children. The simplest way to estimate how many children are represented by a sample estimate is to apply the sample percentage to the figure of 10,000. Allowance should be made for sampling error (see note 1 to chapter). The relationship between population projections from our sample and estimates from the OPCS survey is discussed in Chapter 19.

18.5   Defining levels of residual vision

Early investigations showed that the records provided by the LEAs could not be relied on as a source of ophthalmic information on each child. The best information we have comes from the survey itself; that is from the replies to questions designed to establish levels of residual vision.

Four questions were selected which between them define five levels of residual vision as follows:

Level 0
Cannot tell by the light where the windows are (S2Q1).

Level 1
Cannot see well enough to recognise someone he/she knows close to his/her face (S2Q3).

Level 2
Cannot see well enough to recognise someone he/she knows across a room (S2Q8).

Level 3
Cannot see well enough to recognise someone he/she knows across a road (S2Q9).

Level 4
Can see well enough to recognise someone he/she knows across a road (S2Q9).

Table 18.1 shows the distribution of the sample over these five levels.

We selected these four questions on two grounds. Firstly, between them they constitute a scale spanning five steps in the range of visual loss, from the most severe – no light perception (Level 0) – to a level where any loss is only slight – ability to see well enough to recognise someone across a road (level 4 on the scale). Secondly, these same

Table 18.1 Distribution of RNIB sample over the five levels of residual vision

Level of residual vision	Distribution
	%
0	10
1	14
2	35
3	17
4	24
Total %	100
Base	285

four questions were also asked in the OPCS children's survey, enabling important comparisons to be made between the two surveys (see section 18.7).

18.6 Definition of high and low residual vision

For analysis purposes it is convenient to have just one question which will divide the sample in about equal proportions between those with high and low residual vision.

The purposes of the present survey are best met if this can also be a question which can be expected to relate to the visual acuity levels required for reading print. At the same time it needs to be a question which can be used to assess all the children in the sample irrespective of either their chronological age or reading ability. Question S2Q7, shown in Table 18.2, was selected to meet these criteria.

Table 18.2 Question S2Q7 tabulated against the residual vision scale

'Can . . . (child) see well enough to pick out a small object like a coin from a table without having to feel for it first?' (S2Q7)

Residual vision scale	Yes (High)	No (Low)	Total
	%	%	%
0	0	21	10
1	0	27	14
2	19	52	35
3	35	0	17
4	46	0	24
Total %	100	100	100
Base	145	140	285

Table 18.2 shows the answers to S2Q7 tabulated against the five-point residual vision scale. The breakdown shows that S2Q7 meets the above

criteria very well. The yes/no answers divide the available 285 sample almost exactly in half (145/140), those saying 'yes' or 'no' falling predominantly into either the high or low levels, respectively, on the scale of residual vision.

For convenience of analysis and description, therefore, throughout this survey, unless otherwise specified, high and low residual vision have been defined in terms of those saying 'yes' or 'no' to question S2Q7.

The functional value of this two-way split is demonstrated in Chapter 11 in relation to the ability to read print. Sixty-three percent of children with high residual vision were reported as being able to read print of ordinary size as compared with only 18% of children with low residual vision. In other words, this easily applied method of classification has proved reasonably reliable in subsequently distinguishing between children who could and could not read print of ordinary size.

18.7 Comparison of residual vision levels in the OPCS and RNIB surveys

As noted in section 18.5 there are four questions in common used to measure residual vision levels in the OPCS and RNIB surveys.

Computations based on the OPCS data (see note 2) allow comparisons to be made, as in Table 18.3, between the range of residual vision covered in the two surveys.

Table 18.3 Comparing the sample distribution over residual vision levels in the RNIB and OPCS surveys

Residual vision level	Sample from RNIB	Sample from OPCS
	%	%
0	10	8
1	14	17
2	35	41
3	17	33
4	24	0
Total %	100	100
Base number interviewed	285	82

What emerges most strikingly from the comparison in Table 18.3 is that while the RNIB sample has 24% at level 4, the OPCS sample has no children at all at this level. The range of residual vision in the OPCS survey ends at level 3.

This result emerges from the way in which the population samples were defined and delimited in the two surveys. Level 4 consists of 'those who can see well enough to recognise someone he/she knows across a road'. This item was used to define the threshold for seeing disability in the OPCS survey. Those who can see at this level were defined as not having a seeing disability.

Whereas OPCS used this relatively sharp cut-off for their definition of the child population with a seeing disability, any child recorded as visually impaired on the pro formas returned by the LEAs was eligible for inclusion in the RNIB sample. The pro forma itself, and the guidelines for completion sent with it (see appendix to Chapter 20) were designed to maximise consistency across all the LEAs. Even so it is evident that the recording of visual impairment on LEA records is based on an assessment of educational needs, and the recording procedure varies considerably between LEAs.

18.8   Residual vision levels and registration status

Table 18.4 provides further evidence that the threshold value in the OPCS survey may have been set too high. In the RNIB sample, among those registered as partially sighted some 17% are at level 4. Thus elimination of level 4 in the OPCS definition of seeing disability removes many who would be eligible for registration as partially sighted by the criterion being applied by local social services.

Table 18.4   The residual vision scale and registration status

Residual vision level	Registration status†			Total
	Blind	Partially sighted	Non-registered	
	%	%	%	%
0	33	0	6	10
1	29	10	9	14
2	33	47	33	35
3	5	26	20	17
4	0	17	32	24
Total %	100	100	100	100
Base	58	42	181	281

281 children: 4 gave no information

†Registration status based on questionnaire response

It is notable that some 15% of those not registered were at very low residual vision levels, and among them were 6% who did not even have light perception.

Despite the extension of the LEA records into level 4 on the residual vision scale, there is other evidence, discussed in Chapter 19, that the LEAs are under-recording the numbers of visually impaired children, particularly at partially sighted levels.

Notes to Chapter 18

1 Population estimates

For example, 26% of the childen in the sample had had mobility training. Applying this percentage to the 10,000 figure gives a population estimate of 2,600. The 95% confidence interval for a sample size of 285 is of the order of 26 percent $+/-$ 5 percent, and these percentages can then be applied to the figure of 10,000. It can therefore be said that the chances are 95 in 100 that among children aged between 3 and 19 in private households in Britain noted as visually impaired by the LEAs, the number of children who have had mobility lessons lies between 2,100 and 3,100.

2 Data sources and computation for comparing residual vision levels in the OPCS and RNIB surveys

No information is published directly in the OPCS report on the percentage replies to items S13, S10, S2 and S1, which correspond to items S2Q9, S2Q8, S2Q3 and S2Q1 in the RNIB survey. However, within limits, we can reconstruct fairly closely from the data given what these percentages must have been.

The main source of information is Table 2.12, page 6 in OPCS Report 6 (Meltzer, Smyth and Robus, 1989). This table shows the cumulative proportions with each level of severity in each disability area, including seeing. The severity scale for which data are given is the OPCS general scale of overall severity; the scale runs from 0 to 14. This is much more elaborate than the residual vision scale that can be constructed from the four questionnaire items that are common to the two surveys. But the information given on these items on page 133 (also page 141) of OPCS Report 6 shows the scores of the items in terms of the overall severity scale. Referring this information to the OPCS Table 2.12, we can obtain the cumulative proportions of children at the five levels of seeing disability marked by the items.

Also needed is the information that the total population projection of disabled children from the OPCS sample is 355,000 (see Table 3.3, Report 3, Bone and Meltzer, 1989).

The detail of the working-out of the estimates of the numbers at S1, S2, S10 and S13, and of approximations due to rounding and sample size are given in a working memo (ACMcK to EW) dated 15.3.90. (This and other working documents are available for inspection at the RNIB Reference Library.)

19 Estimates of the Prevalence of Visual Impairment among Children

19.1 Population projections from the OPCS survey

The population projection from the OPCS survey (Bone and Meltzer, 1989) for the number of disabled children living in private households in Britain was 355,000. Of these, 6%, that is, 21,000 were estimated to have a seeing disability (note 1).

The sample for the OPCS survey was based on a representative cross-section of private households. For this reason it forms the best estimate of the number of visually impaired children in private households in Britain. Our data were obtained from LEA records, and as discussed in sections 19.3 and 19.4 there is good reason for thinking that these under-record the prevalence of visual impairment.

19.2 Visually impaired children on the records of local education authorities

Our sampled population was children identified as visually impaired by local education authorities in Britain. The estimate for this population is 10,000 children.

This figure is reached as follows. For the 33 LEAs in our sample the total number of school children was 4,265,300. These 33 LEAs returned pro formas identifying 4,390 children as having some form of visual impairment. This gives a ratio of just over 1 in 1,000. Applying this ratio to all the 9,516,000 children in 110 LEAs yields the estimate of 9,795, or 10,000 rounded.

19.3 The discrepancy between RNIB and OPCS population estimates

After looking at other possible explanations we concluded that the discrepancy arose mainly because large numbers of visually impaired children in LEAs were not being documented as such on their records.

The size and direction of the discrepancy could not be explained by any of the alternative hypotheses, now briefly reviewed.

As the OPCS researchers have been at pains to emphasise, any estimate of the prevalence of disability depends on the definition used, and in particular the threshold on the disability-ability continuum selected to distinguish disability from no disability (Martin et al, 1988). For example, in the RNIB adult survey (Bruce, McKennell and Walker, 1991) the OPCS prevalence estimate for visual disability considerably exceeded that from the RNIB survey solely because the threshold for inclusion was set at much higher levels of residual vision. We therefore looked closely at differences in the range of residual vision covered in the two children's surveys. The data (see Chapter 18) show clearly that the RNIB sample, drawn from the LEA records, covers a wider range of residual vision than the OPCS sample. The threshold for inclusion in the OPCS survey is set lower, and can therefore be ruled out as an explanation of the discrepancy in estimates.

The OPCS survey included all children up to 15 years of age. The RNIB survey covered children in the age range 3 to 19. However, the difference in age coverage must be considered marginal and largely irrelevant as an explanation of the extent of the overall size of the discrepancy in estimates.

In short, we think those children who constitute the discrepancy between the estimates from the LEA records and the OPCS survey are simply those who have not been identified by the LEAs. The possibility of inferences from our sample to the larger OPCS estimated visually impaired population is discussed in note 3.

19.4 Variation between LEAs in reported prevalence

As noted in section 19.2, the ratio of children identified as visually impaired in the school population was of the order of 1 in 1,000 for the 33 LEAs in our sample. This is an overall figure, or average, for the 33 LEAs. We found immense variation about this average. The highest reporting authority had a prevalence ratio of 2.6 per 1,000, more than fourteen times that of the lowest at 0.18 per 1,000 (details in Chapter 20).

Whatever natural geographical variation there may be in the prevalence of visual disability between the regions represented by the LEAs, there is little reason for thinking it could account for the massive variation encountered in our data. The finding would seem to be predominantly a reflection of the variation in the extent to which the LEAs identify and record visually impaired children as needing support in their area.

It is worth noting that the prevalence ratio does not show the same variation if we take larger geographical regions. LEAs in the sample were drawn from eight larger regional strata. We sampled about 4 LEAs within each region, but it is very noticeable how the average ratio tends

Table 19.1 Visually impaired/10,000 child population

Region	Average of the separate LEA ratios
1. Scotland and Northern England	14.6
2. Yorkshire and Humberside	11.9
3. North West	11.6
4. West Midlands	11.3
5. East Midlands and East Anglia	11.2
6. Wales and South West	10.0
7. South East	13.5
8. ILEA and London Boroughs	12.4

to be much less variable between regions than within. (See Table 19.1: details of the variation within the eight regions are given in Chapter 20.) The visually impaired ratios for the eight larger regions tend to exceed 1 in 1,000, but only marginally. We are still a long way from the 2 per 1,000 estimate obtained in the OPCS survey. Nationally we still have a picture of under-recording of the prevalence of visual impairment by the LEAs. It is meaningful to regard the present survey as establishing an average figure which reflects the extent of this under-recording nationally and round which the LEAs vary.

Another way of looking at these data is to consider that the LEA with the highest prevalence ratio provides a guide to what would be obtained if all LEAs were equally rigorous in identifying visually impaired children in their area. The highest prevalence ratio found was 2.6 per 1,000. Applying this figure to the 9,516,000 schoolchildren in 110 LEAs yields an estimate of 25,000 visually impaired children nationally. This exceeds the 21,000 estimate from the OPCS survey, but seems reasonable when we consider the evidence, discussed in sections 19.2 and 19.3, that 24% of the children identified as visually impaired by LEAs are at residual vision levels above the threshold level used in the OPCS definition of seeing disability.

Notes to Chapter 19

1. The six percent estimate from the OPCS survey is subject to sampling variation. If we take the numbers in the OPCS sample as 1,395 (Table 5.2, OPCS report 3, Bone and Meltzer, 1989) a first approximation to the allowance to be made for sampling (see section 20.5) would be +/− 1. That is, there is 95% certainty that the true population figure can be taken as lying between 5 and 7 percent of all disabled children.

2. The number of visually impaired children available for refined analyses is limited in the OPCS survey. OPCS interviewed the parents of 1,359 disabled children but only 6% of these, that is 82 children, were visually impaired. While our sample covers only children in private households, the OPCS obtained estimates of the population living permanently in

communal establishments. These were found to be only a small proportion of the total number of children. Only about 1 in 100 disabled children are in communal establishments. For visually impaired children the proportion is higher, about 4 in 100 (Table 3.9, OPCS Report 3, Bone and Meltzer, 1989).

3.　Any inferences beyond the LEA records must be made cautiously. The use of the larger OPCS derived figure as a basis for estimation involves the assumption that those children not recorded by the LEA as visually impaired are otherwise similar with respect to the characteristic being estimated. This assumption is hardly likely to be correct for any characteristic associated with the educational process, for instance the type of school attended, or the instruction received.

For other characteristics the larger figure may still provide a guide to the numbers in the total population, including those not recorded as visually impaired by the LEAs. If we judged, for example, that having mobility lessons is not at all associated with being on the LEA records as visually impaired, then 26% of those not on LEA records would also have had mobility lessons. On this assumption, the 26% sample figure could be applied to the 21,000 base. The 95% confidence interval for the total number of visually impaired children who have had mobility lessons would then lie between 4,410 and 6,510. These would be overestimates to the extent that the visually impaired children who do get on to the LEA records are more likely to have had mobility lessons. Perhaps one way of proceeding would be to accept projections based on the 10,000 as the conservative estimate, while leaving open the possibility that this may well be exceeded for characteristics which are unrelated to the LEA recording practices.

For most characteristics there will be no independent national figures against which a check can be made. Registration as visually impaired is an exception. We found that by using informants' own statements that their children were registered blind, the sample projection based on 10,000 agreed exactly with published DOH figures (see note to Chapter 5). Here it would seem to be the case that all registered blind children do get on to the LEA records (although about 1 in 5 are not recorded as registered). In the case of partially sighted registration, projection on the 10,000 basis led to a considerable (30%) shortfall from the published DOH figures. This could be because the fact of registration is either not recorded on these records or is not known to the parents. However if, as seems likely, parents would know whether or not their child is registered with the local authorities as partially sighted, the inference would be that many registered partially sighted children are not being included among those identified by the LEA as visually impaired.

Projection on the basis of 21,000, however, leads to a considerable (30%) overestimation of the numbers registered as partially sighted.

20 Methodological Appendix

20.1 Technical aspects of sample design and selection

The sample of children included in the survey was selected from local education authority (LEA) records based on the procedures outlined below.

20.1.1 Sampling frame of LEAs

The LEAs within England, Wales and Scotland were first grouped into geographical regions. A few low density Scottish areas were omitted (Dumfries and Galloway, Orkney, Shetland Isles, Borders, Western Isles and Highland). Northern Ireland was also excluded. The Scottish areas were excluded partly because of the cost and difficulty of sending an RNIB employee to those areas to help with the listing of administrative records, should that have proved necessary. The area also had a negligible number of children in special education. Northern Ireland was excluded on cost grounds alone.

The regional grouping and the total number of school children in each region is shown in Table 20.1. The grouping was designed to provide main strata of sufficient size so that each region could be sampled independently from the other regions. With the exception of the large South East region, the other regions each contained approximately 1,000,000 school children, i.e. 10% or more of the total.

Table 20.1 School age population of the eight sample regions

	School age population	%
Region		
Scotland	1,292,314	13.6
Yorkshire and Humberside	931,552	9.8
North West	1,226,688	12.9
West Midlands	991,406	10.4
East Midlands and East Anglia	1,030,425	10.8
Wales and South West	1,249,275	13.1
South East	1,723,696	18.1
ILEA and London Boroughs	1,071,058	11.3
Total	9,516,414	100.0

Within each region the LEAs were first grouped into metropolitan or county areas. Within each of these groups they were then arranged in order according to educational policy criteria. Finally, within each small grouping formed from these two stratification factors, the LEAs were ordered in terms of total population density. Thus, in total, there were four stratification factors. In descending order of importance these were:

Region
Metropolitan or county area
Educational policy
Population density

This procedure was modified slightly in London where the final stratification was a geographical one instead of population density.

The educational policy stratification variable – related to the integration of visually impaired children in schools – was devised within RNIB. Each area was allocated to one of six categories based on the following definitions and the knowledge of the area among staff in RNIB's Education and Leisure Division. The policy categories related to the education of visually impaired children in the area are as follows:

0.   No knowledge to date of the policy for the education of visually impaired children;

1.   A generic special needs service, having some integration, but with no specific service for visually impaired children – indicated by the absence of any named officer having overall responsibility for visually impaired children;

2.   Some service (see note 1) specifically for visually impaired children with integration into mainstream, but placements continue to be made in out-county special schools where this is recommended. For example, many London Boroughs regularly 'buy-into' one of the three schools for visually impaired children near London;

3.   Some service (see note 1) as above, but placements are made at in-county special schools for visually impaired children, which may also be developing into resource centres as integration increases;

4.   A well-established service (see note 1), integrating wherever possible, with considerable back-up and support from a peripatetic service and occasionally making out-county placements if this is in the best interests of the child;

5.   As category 4 but individual placements are at in-county schools, units or resource centres.

20.1.2 Pilot survey selection

The stratified sampling frame was used to select the sample of LEAs from which an initial selection of 10 areas was made as a small pilot survey to test the methodology of identifying and selecting visually impaired children within each area. The 10 areas selected for the pilot survey provided a balanced sample across regions, metropolitan/county areas and areas with different educational policies towards integration. Figure 1 shows the 10 pilot survey areas.

Figure 1 Ten pilot areas used and the sample stratification factors

Lothian	(County – policy 1)
Leeds	(Metropolitan – policy 4)
Wirral	(Metropolitan – policy 2)
Walsall	(Metropolitan – policy 3)
Nottinghamshire	(County – no information on policy)
Clywd	(County – policy 2)
Dorset	(County – policy 1)
Hampshire	(County – policy 4)
London Borough of Brent	(London – policy 2)
London Borough of Redbridge	(London – no information on policy)

20.1.3 Selection of the main sample of LEAs

Based on the experience of the pilot survey a total sample of 38 LEAs was selected (including the 10 used for the pilot survey), with probability proportional to the total number of school children in each area (see note 2). The sample was selected independently within regions. This meant that a fixed number of visually impaired children could then be selected from within each LEA in a region, thereby giving each visually impaired child a chance of selection proportionate to the total number of school children in the area.

Initially it had been intended to use the total number of children identified as visually impaired within selected LEAs to introduce corrective weighting in the final data analysis. Strictly speaking, the sample of areas should have been selected with probability proportional to the number of visually impaired children in each area (data which were not available) rather than proportional to the total number of school children. However, after the event, it became clear that the size of the lists of children identified as visually impaired within the different areas varied considerably more than one would expect in relation to regional differences in the proportion of visually impaired children. The variation in the listing between areas was probably due to policy differences rather than real differences in the number of visually impaired children, so that source of information could not provide us with a valid basis for adjusting selection probabilities. No reweighting was introduced in the final analysis which means, in effect, that visually impaired children included in the survey were included in proportion to the total children in their areas, rather than to the number of visually impaired children. Although the ratio of visually impaired children to the total number of school-aged children does vary between areas, for the reasons above, the difference is unlikely to have created a serious bias in the survey results (see also section 20.1.9).

The list of areas initially selected for the survey is given in figure 2.

Figure 2 LEAs initially selected

Grampian	Lothian (pilot)
Strathclyde	Newcastle upon Tyne
Leeds (pilot)	Barnsley
Bradford	Humberside
Cheshire	Lancashire
Wirral (pilot)	Stockport
Tameside	Birmingham
Walsall (pilot)	Staffordshire
Hereford and Worcestershire	Nottinghamshire (pilot)
Derbyshire	Lincolnshire
Cambridgeshire	Mid Glamorgan
Avon	Clywd (pilot)
Dorset (pilot)	Cornwall
Berkshire	West Sussex
Kent	Essex
Hertfordshire	Surrey
Hampshire (pilot)	Brent (pilot)
Croydon	Redbridge (pilot)
ILEA	

20.1.4 Postal survey among the selected LEAs

A letter was sent to each selected LEA asking them to provide details of visually impaired children, on record sheets (pro formas) prepared by RNIB. The selection excluded children permanently in institutions. At that stage each child was identified by a serial number allocated by the LEA so that personal details were not identifiable outside the authority.

An offer was made by RNIB to assist in the preparation of the pro formas but it was rarely taken up; this stage was usually conducted by letter.

The record form for each child asked for details of sex, age, sight level, registration, prognosis, other handicaps and type of school attended.

Because some LEAs were unable or unwilling to provide details of children in their areas it was necessary to substitute other areas in their place. These substitutions were made from within the stratified sampling frame so that closely matching areas were included as replacements for the original LEAs.

In the closing stages for the receipt of completed forms, too late to introduce further substitutions, it became clear that four additional areas were not in a position to produce their data. Because of these exclusions, the sample which would have been allocated to those areas was redistributed to LEAs selected within the sample geographical region.

20.1.5 Variation in the ratio of identified visually impaired children in LEAs

Table 20.2.a. shows an anonymised list of the LEAs which provided data. The number of visually impaired children identified by each LEA is given in the second column. Table 20.2.a. shows the very varied ratio of visually impaired children to the total number of school children between areas. Table 20.2.b. shows the smaller variations between individual LEAs when grouped into regions.

20.1.6 Sample selection

Children aged 2 or less or 19 years and over were excluded prior to selection. Also excluded were an additional 195 children for whom no details of sight were available. After these exclusions there were around 4,000 children from which to select the final sample.

A sample of 500 children was then selected so that each area within a region had approximately the same number of children (subject only to minor variations to adjust for non-response in a few areas, as discussed in section 20.1.4).

Prior to selection, the children within each LEA were stratified by sight level (based on the data from the pro formas) and a systematic random selection was then made. In most LEAs the number of children selected varied between 12 to 14. In areas in which the numbers were enlarged to compensate for non-response the selection increased to a maximum of 20. In one LEA 27 children were selected because this LEA came up twice in the area selection and required the equivalent of two samples of children to balance the probabilities.

The selection of 500 children was made to allow for non-response both at the initial parental consent stage and later at the fieldwork stage. The target was to achieve 300 completed interviews.

Table 20.2.a Anonymised list of LEAs showing the variation in the ratio of visually impaired children to the school aged population

LEA Area	School children ('00)	Number VI	Ratio VI/10,000
A	473	124	26.2
B	1,765	390	22.1
C	700	132	18.9
D	453	85	18.8
E	348	60	17.2
F	536	91	17.0
G	1,466	239	16.3
H	529	85	16.1
I	2,632	391	14.9
J	1,679	216	12.9
K	1,098	141	12.8
L	1,014	130	12.8
M	2,574	312	12.1
N	1,003	117	11.7
O	1,032	121	11.7
P	1,214	138	11.4
Q	1,794	190	10.6
R	729	70	9.6
S	273	26	9.5
T	732	68	9.3
U	958	88	9.2
V	2,500	209	8.4
W	1,918	160	8.3
X	1,979	155	7.8
Y	1,514	115	7.6
Z	628	42	6.7
A1	882	56	6.3
B1	3,428	206	6.0
C1	1,106	65	5.9
D1	1,015	56	5.5
E1	538	25	4.6
F1	425	19	4.5
G1	3,718	68	1.8
Total	42,653	4,390	10.3

Table 20.2.b Anonymised list of LEAs showing the smaller variation within regions in the ratio of visually impaired children

LEAs within Regions	Regions	School children ('00)	Number VI	Ratio VI/10,000
A	1	473	124	26.2
B		700	132	18.9
C		1,241	138	11.4
D		3,718	68	1.8
E	2	453	85	18.8
F		1,679	216	12.9
G		729	70	9.6
H		882	56	6.3
I	3	1,765	390	22.1
J		2,500	209	8.4
K		628	42	6.7
L		538	25	4.6
M		425	19	4.5
N	4	529	85	16.1
O		1,098	141	12.8
P		1,918	160	8.3
Q		1,979	155	7.8
R	5	1,014	130	12.8
S		1,032	121	11.7
T		958	88	9.2
U	6	1,466	239	16.3
V		732	68	9.3
W		1,106	65	5.9
Y		1,514	115	7.6
Z	7	2,632	391	14.9
A1		2,574	312	12.1
B1		1,003	117	11.7
C1		1,794	190	10.6
D1		1,015	56	5.5
F1	8	348	60	17.2
G1		536	91	17.0
H1		273	26	9.5
J1		3,428	206	6.0
Total		42,653	4,390	10.3

The initial stage at which non-response could occur was when RNIB sent each LEA the list of selected serial numbers. The LEAs then had to write to parents to seek permission for an interview.

The target number of interviews to be achieved within each region and the final achieved sample is given in Table 20.3. BMRB, the agency carrying out the fieldwork, issued 422 addresses and contacted 357 parents to achieve the 300 interviews. The interview success rate was 84% of contacts.

Table 20.3 The interview targets set and achieved in each region

Region	Target	Achieved
Scotland and North	41	41
Yorkshire and Humberside	30	31
North West	39	39
West Midlands	31	28
East Midlands and East Anglia	32	31
Wales and South West	39	41
South East	54	56
ILEA and London Boroughs	34	33
Total	300	300

20.1.7 Non-response

The 57 non-responses selected without interviews taking place break down as in Table 20.4.

Table 20.4 Reasons for non-response

	%
Contact established, but not carried through due to interviewer already filling quota	28
House empty/wrong address/moved	26
No reply, no contact, out at all contacts	25
Interview refused	5
Child claimed not to have sight problem	4
Away during fieldwork	4
Respondent or respondent's family not well	4
Appointment not kept	2
Child in care	2
Respondent did not speak English	2
Total %	100
Number of non-response cases	57

20.1.8 Supplementary sample of blind children in ordinary schools

Of special interest in the survey was a group of children identified as registered blind (or thought to be blind) by the LEAs who were in ordinary schools. There were 56 such children and 25 of these were selected to form a special supplementary sample. A further 8 of these children were (already) included in the main sample as part of the random selection process. The supplementary sample has not been included in the main analysis of the survey so it does not interfere with selection probabilities.

20.1.9 Representativeness

The sample design set out to achieve a regionally distributed sample of visually impaired children in proportion to the total number of school children in each region (see section 20.1.1). The final achieved sample was almost a perfect match to the target distribution, and the response rate in the field was so high that it is unlikely that serious errors or bias occurred through fieldwork non-response.

There were 37 LEAs initially selected, of which 10 were substituted and four did not co-operate. The substitutions were carefully matched so that the distribution by region, type of area and integration policy was maintained. It is unlikely that serious error or bias arose as a result of the substitutions and non-response.

A further possible source of bias could have arisen from lack of parental consent in correspondence between the LEAs and families selected. It was at that stage that parents had to agree to the LEA providing us with names and addresses. Here too, the cooperation was very high, sufficient for us to be confident that serious bias was avoided.

Finally, errors could have arisen through incomplete identification and listing of visually impaired children in some areas. It was not possible to instruct LEAs to use a uniform definition of visual impairment across all areas. As already pointed out (section 20.1.5), the ratio of visually impaired to total school children varied considerably between areas based on each of the LEA returns. For example, in LEA 'G1', from Table 20.2.a., it was 1.8 in 10,000 whereas in LEA 'A' it was 26.2. It is unlikely that such a wide variation reflects a real difference in the ratio between areas. It seems more probable that areas used different definitions or provided us in some cases with incomplete lists.

20.2 Stratification of the sample by sight data from the completed pro formas

The sampling frame for the second stage consisted of the set of LEA records. We wanted to stratify this frame by sight level in order to improve the precision of the second stage sample. Pilot studies showed we could not rely on the LEA's records to get sight test information on the children. We therefore designed the pro forma to obtain the best information available on the children's sight level. Columns 9 and 10 of the pro forma were designed with this in mind.

Stratification was on the following basis:

> Strata 1: Registered blind (9.1 i.e. Col 9, code 1 on the pro forma)
> Strata 2: No vision or limited useful vision (10.1 or 10.2 and also 9.3 or 9.4)
> Strata 3: Registered partially sighted (9.2)
> Strata 4: Some useful vision (10.3)
> Strata 5: Less serious sight problems (10.4)

Records with no information (10.5) were also classified as strata 5. Only three such records were drawn in the 300 sample.

During analysis we were able to compare the effectiveness of this stratification with the more detailed questionnaire information on residual vision, with the following results shown in Table 20.5.

Table 20.5 Comparing the sight data collected from the LEAs with the high and low residual vision level definition from the questionnaire

	Questionnaire information† on residual vision		
	High	Low	Total
	%	%	%
Pro forma strata			
Strata 1	4	29	16
Strata 2	4	20	18
Strata 3	20	17	12
Strata 4	47	25	37
Strata 5	25	9	17
Total %	100	100	100
Base for %	145	140	285

† Based on S2Q7: see Section 18.6.

It can be seen that the stratification was very effective in distributing the sample over residual vision levels. We did consider weighting the sample to give more respondents at low residual vision levels, but this would have meant weighting back the data at the analysis stage to give a balanced sample, and we decided the complications introduced would not be worth the gains.

20.3 Pro forma and letter sent to the LEAs

A copy of the pro forma sent to the LEAs and the accompanying letter explaining how to complete it are included in the appendix to this chapter. Also in the appendix are copies of the letters to Chief Education Officers and parents.

20.4 Questionnaire sections

Questions are identified in the report by giving the section number followed by the number of the question in that section. For example, 'S2Q5' refers to Section 2, Question 5. See Figure 3 for details.

Figure 3   Questionnaire sections

Section	Colour	Identifying prefix
1. Sample details	White	S1
2. Residual vision	Pink	S2
3. Onset	Blue	S3
4. Registration	Green	S4
5. Other handicap and health	Buff	S5
6. Counselling	White	S6
7. Mobility	Pink	S7
8. Daily living skills	Blue	S8
9. School and careers	Green	S9
10. Accommodation	Buff	S10
11. Reading and writing	White	S11
12. Radio, television tapes and telephones	Pink	S12
13. Toys	Blue	S13
14. Leisure/holidays	Green	S14
15. Information	Buff	S15
16. Closing details	White	S16
17. Other sample details	White	S17
18. Pro forma details	–	S18

20.5 Significance tests

Sample survey estimates of population parameters (for example, percentages) always contain errors due to random (chance) variations termed 'sampling error'. When the sample has been drawn by strict probability methods it is possible to compute the likelihood of an error of any given size occurring. The essential aim is to avoid the danger of misinterpreting information from the survey by taking seriously small differences that are mostly the results of chance variations in the sampling. In the use made of policy surveys, where readers are often searching for differences, this is a more likely source of error than the opposite one of ignoring differences which may be indicative of important contrasts.

This section of the methodological appendix is written to help the non-technical reader who wants some guidance as to when he or she should consider a difference between any two percentages significant – that is to say a real difference, not one due to chance. Also, since population estimates are made as routine from the percentages in our survey, guidance is necessary in the allowance that should be made, that is in 'the confidence interval' that should be set around the percentage value as an estimate of the true percentage in the population. Although related in probability theory these two aspects can be considered separately, and are discussed under (a) and (b) below.

a. Differences between percentages

Small differences between percentages can often be dismissed as 'statistically insignificant' at a given probability level. For example, non-significance at the 0.05 probability level means that such a difference could be expected to occur by chance more than 5 times in a hundred, or more than 1 in 20 times even when there is not any real or underlying difference. A statistically significant result at the 0.05 probability level would be one which could be expected to occur not more than 5 times in a hundred. At this level the probability that the finding has occurred by chance can be ignored with 95% confidence.

Statistical significance depends on the size of the samples or sub-samples on which the percentages are based as well as on the actual size of the observed difference between them. Technically a numerical measure of the variation due to sampling is provided by the quantity known as the standard error, the size of which varies as the square root of the sample, or sub-sample sizes, and is also affected by other factors such as the use made of weighting and the type of sample design (see note 3).

The entries in the following tabulations may be of help in providing an intuitive grasp of the kind of percentage difference that would or would not pass this screening for statistical significance.

Table 20.6 is read as follows: for percentages in the region of 50 based on samples of size 250, a difference of 9 could be accepted (with 95%

Table 20.6 Examples of 95% confidence intervals when comparing two percentages (based on random samples)

Sample sizes		Region of percentages being compared		
n1	n2	50	40/60	10/90
250	250	9	7	5
250	100	12	9	7
100	100	14	11	8
100	50	16	12	8
50	50	18	13	9

confidence) as existing in the population from which the samples were drawn. Thus two percentages of 50 and 59 would be accepted as significantly different. Percentages of 50 and 57 would not be accepted as statistically significant.

The confidence interval decreases somewhat as percentages depart from 50. For percentages in the region of 10, or 90, for example, a difference of as little as 5% would be significant on samples of 250.

As the sample size gets smaller the allowance that must be made for chance differences increases. For example, with sample sizes of 50 the difference must be as large as 18 for statistical significance for percentages in the region of 50. For percentages in the region of 10 it is to be noted that the difference has to be as large as 9 for sample sizes of 50.

In presenting tables in the text we have used these estimates as a rough guide, and have not as a rule commented on the differences between sub-groups, where any differences would fall well below statistical significance. Where we have departed from this rule, for example where only small sample bases are available for important comparisons, we have pointed out the smallness of the bases and the need for caution in interpretation because of the possibility that the differences observed could be statistically non-significant, that is they could have arisen by chance.

b. Confidence limits for a single percentage

Table 20.7 is read as follows. An allowance of $+/-4$ should be made for a percentage finding of 50% on a sample size of 500. This means that the population value can be taken as lying between 46 and 54 percent for this sample size with 95% confidence (i.e. there is still 5% or 1 in 20 chance that the population value could be outside these limits). For a sample size of 100 the (95%) confidence limits would be $+/-10$ on a finding of 50% giving a confidence interval between 40 and 60 percent.

Table 20.7 The 95% confidence limits ($+/-$) for percentage findings on a given sample size

Sample size	Percentage finding		
	50	70/30	90/10
500	4	4	3
400	5	4	3
300	6	5	3
200	7	6	4
150	8	6	5
100	10	8	6
50	14	11	8

As percentages depart either side of 50, the confidence limits narrow somewhat for a given sample size. Thus for a 90% finding based on a sample of 100 the allowance would be $+/-6\%$, giving an expected population value between 84 to 96 percent. The allowance for a 10% finding would be the same, $+/-6\%$, but in this case the population values would be expected (with 95% confidence) to fall in the range 4 to 16 percent.

Notes to Chapter 20

1. Some service or a well established service is taken to mean that a named officer or qualified peripatetic teacher has responsibility for the placement of visually impaired children.

2. As one LEA was selected twice within the sample there were actually 37 different LEAs included. In this area a double sample of children was included.

3. The values in the tables on confidence intervals are based on the simplifying assumption of a simple random sample in which the 95% confidence limits are taken as $+/-1.96$ times the standard error. A common practice with stratified multi-stage samples has been to assume that standard errors, and hence confidence intervals, are 1.5 times those calculated from the simple formula (Stuart, *Applied Statistics* XII No. 2, page 89). However, while precision is lost through clustering at the first stage of sampling, it is gained through stratification. A heavily stratified sample like the present one will have gained in precision much that is lost in the multi-staging. Recent developments now enable more precise allowance to be made for complex sample designs (*Analysis of Complex Surveys*, eds. Skinner C.J., Holt D., and Smith T.M.F., Wiley, 1990). Our purposes in the present survey, however, have been served by using the values in the above tables as an approximate guide.

Appendix to Chapter 20

A. Pro forma and results

B. Letter explaining completion of pro forma

C. Letter to Chief Education Officer

D. Letter to parents

E. Show card T

F. Show card with school type definitions

A. RNIB NEEDS SURVEY   LEA   Pro forma and results

(Please use a separate pro forma for each child.)

NAME ....

(OR code to identify child at a later date e.g. initials)

		Office Use Only
		1 2
		3 4 5

	RING ONE	6 %
SEX OF CHILD Male 1		60.6
Female 2		39.4

DATE OF BIRTH

Day	Month	Year	7	8

	RING ONE	9
REGISTRATION Registered blind 1		11.9
(This is the registration Registered partially sighted 2		16.0
status with the local Not registered 3		36.1
Social Services.) Registration not shown on records 4		36.1

WHICH ONE OF THESE CATEGORIES BEST FITS INFORMATION TO BE FOUND ON THE CHILD'S RECORDS.

	RING ONE	10
The child is blind/has no useful vision 1		10.2
The child has very limited useful vision 2		15.3
The child has some useful vision/is partially sighted 3		48.8
The child has a less serious sight problem or defect 4		24.0
No information provided on the records 5		1.8

OTHER HANDICAPS   RING ANY THAT APPLY

Hearing impairment/deafness 1	11	5.9
Severe learning difficulty 2	12	
Moderate learning difficulty 3		27.6
Physical handicap 4	13	17.7
Other handicap (specify) 5	14	6.5

SCHOOL ATTENDANCE	RING ONE	15
Day school 1		69.9
Residential (week or term) 2		12.5
Not at school 3		6.9

TYPE OF SCHOOL	RING ONE	16	17
Special school for the visually impaired 01		19.	2
Special school for children with learning difficulty 02		18.9	
Special school for the physically handicapped 03		4.0	
Special school not identified 04		2.9	
Hospital school 05		0.3	
Ordinary school/mainstream 06		39.9	
Special unit for VH in ordinary school 07		3.8	
Other special unit in ordinary school 08		1.9	
Nursery/Pre-school 11		8.2	
Further education 22		0.9	

NAME OF SCHOOL _____ LOCATED AT _____

                                  (Town/City)

18	19

ANY OTHER INFORMATION RELEVANT TO SPECIAL EDUCATION BECAUSE OF VH.

(Please enter visual acuity and/or field of vision information if on the records).

TOTAL SAMPLE   3,280

3 – 18 years

B. Text of letter to LEA contact detailing the completion of the pro forma

Dear –

Thank you very much for agreeing to help us in this survey. This letter provides guidelines to help you complete the forms, and allow consistency across all the LEAs. Also enclosed are copies of the forms to be completed for each child or young person; you can make further copies if required.

The children to be included are those for whom you as a LEA have a legal responsibility. Do NOT include those children from neighbouring LEAs for whom you only provide a service.

We would like details on every child or young person for whom you have records or identified as having a visual handicap, whether 'educationally blind' or 'partially sighted', including those with multiple handicaps. We are trying to assess the total population of visually handicapped children (defined below), so include those children whom you may not have formally assessed, but you acknowledge as meeting the criteria, providing as much information as you have available.

'Educationally blind' means a child or young person requiring education by means not involving the use of sight (i.e. dependent wholly or partly on non-printed materials). 'Partially sighted' denotes someone who, although not blind, requires specialised help or attention, but who can benefit from sighted methods of education.

The following notes may be helpful in completing the form. In this way we hope to achieve consistency across all the LEAs who are helping us in this study. We are aware that collation practices vary from LEA to LEA; we have thus designed the form to collect the necessary information as accurately as possible with this caveat in mind.

A. We have designed the form for ease of completion. In most cases the number that corresponds to the answer simply has to be ringed. Only at 'Other handicaps' can you ring more than one choice.

B. Written details are needed at the 'Name' and 'Date of birth'. The name of the LEA should be placed at the top of each form.

C. You will notice that we have used the term 'child or young people'; this is because we do not wish to exclude any individual for whom you are responsible or is recorded with you. The age range is thus from birth to when you no longer have any educational responsibility for them. Thus individuals catered for outside the LEA boundary or in higher education are to be included.

D.   Where we have asked for the 'School attendance' and 'Type of school' we have also asked for the details of the school. This is especially important so that if you cannot fill in the first two parts of this section we can then look up what type of school the child is going to.

E.   Space is provided at the end of the form for additional information which it may be felt is important. If there is any information as to the remaining sight that the person has this should also be written here i.e. acuity information.

Once you have completed the forms please return them to me here at RNIB, marking the envelopes 'Confidential, Needs Survey'.

Thank you once again for your cooperation in what we hope is a study that will help both RNIB and other service providers plan for an effective provision of service meeting the expressed needs of children with a visual handicap and their parents.

Yours sincerely

Errol Walker
Assistant Survey Director

C.   Text of the letter to Chief Education Officers detailing our request

Dear –

I am writing to ask if you would assist us in RNIB to complete a project which we believe will be of considerable importance for blind people in this country. We are undertaking a major national survey covering all age groups and using data from the survey of disability currently being undertaken by the Office of Population Censuses and Surveys. The OPCS survey, however, does not identify sufficient children with a visual handicap and we have to supplement their sample by going direct to the local education authorities for more information.

I am conscious of the need to handle the operation very carefully in order to avoid any intrusion of privacy or breach of confidentiality. I am writing to CEO's/Directors of Education in ten local authorities to ask if they will let me have a list of all visually handicapped pupils in their authority. I do not require the names of individual children at this stage: it will be sufficient if we can obtain a list from each selected authority which identifies each visually handicapped child separately with a reference number and provides some basic information on age, sex, nature of handicap(s) and schooling. For this purpose I enclose a single sheet which we would like completed for all pupils in your authority.

It is recognised in RNIB that this request will demand time from someone in your authority. Because our initial sample includes only 10 LEAs I would be able, if you wish, to send a colleague to visit your office to help complete the task. The person concerned, Mr. David Griffiths, is a retired advisory teacher who worked for many years with visually handicapped children and young people and is fully conversant with the nature and detail of the RNIB survey.

I would be grateful, therefore, if you contact me personally and let me know whether it will be possible to complete this initial stage in your authority. If you want help with the completion of the lists please confirm and let me have the name of a contact officer with whom Mr. Griffiths can liaise.

I should add that after this limited initial exercise we intend to widen the survey to include many more LEAs and then select a number of children from all areas to yield a nationally representative sample. The final data collection stage will require contact with parents of a handful of children for each authority (no more than 10 for any LEA).

If you require any further details about the survey, please do not hesitate to contact either me or Mrs. Louise Clunies-Ross at RNIB and we will be happy to answer any queries.

Yours sincerely

Tony Lenney
Director of Education and Leisure, RNIB

D. Text of the letter to the selected parents sent on our behalf by the LEAs

Dear Parent,

We have been asked by the Royal National Institute for the Blind (RNIB) for help with a survey they are doing to find out more about the views and needs of parents with children who have a visual handicap. RNIB has asked us to let them know the names and addresses of blind or partially sighted children in this area so that they can arrange to interview the parents.

We consider the RNIB survey could have valuable results and hope that you will be prepared to give an interview. It is not often that the people who receive the services are approached in this way. It is very important for the success of the survey that RNIB should interview everyone in their sample, and hear what the ordinary parent has to say and not just those with very strong views.

But it is not our policy to give out the name and addresses of people without consulting them. Should you not want to participate please inform (INSERT NAME OF PERSON IN YOUR DEPARTMENT DEALING WITH THIS) before DATE XXX. Only if we do not hear from you before DATE XXX will we pass on your name and address to RNIB. They will then contact you after that date to arrange an interview with you at your home about your experiences as a parent of a visually handicapped child. The interview will be arranged at a time that is convenient for you. So if you would like to help in this important work you need not do anything immediately. RNIB will contact you in due course.

Please be assured that any information you give will be in confidence. The information you will give will be pooled with that from other parents RNIB will have spoken to. You will not be identified individually, but what you say could help improve services for visually handicapped children.

Yours sincerely,

Education Officer for the Visually Handicapped

E. **Show card T: Question S9Q72**

Most important thing expect child to get from his/her education

Card T

1. Classwork suited to their own rate of working

2. Low vision aids and braille or large print books

3. A chance to grow up with friends locally

4. Good opportunities to integrate into the community on leaving school

5. Good employment prospects

6. Teachers with understanding of visual handicaps

7. Specialised help from physiotherapists, speech therapists or other specialists

8. Sheltered surroundings where other children also have disabilities

F. Chapter 10 Pink card, school descriptions (S10Q9)

1. **ORDINARY LOCAL SCHOOL**
   An ordinary day school locally with few or no visually handicapped children and no special help for them

2. **ORDINARY LOCAL SCHOOL WITH A LITTLE SUPPORT**
   An ordinary day school locally, but with regular visits by a special teacher and some equipment for the visually handicapped

3. **AREA SCHOOL WITH RESOURCES**
   An ordinary day school, but with more visually handicapped children and special teaching and equipment for them. *But* it would involve a long journey each day

4. **AREA SPECIAL SCHOOL FOR THE VISUALLY HANDICAPPED**
   A school especially for the visually handicapped with special teaching and equipment. There are *no* sighted children. It would involve a long journey each day

5. **A BOARDING SCHOOL SPECIALLY FOR THE VISUALLY HANDICAPPED**
   A boarding school for visually handicapped children with special teaching and equipment. There are no sighted children. However it would be far away, so your child would have to board, at least during the week

6. **AREA SPECIAL SCHOOL FOR ALL HANDICAPS**
   A special day school involving a long journey each day. It would have children with all different types of handicaps.

References

BBC, 1990. *The In Touch Handbook*, Broadcasting Support Services, London

Bone, M. and Meltzer, H., 1989. *OPCS surveys of disability in Great Britain, Report 3: The prevalence of disability among children*, HMSO, London

Bruce, I., McKennell, A.C. and Walker, E.C., 1991. *Blind and partially sighted adults in Britain: the RNIB survey, Volume 1*, HMSO, London

Bruce, I. and McKennell A.C., 1986. 'RNIB general needs survey', *New Beacon*, 70, 830, pp. 165 – 8

Central Statistical Office, 1990. *Social Trends 20*, HMSO, London

Central Statistical Office, 1990. *Annual Abstract of Statistics*, HMSO, London

Colborne-Brown, M.S. and Tobin, M.J., 1983. 'Integration of the educationally blind', *New Beacon*, 67, 795, pp. 281 – 6.

Department of Education and Science, 1978. *Special educational needs: report of the committee of enquiry into the education of handicapped children and young people (The Warnock Report)*, HMSO, London

Department of Health, 1989. *Registered blind and partially sighted persons at March 1988, England*, HMSO, London

Jamieson, M. et al., 1977. *Towards integration*, NFER Publishing Co., Windsor

Langdon, J.N., 1970. 'Parents talking'. *New Beacon*, 54, 643, pp. 282 – 288

Martin, J., Meltzer, H. and Elliott, D., 1988. *OPCS surveys of disability in Great Britain, Report 1: The prevalence of disability among adults*, HMSO, London

Meltzer, H., Smyth, M. and Robus, N., 1989. *OPCS surveys of disabiity in Great Britain, Report 6: Disabled children: services, transport and education,* HMSO, London

OPCS, 1989. *General Household Survey 1987*, HMSO, London

OPCS, 1990. *General Household Survey 1988*, HMSO, London

Skinner, C.J., et. al., 1990. *Analysis of complex surveys*, Wiley, Chichester

Smyth, M. and Robus, N., 1989. *OPCS surveys of disability in Great Britain, Report 5: The financial circumstances of families with disabled children living in private households*, HMSO, London

Stockley, J., 1987. *Vision in the classroom*, RNIB, London

Thomson, O.B., et al., 1985. *Meeting the special educational needs of the visually impaired*, Moray House College, Edinburgh

Printed in the United Kingdom for HMSO
Dd295489 3/92 C15 531/2 10170